Ethical Economy. Studies in Economic Ethics and Philosophy

Volume 53

Ethical Economy describes the theory of the ethical preconditions of the economy and of business as well as the theory of the ethical foundations of economic systems. It analyzes the impact of rules, virtues, and goods or values on economic action and management. *Ethical Economy* understands ethics as a means to increase trust and to reduce transaction costs. It forms a foundational theory for business ethics and business culture.

The Series *Ethical Economy. Studies in Economic Ethics and Philosophy* is devoted to the investigation of interdisciplinary issues concerning economics, management, ethics, and philosophy. These issues fall in the categories of economic ethics, business ethics, management theory, economic culture, and economic philosophy, the latter including the epistemology and ontology of economics. Economic culture comprises cultural and hermeneutic studies of the economy.

One goal of the series is to extend the discussion of the philosophical, ethical, and cultural foundations of economics and economic systems. The series is intended to serve as an international forum for scholarly publications, such as monographs, conference proceedings, and collections of essays. Primary emphasis is placed on originality, clarity, and interdisciplinary synthesis of elements from economics, management theory, ethics, and philosophy.

More information about this series at http://www.springer.com/series/2881

Michaela Haase
Editor

Economic Responsibility

John Maurice Clark - A Classic on Economic Responsibility

Springer

Editor
Michaela Haase
School of Business & Economics
Marketing Department
Freie Universität Berlin
Berlin, Germany

ISSN 2211-2707 ISSN 2211-2723 (electronic)
Ethical Economy
ISBN 978-3-319-52098-8 ISBN 978-3-319-52099-5 (eBook)
DOI 10.1007/978-3-319-52099-5

Library of Congress Control Number: 2017934345

Printed on acid-free paper

This Springer imprint is published by Springer Nature
The registered company is Springer International Publishing AG
The registered company address is: Gewerbestrasse 11, 6330 Cham, Switzerland

Foreword

At the *Global Ethic Institute* in Tübingen, Germany, we were proud to celebrate the centennial of John Maurice Clark's "The Changing Basis of Economic Responsibility" with an academic conference in Clark's honor. Clark expressed a novel insight which is now familiar to many: economic responsibility cannot be confined to individual conduct *within* the sphere of business, but it must address this very sphere itself, reflecting an acute sense of responsibility for the institutional and structural dimensions of the economy. The ethical challenges of the global economy cannot be tackled by isolated individual action. Systematic problems require systemic solutions, a fact easily overlooked by the methodological individualism of conventional economics, which confined the economic responsibility of businesspeople to the letter of the law and shrugged off any and all further considerations with the adage "business is business." Already to John Maurice Clark, it was obvious how this attitude was both theoretically inadequate and practically dangerous. It failed as a *theory* of business because it could not capture the plain reality that "responsibility beyond the law is not an ideal but to a considerable extent a fact," while, in *practice*, it led to an "economics of irresponsibility.".

The past decades have been a confirmation of his assessment. John Maurice Clark's call for economic responsibility hits a nerve, perhaps even more powerfully today than when he issued it a century ago. Moreover, in our age of globality, the question of economic responsibilities necessarily takes on a cosmopolitan dimension (Dierksmeier 2011a). We must not only decide *whether* there are responsibilities specific to the economic sphere but also clarify *which* responsibilities, and *whose* responsibilities, these might be. Notwithstanding the diversity of values across cultures or rather propelled by the differences of customs and conventions all over the world, the quest for parameters which can orient economic decision-making worldwide gathers momentum. Hence, an investigation into the very nature of economic responsibility overlaps with questions such as whether a global consensus on values exists and, if so, which values comprise this cosmopolitan accord.

In order to provide answers to such queries, Hans Küng launched the Global Ethic Project (*Projekt Weltethos*) in 1990 at the University of Tübingen, researching the values common to different nations, regions, and religions. Besides publishing comprehensive studies regarding the ethical and normative commonalities between Judaism (Küng and Homolka 2008), Christianity (Küng 1994), and Islam (Küng 2004) as well as the Indian traditions of Hinduism, Buddhism, and Jainism (Schlensog 2006), Hans Küng and his team of researchers have also investigated value convergence in the fields of world literature (Kuschel 2011) and philosophy (Schönherr-Mann 2010, Schönherr-Mann 2008).

The main result of these studies has been the enumeration of two principles and four basic values which – despite mixed acceptance and adherence throughout the course of history – have been acknowledged as morally binding by all peoples regardless of geographic or temporal location (Küng et al. 2012). Specifically, these principles refer to the "Golden Rule" of reciprocity (known as the directive "Do unto others as you wish done unto yourself") as well as the principle of humanity, i.e., to treat humans humanely, that is, as subjects, not as objects. When applied in everyday life, these two formal principles lead to four basic values – truthfulness, justice, partnership, and peacefulness – that have equally received global acknowledgment, recognition, and acceptance. Together, these principles and values constitute the core of an ethical attitude that has inspired people all over the world to act morally: a global ethos (Küng 2008).

Since these "global ethical values" have found similar expression in dissimilar cultural contexts and therefore seem to be at the core of human self-orientation, so too can they be seen as the core of a realistic-idealistic anthropology. The global ethic, as it were, reflects the heritage of all traditions of humanity: its *tangible multiplicity of cultures* mirrors the *conceptual unity of the ethical nature* of humanity. It shows that people all over the world, regardless of cultural heritage and geographic or ethnic origin, can agree on a set of shared values and that this normative theoretical consensus can serve as the basis for dialogue about practical means of cooperation (Küng 2014).

In order to be universally binding, the values of a global ethic must necessarily address and engage both believers and non-believers. Ample evidence in support of a global ethic and its contention of a global value convergence can be gleaned not only from the world's various religious writings and traditions; a global ethic also finds extensive secular substantiation, as numerous agnostics and atheists have advanced conceptions of a global ethic throughout the course of human history. Despite regional and cultural variations, people have, time and again, agreed upon basic norms of coexistence, in the wisdom traditions and teachings of China and India, in the philosophies of Northern Europe and South America, as well as in the poetry and thought of African cultures (Hasselmann 2005).

It is the common goal of both the *Global Ethic Foundation* and the *Global Ethic Institute* (founded at the University of Tübingen in 2012) to perpetuate and expand on this work in an interculturally inclusive way. The *Global Ethic Project* seeks to emphasize common moral attitudes while celebrating the culturally diverse plethora of humanity's normative systems rather than, as might be feared of a global ethic, overlooking and silencing these differences. In light of the challenges of intercultural cooperation, the abovementioned aim and purpose of a global ethic is of clear importance. It provides a path to avoiding both sweeping relativism and narrow universalism. This is important in particular for businesspeople in need of excelling in stakeholder dialogues across national, ethnic, and religious divides. By adapting and orienting themselves according to a global ethic, businesses are arguably better equipped not only to reduce transaction costs and avoid conflict costs but also to reap additional benefits from heightened goodwill and generosity on the part of their stakeholders. The compass of the Global Ethic Project thus helps firms to navigate the turbulent seas of the global markets.

Hence, the Global Ethic Project has a natural affinity to the questions raised by John Maurice Clark about economic responsibility. Most people, after all, contend that individuals and institutions wielding economic power could and should be held responsible for their actions. This holds true on the micro level of personal decisions as well as on the meso level of activities organized in and through firms or NGOs, and it no less extends to the macro level of national, supranational, and, increasingly, global governance. As all responsibility presupposes freedom, one cannot but conclude that most people believe economic actors on all these levels to be quite capable of ethical decision-making and of shaping their policies accordingly. Practitioners also share this freedom-bound and responsibility-oriented perspective. Businesspeople as well as politicians from all corners of the earth try to justify their economic decisions with ethical arguments and so implicitly accept as valid their respective moral responsibilities (Dierksmeier 2011b).

Given the obvious role of moral accountability in all areas of the *economy*, one could be forgiven for expecting the same prominent role for ethics within *economics* also. Nothing, however, could be further from the truth. In the last two centuries, notions of freedom and responsibility have been marginalized in business and economic education (Brodbeck 1998). Such topics jar with the neoclassical emphasis on certain necessities determining economic outcomes. Conventional economic wisdom highlights how "economic laws" governing relentless market forces allegedly compel individuals and institutions to eliminate from their economic decisions any and all rationales beyond a narrow calculus of costs and benefits (Mirowski 1989). Hence, as a discipline, economics today is struggling to come to terms with the sheer concept of freedom (Dierksmeier and Pirson 2010). In its mechanistic paradigm, freedom appears as something escaping the forces that constitute the very rationality of the discipline of economics. Once human freedom is seen, however, as tantamount to irrationality, it is difficult to do justice to its own rationality, let alone the ethical dimensions and responsibilities deriving from such reasoning. Despite the best efforts of Ludwig von Mises, Friedrich von Hayek, and Amartya Sen, among others, the dismal state of affairs in economics pedagogy addressed by John Maurice Clark – i.e., economic doctrines which obfuscate rather than highlight their own moral implications – has not improved much since Clark set out to write "The Changing Basis of Economic Responsibility." In fact, we have so accustomed ourselves to receive as well as perceive economics in a mechanistic fashion that few are willing or able to question the dominant paradigm and see it for what it is: one mental model among many, and a dangerously limited one at that (Amann 2011).

In recent decades, progress in economics was defined by incremental changes or additions to the extant paradigm. Some dared to take exception to singular tenets, while others questioned its applicability, and still others pondered whether the beliefs it inculcates might have contributed to recent crises and to an overall decline in the ethical mores of business (Elegido 2009). Rare, however, are the individuals and institutions daring to more than adorn the extant with exceptions and amendments. Yet this is precisely what our times need: a paradigm change, a return to the "old normal" of human freedom and responsibility as the bedrock of all things economic (Melé 2003).

For 2400 years (from roughly 400 BCE up to and including the writings of Adam Smith (1723–1790)), economic activity was guided and directed by metaphysical, theological, and moral reflections about the good. Greek philosophers such as Aristotle considered economics to be "life conducive," "life serving," and an integral means of securing the common good of the community. Medieval theologies likewise subordinated economic questions to discourses about the good and pious life, and the philosophers of the Enlightenment pursued economics with the overall goal of emancipating human beings from constraints. Throughout all these centuries, a humanist reflection on *qualitative ends* guided the economic discourse on *quantitative means*. Ethical reflections were at the center of economics (Dierksmeier 2011b).

Around 1800, however, the humanistic focus of economics waned. In the early nineteenth century, advances in physics and mathematical mechanics inspired a fundamental shift in economics. Leading economists of the times (such as Walras, Menger, and Wieser) consciously transformed their discipline from a social discipline based on historical and inductive methods into a *natural* and then a *formal science* based on hypothetico-deductive methodology. Led by the schema of the *homo economicus* (proposed by economists as diverse as Gossen, Jevons, and Mill), which modeled human behavior as a rational maximization of self-interest, the previously dominant vision of the human being as homo sapiens was exiled from economic discourse. No longer did economics investigate what would be right for all people by dint of their human nature; it now asked instead what would benefit given individuals and measured this benefit by instrumental rationality and in materialistic terms alone. The resulting "materialization" of utility into a function of (readily quantifiable) commodity consumption permitted neoclassical economics to translate the social intricacies of qualitative utility evaluations into the simpler formulae of quantitative maximization. This was the decisive turn: economics now operationalized (moral) concerns of "better" versus "worse" into a (technical) calculus of "more" versus "less." It is from this development that all subsequent business education has received its mechanistic tint and that all cost-benefit analyses still take their cue.

As we have seen, however, in the long history of economic ideas, the mechanistic paradigm is merely an exception to the rule of a humanistic economics. And so the mechanistic doctrines of neoclassical economics must be treated not as the norm but as a deviation, not as what provides the framework but as what is in need of justification. Only once we shift the burden of proof from humanistic to mechanistic economics can we make a sober use of the models and methods of neoclassical authors without falling prey to their ideology. As soon as we realize the mental models of neoclassical economics for what they are – lenses that allow us to focus on certain aspects of economic life while occluding our vision of others – we will be able to make a better use of them. The more critical we behold the neoclassical axioms, the less we are beholden to them.

"We need an economics of responsibility, developed and embodied in our working business ethics," asserted Clark. Indeed, once we too realize that the present "scope of personal responsibility is broader than ever before," comprising also "causes of a social and environmental sort," our theories must be brought into convergence with practical experience. Rather than continuing to build economic models based on the fictional anthropology of the *homo economicus*, today's economics should be informed and inspired by what constitutes the real *conditio humana*. Many are the sciences which must inform this much more comprehensive account, and, certainly, the currently trending disciplines of behavioral and neuro-economics will have their say in this regard. Likewise, the values and virtues espoused by people all across the globe, as enumerated by the Global Ethic Project, deserve close consideration. The economic anthropology of yesterday failed to be realistic enough as it was too timid to be idealistic enough. Let us not repeat that mistake.

There is clearly a business case for economic responsibility at large and for business ethics in particular, and it deserves to be made. Nonetheless, this is not to say ethics has to justify itself in the narrow terms of neoclassical economics. Rather the opposite holds true. The use of positivistic economic methods remains in need of ethical justification and can be validated in moral terms only, insofar as such methods afford us the conceptual tools needed to pursue specific social goals. It is time, therefore, for a "new normal": a humanistic economics.

Weltethos Institute at University of Tübingen
Tübingen, Germany
Claus Dierksmeier

References

Amann, Wolfgang, Michael Pirson, Claus Dierksmeier, Ernst von Kimakowitz and Heiko Spitzeck. 2011. *Business schools under fire: Humanistic management education as the way forward.* Houndmills/Basingstoke/Hampshire: Palgrave Macmillan.

Brodbeck, Karl-Heinz. 1998. *Die fragwürdigen Grundlagen der Ökonomie: eine philosophische Kritik der modernen Wirtschaftswissenschaften.* Darmstadt: Wissenschaftliche Buchgesellschaft.

Clark, John M. 1916. The changing basis of economic responsibility. *The Journal of Political Economy* 24(3): 209–229.

Dierksmeier, C. 2011a. *Humanistic ethics in the age of globality.* Basingstoke: Palgrave Macmillan.

Dierksmeier, C. 2011b. The freedom-responsibility nexus in management philosophy and business ethics. *Journal of Business Ethics* 101(2): 263–283.

Dierksmeier, Claus, and Michael Pirson. 2010. The modern corporation and the idea of freedom. *Philosophy of Management* 9(3): 5–25.

Elegido, Juan M. 2009. Business education and erosion of Character. *African Journal of Business Ethics* 4(1): 16–21.

Hasselmann, Christel. 2005. *Hans Küngs Projekt Weltethos interkulturell gelesen*. Nordhausen: Bautz.
Küng, Hans. 1994. *Das Christentum: Wesen und Geschichte*. München: Piper.
Küng, Hans. 2004. *Der Islam: Geschichte, Gegenwart, Zukunft*. München: Piper.
Küng, Hans. 2008. *Spurensuche: Die Weltreligionen auf dem Weg 1 und 2: Stammesreligionen, Hinduismus, chinesische Religion, Buddhismus, Judentum, Christentum, Islam*. München/Zürich: Piper.
Küng, Hans. 2012. *Handbuch Weltethos: Eine Vision und ihre Umsetzung*. München/Zürich: Piper.
Küng, Hans. 2014. We need bridge-builders – no survival for the world without a global ethic. In *East-West divan. In memory of Werner Mark Linz*, ed. Aran Byrne, 3–7. Chicago: The University of Chicago Press.
Küng, Hans, and Walter Homolka. 2008. *Weltethos aus den Quellen des Judentums*. Freiburg: Herder.
Kuschel, Karl-Josef. 2011. *Im Ringen um den wahren Ring: Lessings "Nathan der Weise" – eine Herausforderung der Religionen*. Ostfildern: Patmos.
Melé, Dominic. 2003. The challenge of humanistic management. *Journal of Business Ethics* 44(1): 77–88.
Mirowski, Philip. 1989. *More heat than light: Economics as social physics, physics as nature's economics*. Cambridge, MA/New York: Cambridge University Press.
Schlensog, Stefan. 2006. *Der Hinduismus: Glaube, Geschichte, Ethos*. München: Piper.
Schönherr-Mann, Hans-Martin. 2008. *Miteinander leben lernen: Die Philosophie und der Kampf der Kulturen*. München/Zürich: Piper.
Schönherr-Mann, Hans-Martin. 2010. *Globale Normen und individuelles Handeln: die Idee des Weltethos aus emanzipatorischer Perspektive*. Würzburg: Königshausen & Neumann.

Preface and Acknowledgments

The publication of this book is an important step that accomplishes a process having its first formal expression in 2013. In the following, I would like to shed some light on the process and to thank the persons and organizations who made this project possible for their support.

In 2013, at the annual meeting of the committee "Wirtschaftswissenschaften und Ethik" (Economics and Ethics) in the "Verein für Socialpolitik," I got the chance to give a presentation titled *Economic Responsibility in the Light of the Ethic of Responsibility* at the "Stiftung Leucorea" (Leucorea Foundation) in Wittenberg, Germany. In Wittenberg, I also had the opportunity to discuss the idea to launch a book project related to John Maurice Clark's article "The Changing Basis of Economic Responsibility". I would like to thank the committee members for stimulating and encouraging discussions in Wittenberg, as well as for the very practical support for the book project as authors, reviewers, workshop participants, and panel members.

In the same year, the first call for papers titled "The Changing Basis of Economic Responsibility: A Look from the Perspective of Today" was issued. Launched by Katharina Hoegl at the Weltethos Institute and myself, this call for papers was an expression of a joint endeavor by the Weltethos Institute at the University of Tübingen, the Freie Universität Berlin, and Springer's Book Series *Studies in Economic Ethics and Philosophy* (SEEP).

Part of the preparation process of the book was a workshop conducted at the Weltethos Institute in Tübingen in February 2014. The director of the Weltethos Institute had invited the authors of the submitted articles to give them the opportunity for the presentation and discussion of their contributions. Part of this workshop was a public panel discussion, with Ingo Pies, Carsten Herrmann-Pillath, and Richard Sturn on the panel, the workshop participants, and the broader public. After the end of the workshop, the Weltethos Institute was also hosting a meeting of the committee "Wirtschaftswissenschaften und Ethik" (Economic and Ethics) in the "Verein für Socialpolitik." I would like to thank the Weltethos Institute, especially its director Claus Dierksmeier, for hosting the workshop. Special thanks go to Katharina Hoegl and her team at the Weltethos Institute for the preparation of the workshop and their friendly, professional, and continuous support in these days. I have to emphasize that the support of the Weltethos Institute was not only on the organizational and resource part but also, and more importantly, on the encouraging and motivating part of the project. My thanks go also to the participants in the workshop at the Weltethos Institute in Tübingen, the panelists, and the attendants participating in the public panel discussion.

Important parts in the preparation of a book are played by the authors and the reviewers. I am grateful to the contributions of the authors and their cooperation and to the reviewers of the submitted articles. I acknowledge the support of all reviewers of manuscripts submitted to the book. These are, in alphabetical order:

Michael Aßländer
Damian Bäumlisberger
Ingrid Becker
Leonard Dobusch
Uwe Fachinger
Steffen W. Groß
Diana Grosse
Jessica Heesen
Florian Krause
Hans Lenk
Helge Löbler
Wenzel Matiaske
Hermann Sautter
Bernd Schauenberg
Ute Schmiel
Richard Sturn
Gotlind Ulshöfer
Gerrit de Vylder
Stephen J. Ward

I would also like to mention the support of the Springer Publishing House. Springer hosts the book series *Studies in Economic Ethics and Philosophy*, launched by Peter Koslowski, who functioned as the series editor until his sudden death in May 2012. From the very beginning, Springer was in favor of including this book intc the book series. Thanks to the team at the Springer Publishing House for their continuous support and cooperation throughout the preparation of the book, in particular to Christopher C. Wilby, Floor Oosting, and Diana Nijenhuijzen. To this book, we added a reprint of John Maurice Clark's article "The Changing Basis of Economic Responsibility," originally published in the *Journal of Political Economy* (Vol. 24, No. 3, 1916), and we would like to thank the University of Chicago Press for their cooperation.

Special thanks go to William Redmond for his constructive criticism on the book manuscript and two anonymous reviewers of the book series for their helpful comments.

Last but not least, I would like to thank the Marketing Department at the Freie Universität Berlin that enabled me to realize this project and provided helpful support in the final phase of the preparation of the book manuscript, in particular Charlotte Weber and Maximilian Hoechst.

Berlin, Germany
November 2016

Michaela Haase

Contents

Chapter 1
From the Economics of Responsibility to Economic Responsibility: Introduction

Michaela Haase

Abstract This introduction provides an overview on the content of John Maurice Clark's article *The Changing Basis of Economic Responsibility* and the contributions to the book *Economic Responsibility – John Maurice Clark: A Classic on Economic Responsibility*. At the beginning, the introduction provides reasons for the specification of a concept of economic responsibility that stems from economic theory. Taking Clark's perspective, it analyzes the social and economic changes in the US at the turn of the last century and their consequences for economic theory and practice. Clark was striving for the development of an economics of responsibility and a change in the working business ethics. The social and economic changes Clark faced in the US are described with respect to metaphysics, loci of responsibility, and social responsibility. Differences in the understanding of individual, collective, and social responsibility are addressed as well. This introduction further devotes attention to the close relationship of Clark's works on economic responsibility and social value; economic value and social value; and individual control and public control. The final section introduces the reader to the articles in the collected volume.

1.1 Reasons for the Book

2016 was the hundredth anniversary of the publication of John Maurice Clark's article *The Changing Basis of Economic Responsibility* in the Journal of Political Economy. Clark (1884–1963), a representative of institutional economics and of the First Chicago School in economics (Rutherford 2015), was a profound pioneer of what he called the *economics of responsibility*. There are two reasons for our interest in the anniversary and the topic of Clark's article, economic responsibility. First, Clark was addressing an issue of major importance for the discipline of economics: *economic* responsibility, that is, the responsibility of economics for the study of complex and changing economic phenomena and the responsibility of actors for

M. Haase (✉)
School of Business & Economics, Marketing Department,
Freie Universität Berlin, Berlin, Germany
e-mail: michaela.haase@fu-berlin.de

M. Haase (ed.), *Economic Responsibility*, Ethical Economy 53,
DOI 10.1007/978-3-319-52099-5_1

their economic affairs. As the recent financial and economic crisis has shown, the importance of these two kinds of responsibilities has not changed in the last hundred years. The second reason for our interest in economic responsibility could not have been foreseen by Clark and his contemporaries: the development of business ethics and Corporate Social Responsibility (CSR) as fields of study in the second half of the last century and their understanding of "economic responsibility."

In business ethics, CSR studies and beyond, Caroll's models of social responsibility (Caroll 1979, 1991) attracted exceptional attention (Caroll and Shabana 2010). These models identify four dimensions of social responsibility: economic, legal, ethical, and discretionary or philanthropic responsibility. In the graphic presentation of these dimensions, that is, the CSR pyramid, economic responsibility is the basic "layer"; the other dimensions are built on it in the above-listed order. Both articles include a discussion of each dimension; in case of economic responsibility one short-cut formulation won out over other interpretations of economic responsibility – viz. the equation of "economic responsibility" with "be profitable."

This equation expresses a certain view on economic activities and their objectives that is falling short from our perspective. One reason for that is that Caroll's models do not draw on economic theory; thus, "economic responsibility" in these models is not what economics (in case of Clark's work) had or (with respect to future work) has to say on the issue. As Clark's article makes clear, economics has more to say about economic responsibility than what is expressed in the equation of "economic responsibility" and "profitability." If John Maurice Clark had a chance to get knowledge about the interpretation of "economic responsibility" in business ethics and CSR, he would probably turn in his grave. He may wonder why the majority of scholars in the above-mentioned fields of study did not oppose this equation. One reason for this is perhaps that, with respect to CSR, "distorting ideology" (Jones 1996, p. 33) characterizes the views of even those who oppose CSR as the Band-Aid of capitalism (Fleming and Jones 2013). A second issue would not amuse John Maurice Clark as well: concerning the development of an economics of responsibility, he is a pioneer without followers.

For Clark, the institutional economist, it is an explicit objective to develop an *economics of responsibility* from the institutional-economic point of view. This can be considered a task of the economic scientific community; it can be considered a responsibility of this community as well. Scientific communities have been conceived of as epistemic subjects (Kuhn 1962), and as such, they are responsible for the knowledge they create and the ways they impart it to academic offspring and other groups. In this case, the development of an economics of responsibility would be an issue in academic ethics. A concept of economic responsibility would then result from the conceptual work of the scientific community and it is no surprise that this concept would be based on the analysis and normative assessment of economic action and economic affairs. Clark outlined this structure and provided it with content, but the framework has not been completed yet. As a general rule, but in particular after a hundred years, both structure and content have to be critically reflected upon. A topic open to discussion is also whether there is still a need for an economics of responsibility and an explication of the concept of economic responsibility. Figure 1.1 expresses a reconstruction of Clark's approach to economic responsibility:

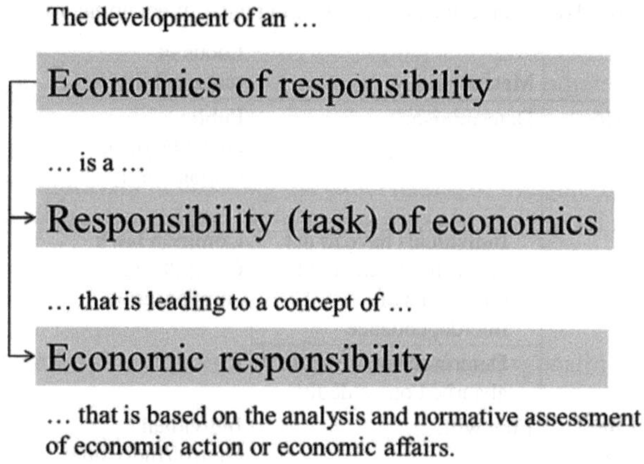

Fig. 1.1 Clark's approach to economic responsibility

1.2 The Article

The Changing Basis of Economic Responsibility was published in 1916, one year after Clark accepted an appointment at the University of Chicago. Clark was one of the leading figures of institutional economics; and he was a recognized scholar beyond that economic school (Rutherford 2000). *The Changing Basis of Economic Responsibility* was written by a young scholar (in the year of publication of the article, Clark turned 32) who just began to mark his territory within the discipline. Clark did this by looking back, by addressing the changes in the economy that took place in the two decades prior to 1916; by appraising the performance of contemporary mainstream economics; and by looking forward and creating milestones for the further development of the discipline. In a nutshell, Clark announced an academic project: the development of an economics of responsibility.

1.2.1 The Changes in the Economy

Clark analyzed the changes in the economy that took place between 1886 and 1916 in the USA. Table 1.1 summarizes these changes with respect to metaphysics, the locus of responsibility, and the understanding of social responsibility.

1.2.1.1 Metaphysics and Loci of Responsibility

In 1916, compared with the previous two decades, the starting point of economic analysis had changed: Prior to the change, the self-reliable and self-dependent individual was seen as being responsible for his own affairs, whereas after the change, individual responsibility was seen as liable to become absorbed by the influence of "societal forces": "We have swung far away from narrow individualism toward a of objective social value or a systematic explication of any consistent set of laws comprising and reconciling the *raisons d'être* of both free exchange and social reform" (Rohrlich 1981, p. 347; italics in the original); second, the impartment of knowledge to those who can use it in their endeavor to conduct control over their individual and collective actions.

The Changing Basis of Economic Responsibility is a starting point for the attempt to re-address the meaning of "economic responsibility" on the basis of an economics of responsibility. It is questionable, or open to debate, if, after the Clarkean economics, a further strand of economics addressing this field of study has developed. However, that there is (beyond Clark's approach) no economics of responsibility yet does not mean that there is no connection between economics and ethics at all. If one examines the types of problems addressed in economics, then numerous works that could be subsumed under "economic ethics" come into sight. The volumes published in the book series *Studies in Economic Ethics and Philosophy* are an example for that. Accordingly, contemporary economics addresses many problems at the intersection of economics and ethics. Take, for example, Serge-Christophe Kolm's introductory sentences to his entry titled "justice" in the *Handbook of Economics and Ethics* (Van Staveren and Peil 2009): "Economics is a moral and normative science. It always has been. A large part of economics is ethics, applied ethics and often pure ethics as with social choice, theories of economic fairness or justice and concepts of economic inequality and poverty" (Kolm 2009, p. 291).

As has been argued above, Clark's framework may be in need of adaptation or further development. In this regard, the implementation of a cooperation between economics and the ethic of responsibility may be indicated (for a fundamental approach to the cooperation between ethics and social science, see Birnbacher 1999). The Handbook of Economics and Ethics (Peil and van Staveren 2009) however does not include an entry on economic responsibility. The word "responsibility" does not appear in the index of the handbook at all.

1.4 The Contributions to the Book

The authors of the articles collected in this book dedicated their work to the celebration of the hundredth anniversary of *The Changing Basis of Economic Responsibility*. The articles in the book draw on various scholarly backgrounds, research foci, and experiences. They are divided into three groups. The three articles in the first group are headed by "Theories and frameworks: interdependence and complexity." These three articles address the complexity and interdependence of human action in a modern society[8]; and they provide a theoretical framework that they apply to the

[8] The attribute of modernity was attached to Clarkean economics as well, for example by William H. Spencer in his foreword as the editor of the second edition of *Social Control of Business* (Clark 1926 [1939]).

study of these phenomena. In addition, these articles reflect on *The Changing Basis of Economic Responsibility* from the point of view of their respective theoretical framework, and work out the strengths and weaknesses of Clark's approach from their contemporary perspectives. These frameworks draw on different approaches stemming from economics (ordo-economics, institutional theories), philosophy and ethics (Hegel, Kant, theory of justice, ethic of responsibility), and cybernetics, systems theory, and social constructivism – a list not complete.

John Maurice Clark: An Early Classic of Ordo Responsibility (Ingo Pies) is the first article in this group. Pies sketches the ordonomic approach to business ethics and applies this approach in his analysis of Clark's article aiming at "a modern interpretation" (Pies, p. 25). Pies develops his argumentation in four main sections. He begins with "some ordonomic concepts." In the light of the ordonomic approach, Clark was arguing for an "orthogonal perspective," that is, the relation between individual responsibility and social responsibility is seen as being contingent. Thus, Clark rejects the idea of a trade-off between the two responsibilities (Fig. 2.1). Pies then introduces two different areas of action and, with it, (private) "choice within rules," and (public) "choice among rules." The first relates to "responsibility *in* a game" and the second to "responsibility *for* a game" (Pies, p. 27). Social responsibility includes the responsibility of actors for the institutions that set the rules of the game and for their behavior as players playing the game. Pies distinguishes two types of subjects of responsibility (the individual and the group) and two types of objects of responsibility (responsibility for the way one – individual or group – plays the game and responsibility for the rules of the game). Regarding the responsibility for the rules of the game, the author reserves the expression "joint ordo responsibility" while a group's moves in the game are called "collective responsibility" (Figure 2.2). In this vein, Clark introduced "a new sphere of moral obligation" that can be interpreted as a "joint ordo responsibility" (Pies, p. 28).

In the next section of the article, Pies introduces Clark's line of thought in more detail. Based on a two-by-two matrix, social structure and semantics (two core concepts of the ordonomic approach) are discussed with respect to the orthogonal position and the trade-off position. Pies outlines the role of economics in the process of furthering the actors' awareness of the need to act in accord with the objective of social responsibility and their faculty of acting consequently. He discusses the juxtaposition of market and state in laissez-faire economics and explains how Clark's views differ from that. The fourth section is devoted to the strengths of Clark's article. Pies explains in detail three characteristics which, from the ordonomic perspective, are strengths of Clark's article: First, the moral orientation and the relevance of information for the identification of what is right or wrong. Second, economic theory (the economics of responsibility) is part of the solution of the problems accruing from the "working business ethics" (Clark 1916, p. 210). Third, Clark's "vanishing point … was the democratic ideal of self-governance" (Pies, p. 34). After that (section five), Pies elaborates on the weaknesses of Clark's article from the ordonomic point of view. Here again three points are brought to the fore: First, Clark came "close to appealing morally" and expressing "the need of a public spirit" (Pies, p. 37). Second, Clark "underestimates the potential for corporate responsibility" and third, he had only "little or nothing to say about the free press or civil society organizations for the 'social interpretation' as well as for the 'social management' of modern affairs" (Pies, p. 38). Pies concludes with "Lessons (to be) learnt:" First, there is a lesson (to be) learnt concerning the semantics of responsibility theories: "Taking *social* responsibility can provide an enabling environment for taking *individual* responsibility" (Pies, p. 42; italics in the original). Second, further insights relate to the role assigned to theory in the process of exercising responsibility: it provides information and helps the actors to get rid of superfluous, harmful, or inadequate semantics. Third and finally, the conceptual weaknesses of Clark's approach are again reflected upon, and the Clarkean framework is conclusively compared with the ordonomic approach.

The next article in the group, *Externalities, Complexity and Justice: Exploring the New Paradigm of 'Deliberative Trade Policy'* (Carsten Herrmann-Pillath), relates to Pies' article in several respects. Like Ingo Pies, Carsten Herrmann-Pillath interprets Clark from an institutional-economic perspective. However, this author does not address Clark's article in similar depth as Pies; rather, he picks up important topics such as externalities and the state-market dualism rejected by Clark and makes them the subjects to be considered in the development of his new paradigm. Herrmann-Pillath's article can be read as well as providing evidence for the importance of one of the categories that, according to Pies, Clark should have paid more attention to: civil society. Herrmann-Pillath's article begins with a section on complexity and interdependence, in which he outlines challenges to global trade policy. He continues by addressing the central role of externalities for the understanding of the impact of trade policy institutions (section two) and, then, rethinks the idea or concept of free trade (section three). Kant and Hegel are the origin of the "perspectives in use" by Herrmann-Pillath. In this section, Herrmann-Pillath describes in detail and with respect to the TRIPS[9] agreement as exemplary case, the three pillars of free trade from a Hegelian perspective: personal freedom, moral freedom, and social freedom. While the Kantian approach shapes the contemporary conceptualization of trade relationships and the design of trade-related agreements, Herrmann-Pillath elaborates on the alternative Hegelian view in his article. Proponents of both views can use the same words, for example, "free trade," that then mean different things in the one or the other approach. The author includes the World Trade Organization (WTO) and several institutional arrangements in his analysis, particularly the GATT[10] and the TRIPS. At the end of section three, he proposes "a radical rethinking of the idea of trade liberalization which is based on Hegel's analysis of freedom" (p. 70). In addition, Hegel's approach provides a foundation for realization-

[9] "TRIPS" stands for "(The Agreement on) Trade-Related Aspects of Intellectual Property Rights" – an international agreement administered by the World Trade Organization (WTO). For further information, see https://www.wto.org/english/tratop_e/trips_e/trips_e.htm. Accessed 15 March 2016.

[10] "GATT" stands for "General Agreement on Tariffs and Trade" that covers the international trade in goods. For further information, see https://www.wto.org/english/tratop_e/gatt_e/gatt_e.htm. Accessed 15 March 2016.

focused comparisons that already take place at the WTO and ultimately aim at internalizing externalities accruing from trade relationships. This potential of the Hegelian approach is unfolded in section four. In the fifth section, the author concludes that, in the light of the Hegelian idea of "wisdom of history," the WTO has already changed its practices and follows a track characterized by realization-focused comparisons. In the following, the author sketches what is needed for "a fully-fledged institutional elaboration of these developments" and argues that efficiency and justice "are no longer concepts staying in tension" (p. 78).

Herrmann-Pillath's article relates in three substantial aspects to Clark's article: complexity and interdependence are main characteristics of international trade relationships; externalities give rise to questions of responsibility and justice; and the state-versus-market dualism, according to which business is responsible for doing business and governments are responsible for the regulation of the business. These three aspects are related today and were related at the time Clark was writing his article. Although Clark did not use the word "externality,"[11] he took account of negative externalities in his analysis. Externalities are an expression of interdependence and, against the backdrop of the state-versus-market dualism, it is the task (the responsibility) of the state (the ruler) to establish and enforce institutions or rules that have the wished-for effect on negative externalities. As Herrmann-Pillath (p. 56) emphasizes, "internalization of externalities is a central concern of institutional design" and the evaluation of institutions designed to influence the appearance of externalities is a central issue as well. According to Amartya Sen (Sen 2009), on whom Herrmann-Pillath draws in this regard, there are two different evaluation modes: transcendental institutionalism and realization-focused comparisons. In the light of the former view, every deviation from the single coherent framework of international trade policy is negatively assessed as haggling over special interests without having the one great standard in view. Herrmann-Pillath examines the analytical fruitfulness and explanatory power of the Kantian approach and concludes that the practice of the WTO has ceased to fit the Kantian theoretical underpinning. Thus, the WTO's constitutional-level rules fail to internalize externalities; worse, they are yet another source of the terms-of-trade externalities. The author distinguishes four kinds of externalities: technological, regulatory, terms of trade, contingent and systematic externalities on markets for market access.

Herrmann-Pillath outlines an economic framework for the domain of international trade relationships based on Hegel's critique of Kant. While the Kantian approach highlights efficiency and draws on an – with respect to those affected by trade relationships or agreements – external standpoint for the evaluation of efficiency, the other approach, drawing on Hegel, emphasizes the internal standpoint accruing from comparisons and deliberations about the results of these comparisons. Three pillars are elementary for this framework: enhancing the inclusion of responsible actors in the trade process; inclusion of the civil society (based on the

[11] Clark used various formulations for what was later called "negative externalities," among them: "We have begun to realize the many inappropriable values that are created and the many unpaid damages that are inflicted in the course of business exchanges" (Clark 1916, p. 218).

adoption of a wide or particular concept of civil society that re-vitalizes Hegel's view of the market as a driver of change and, with it, of identifying the civil society with a market society); and the inclusion of environmental (ecological) issues.

The article *The regulative idea of recursive operations: a second-order cybernetic approach to responsibility* (Stefan Hielscher and Helge Löbler) presents a short outline and critique of what the authors refer to as "first-order responsibility" (Fig. 4.1). In the light of the problems resulting from the conditions and consequences of social interaction in our modern societies or the "complex structures of interdependent social interaction" (p. 83), the authors discuss the shortcomings of first-order approaches and outline the basic structure of an alternative approach to "responsibility," that is, second-order responsibility and the role it may play in contemporary modern societies.

In their introduction ("Responsibility in Modern Societies"), Hielscher and Löbler criticize what they call the standard model of responsibility, which relates descriptions and interpretations with normative assessments. This model tells a story about task requirements, obligations, duties, norms, values, and valuations and draws on actors, actions, and action consequences as basic elements. As Clark's article testifies, changes in the economy have led to the erosion of the applicability conditions of the standard (or classical) model of responsibility. In section two, the authors bring "The Threat of Erosion in the Standard Model of Responsibility" to the fore and discuss recent adaptations of the model. Scholars have modified the model to alleviate its shortcomings and to adapt it to the "conditions of modernity" (see Bayertz 1995). For example, they introduced collective actions units (organizations) and amended the backward looking perspective by a forward looking one. Yet, Hielscher and Löbler don't try to extend or adapt the standard model of responsibility to the conditions of modernity; instead, they invoke an alternative approach, a "Second-Order Cybernetic Approach to Responsibility" (section three). A second level of analysis is introduced through the application of the concept of responsibility in a recursive manner to itself in order to identify the so-called Eigenform of the concept of responsibility. After the introduction to second-order cybernetics, the authors substantiate their distinction between first order and second-order responsibility. Based on examples from mathematics and the use of the Google translator they show that a recursively-conducted operation can lead to stable interpretations or results, even if the operation continues. As the authors argue, "using the idea of recursive operations means to think about the consequences of applying responsibility to responsibility itself" (p. 92). According to the authors, both the classical model of responsibility and its adaptation express a misleading way to state the problem, while second-order responsibility is considered as a way "to think out of the box." Instead, the goal of responsibility looks to the process of negotiations as a recursive operation. Pluralism of values, negotiation, and agreement characterize a process that is based on the engagement of actors and groups to participate in such a process; and this can be related to what Clark (1916, p. 226) called "public spirit" and "social responsibility." The article ends with "Implications and Conclusion." Here, the authors discuss the advantages of their second-order approach over the standard model and relate the insights gained from this discussion with theory traditions in cybernetics and economics. In essence, this article calls for "a perspective worth thinking about" (p. 94). To proceed always in the same manner in the attempt to solve a problem, or to adapt an approach to the requirements of modernity, may not be successful for systematic reasons. A paradigm change, a Gestalt shift, may lead to solutions which have previously not been in "sight" – simply because they are located on the blank area of the map. Thus, it makes sense to change the map and to see how successful travels may be made by using a new map. This article makes the traveler aware of this opportunity. As the authors argue, their approach is in "need for further elaboration" (p. 96).

The next group of articles, titled by "Topics: Problematic Online Advertising and Female Homeworkers in a Global Supply Chain," consists of two contributions. The first article titled *Who is Responsible? Institutions for Self-Control and the Spread of Problematic Online Advertising* is authored by a group of scholars (Jutta Krautter, Markus Feiks, Uta Müller and Guido Zurstiege) responsible for the DFG-funded project "Ethics and Advertising" at the University of Tübingen (Germany). This article addresses ethical problems in online advertising and, with it, in the use of a communication or social medium that was definitely not available hundred years ago: the internet. Notwithstanding, the authors address an issue of major importance for Clarkean economics in general and *The Changing Basis of Responsibility* in particular: tolerable social control: "We are in an economy of control with which our intellectual inheritance fits but awkwardly. To make control really tolerable we need something more; something which is still in its infancy. We need an economics of responsibility, developed and embodied in our working business ethics" (Clark 1916, p. 210). As the authors point out, in the case of problematic online advertising, there are different actors who can and actually do exert different kinds and amounts of social control, that is, "control exercised by or in behalf of the entity we call 'society'" (Clark 1926 [939], p. 7).

In their introduction the authors relate their research question and statement of the problem to Clark's article: diffusion of responsibility among different actors, interdependency and interconnectedness via the "*inter*-net" (p. 102). Part of the problem statement is that "producers of internet content and therefore also ads, have hence increasingly lost control over their 'products'" (p. 102) and the exaggerated "hyper-semantics" often in use in digital media. In section two, the authors discuss pros and cons of advertising in general and introduce advertising ethics with reference to marketing ethics and media ethics. In the light of the poor image of advertising and the attempts to exercise public control of it, self-regulatory institutions have been established "to prevent the development of further legal regulations that may result from (…) complaints, and to generally improve the image of the advertising business" (p. 104). The next section (section three) is devoted to the development and challenges of digitalization. After having presented some general remarks on the topic, the authors address digital advertising. For their line of argumentation, it is important that they state "the internet is uncontrollable when it comes to any kind of data and information, and whatever goes public becomes uncontrollable" (p. 107). Notice that the authors do not relate their work to authoritarian and dictatorial regimes that attempt to prohibit the use of the internet. Consequently, in case of nomic responsibility. According to Clark, social responsibility is individual (or business) responsibility extended to the social sphere (sub-section one). Clark does not reject the influence of the social environment on individuals, but this does not mean that actors have completely lost control of their action consequences. Empowered by theory-based causal knowledge, they "do not stand entirely helpless" (Clark 1916, p. 214). There is thus a joint or collective responsibility for the social sphere. Drawing on his approach to social value, Clark promoted an ideal of responsible economic action that leads every actor to include the value to society into his or her action calculus. The views promoted by laissez-faire economics stand in the way of such a "working business ethics" (Clark 1916, p. 210). Economic actors need support by an economics of responsibility, that is a dynamic economic approach dealing with, among others, the identification of significant and responsible causes, the furthering of willing cooperation, and the establishment of reasonable and moderate public control (sub-section two). The article continues on the basis of the conjecture that, for an explication of the concept of economic responsibility as well as for the development of an economics of responsibility, a broader framework of analysis composed of empirical, philosophical, or ethical theories may be necessary (sub-section three). This section ends with a brief comparison of Caroll's and Clark's approaches to social responsibility. The last section offers concluding remarks.

References

Abramovitz, Moses, and Eli Ginzberg. 1936. Introduction. In *Preface to social economics: Essays in economic theory and social problems*, ed. John M. Clark, ix–xxi. New York: Farrar & Rinehart.

Arruñada, Benito, and Veneta Andronova. 2008. Market institutions and judicial rulemaking. In *Handbook of new institutional economics*, ed. Claude Ménard and Mary Shirley, 229–250. Berlin/Heidelberg: Springer.

Bayertz, Kurt. 1995. Eine kurze Geschichte der Herkunft der Verantwortung. In *Verantwortung: Prinzip oder Problem?* ed. Kurt Bayertz, 3–71. Darmstadt: Wissenschaftliche Buchgesellschaft.

Birnbacher, Dieter. 1999. Ethics and social science: Which kind of co-operation? *Ethical Theory and Moral Practice* 2: 319–336.

Caroll, Archie B. 1979. A three-dimensional conceptual model of corporate performance. *Academy of Management Review* 4(4): 497–505.

———. 1991. The pyramid of corporate social responsibility: Toward the moral management of organizational stakeholders. *Business Horizons* 34: 39–48.

Caroll, Archie B., and Kareem N. Shabana. 2010. The business case for corporate social responsibility: A review of concepts, research and practice. *International Journal of Management Reviews* 12(1): 85–105.

Clark, John M. 1915. The concept of value. *The Quarterly Journal of Economics* 29: 663–673.

———. 1916. The changing basis of economic responsibility. *Journal of Political Economy* 24(3): 209–229.

———. 1926. *Social control of business*. New York/London: McGraw-Hill.

———. 1936. *Preface to social economics: Essays in economic theory and social problems*. New York: Farrar & Rinehart.

Da Fonseca, Eduardo G. 1991. *Beliefs in action: Economic philosophy and social change*. Cambridge: Cambridge University Press.

Fiorito, Luca, and Massimiliano Vatiero. 2011. Beyond legal relations: Wesley Newcomb Hohfeld's influence on American institutionalism. *Journal of Economic Issues* 45(1): 199–222.

Fleming, Peter, and Marc T. Jones. 2013. *The end of corporate social responsibility: Crisis and critique*. Los Angeles: SAGE.

Friedman, Milton. 1970. The social responsibility of business is to increase its profits. *New York Times Magazine*. September 13.

Haase, Michaela, Ingrid Becker, Alexander Nill, Shultz II, Clifford J, and James W. Gentry. 2016. Male breadwinner ideology and the inclination to establish market relationships: Model development using data from Germany and a mixed-methods research strategy. *Journal of Macroeconomics* 36(2): 149–167.

Jones, Marc T. 1996. Missing the forrest for the trees. *Business & Society* 35(1): 7–41.

Kolm, Serge-Christophe. 2009. Justice. In *Handbook of economics and ethics*, ed. Jan Peil and Irene van Staveren, 291–300. Cheltenham/Northampton: Edward Elgar.

Kuhn, Thomas S. 1962. *The structure of scientific revolutions*. Chicago: University of Chicago Press.

Lutz, Mark A. 1990. An essay on the nature and significance of social economics. In *Social economics: Retrospect and prospect*, ed. Mark A. Lutz, 407–422. Boston/Dordrecht/London: Kluwer.

Moneta, Alessio, and Federica Russo. 2014. Causal models and evidential pluralism in econometrics. *Journal of Economic Methodology* 21(1): 54–76.

Rohrlich, George F. 1981. John Maurice Clark's unmet challenge. *Review of Social Economy* 39(3): 343–348.

Rutherford, Malcolm. 2000. Understanding institutional economics: 1918–1929. *Journal of the History of Economic Thought* 22(3): 277–308.

———. 2015. Chicago and institutional economics. *Becker Friedman Institute for Research in Economics Working Paper.* SSRN. http://ssrn.com/abstract=2714082. Accessed 28 Jan 2016.

Sen, Amartya. 2009. *The idea of justice*. London/Cambridge, MA: Allen Lane/Harvard University Press.

Stanfield, J. Ron. 1981. The instructive vision of John Maurice Clark. *Review of Social Economy* 39(3): 279–287.

Van Staveren, Irene, and Jan Peil. 2009a. Introduction. In *Handbook of economics and ethics*, ed. Jan Peil and Irene van Staveren, xvi–xviii. Cheltenham/Northampton: Edward Elgar.

Young, Iris M. 2004. Responsibility and global labor justice. *The Journal of Political Philosophy* 12 (4): 365–388.

Part I
Theories and Frameworks: Interdependence and Complexity

- Cell III is the sphere of "individual" responsibility as traditionally conceived: In a given situation, an actor is accountable for his own behavior.
- Cell IV is the sphere of "collective" responsibility: A group of actors is jointly accountable for their behavior. This may give rise to a free-riding problem: Although everybody is expected to behave responsibly, people may lack the incentives to do so, so that actually no one fulfills the attendant expectations. Since "collective" responsibility is characterized by what Mancur Olson called the "logic of collective action" (compare Olson 1965, p. 1971)—or, more precisely, by the logic of collective inaction—it is likely that this moral obligation is rather difficult to meet.
- Changing the level of perspective from the moves *in* a game to the rules *of* the game, i.e. moving from the left side of the matrix to the right side, cells I and II mark the sphere of "ordo" responsibility.
- The schematic overview reveals an ambiguity in the notion of "social" responsibility, which refers to the upper part of the matrix, comprising both cells I and IV. The term thus covers two cases: a collective responsibility for the moves in a game (cell IV) and a joint responsibility for the rules of a game (cell I).
- Cell I marks the overlap of "social" responsibility and "ordo" responsibility. It could be called "joint ordo responsibility". Obviously, this is the cell that Clark has in mind when he draws attention to the possibility (and requirement) that in his era the moral obligations of economic actors have to be redefined in order to be more encompassing.

With the help of Fig. 2.2, it becomes easy to identify John Maurice Clark as an early classic of the idea of "ordo" responsibility, although, of course, he does not use this term, which has been introduced rather recently: His essay in conceptual

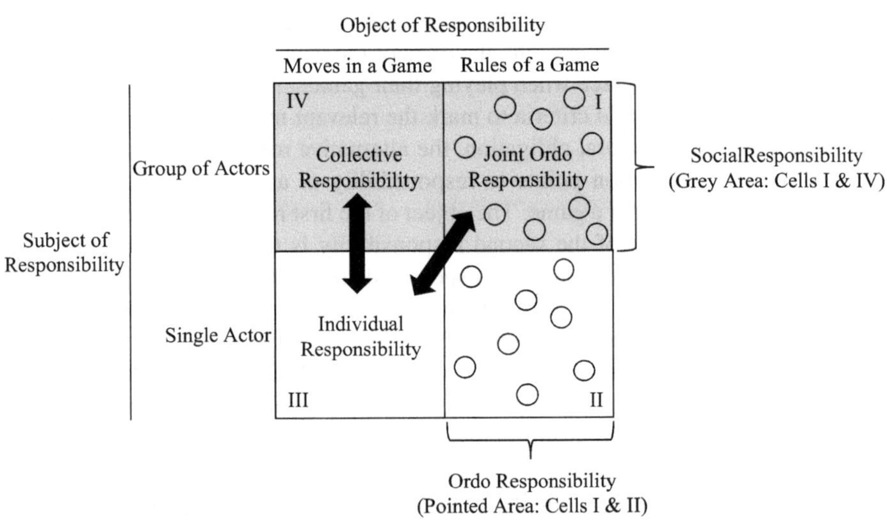

Fig. 2.2 Schematic overview: individual, collective, social, and ordo responsibility

clarification concedes that the relatively new notion of "social" responsibility, conceived as "collective" responsibility (cell IV), may conflict with the traditional notion of "individual" responsibility (cell III). This is graphically represented by the left arrow in Fig. 2.2. However, Clark's innovative contribution is graphically represented by the right arrow in Fig. 2.2. Clark strongly argues that "social" responsibility is not identical with "collective" responsibility. He thus points to the possibility that "social" responsibility, conceived as "joint ordo responsibility" (cell I), may be in harmony with the traditional notion of "individual" responsibility (cell III).

((3)) Summing up: The ordonomic concepts of a multi-level distinction and a radical shift in perception help to assess in retrospect an important achievement of Clark's 1916 article: He shows that—contrary to popular perceptions—there is not necessarily a tradeoff between individual responsibility and social responsibility. In fact, what he proposes can be interpreted as an "orthogonal position" that transcends this tradeoff by changing the perspective and the underlying framework of perception.

Figure 2.1 helps to explain this: Perceived within a tradeoff framework, graphically represented by the negatively sloped line, social responsibility necessarily weakens individual responsibility, and vice versa. Clark criticizes this popular notion. He takes the view, graphically represented in the right diagram, that this tradeoff framework can be transcended. He changes the direction of thought by 90°, thus switching from a one-dimensional to a two-dimensional paradigm of perception, graphically represented by the grey arrow that points north-east. Via this "orthogonal position", Clark escapes the notion that individual and social responsibility necessarily weaken each other.

Figure 2.2 helps to better understand his essay in conceptual clarification. Clark strongly argues that the modern era makes it necessary to enlarge the scope of moral obligations for economic actors. Traditionally, these moral obligations have been confined to the notion of "individual" responsibility (cell III). The popular movement that calls for more responsibilities amounts to an upward shift in the matrix. This gives rise to potential conflicts between "individual" responsibilities and "collective" responsibilities (cell IV). In order to avoid such conflicts, Clark argues that what is also needed is a shift from the left part to the right part of the matrix. He thereby identifies a new sphere of moral obligations (cell I). Without using this term, he in fact proposes "joint ordo responsibility" as the core idea of the new notion of "social" responsibility.

Looking at Clark's article through an ordonomic lens immediately identifies his innovative contribution. His essay in conceptual clarification offers to reconcile a potential conflict within the normative semantics of responsibility. Clark recommends to search for and cultivate forms of "social" responsibility that should not weaken but instead strengthen "individual" responsibility. In retrospect, this recommendation qualifies as an "orthogonal position", especially since it rests on a two-level distinction between the rules and moves of a game. Against this background, Clark's key insight can be formulated as follows: *In the "new era" of modern society it belongs to a (business) person's "social" responsibility to take* well be characterized as the economics of irresponsibility, and the business system of free contract is also a system of irresponsibility when judged by the same standard (ibid., pp. 217 f.).

((3)) Against this background, Clark proposes a change in perspective. Instead of perceiving market and state as substitutes, he suggests perceiving them as complements, in the sense that more (or better) state activities might enlarge the space for more (and improved) market activities:

> [T]he demand for control has grown with amazing speed, and in every direction experiments are being tried. This should properly be regarded as a recognition of special kinds of responsibility which the business economics leaves out of account and which the machinery of free contract furnishes no way of bringing home to the proper persons (ibid., p. 219).

For Clark, it is possible that state regulation does not inhibit but improve the working conditions of markets. He discusses numerous examples. Among others, one example refers to the environmental externalities of forestry,[2] another to the emergence of economic crises (including banking panics),[3] still another to patterns of consumption that lead to seasonal unemployment,[4] a fourth one to safety regulation in the workplace.[5] All of these examples have something in common. They point to deficiencies in the institutional framework of markets and thus make

[2] "Every lumberman in the Mississippi Basin is jointly with others a cause of the new flood conditions that are inflicting so much damage and calling for so much expenditure of money and thought to devise methods of prevention" (Clark 1916, p. 223).

[3] Long before John Maynard Keynes, Clark (1916, pp. 214 f.) develops a business cycle argument of a truly Keynesian nature. He writes: "[T]he essential thing seems to be that we have an industrial system in which misfits work cumulatively, regardless of the source from which the original disturbance arises. In a system of private production with enormous use of capital, involving the staking of industrial fortunes on a distant future, any irregularity is intensified in some quarters. An unexpected weakening of demand is felt more keenly by wholesalers than by retailers, since the retailer not only has sold fewer goods, but is allowing his stock to diminish. For the time being he buys even less than he sells. For the same reason the manufacturer feels the slackening of demand more keenly still, and the machine industries and construction industries most of all, since new construction is suspended and even maintenance is likely to be postponed. Those engaged in these industries can buy less, and this may lead to a slackening of demand for many products. Even in active times contractors may be squeezed by a rise in the price of their materials, and their profits turned to losses. Their failures, in turn, embarrass their creditors and may spread a feeling of panic to the whole financial community. The part played by banks in making both expansion and contraction cumulative is too well known to call for comment here."

[4] "Unemployment used to be considered largely a matter of personal fitness and willingness to work; now it is spoken of as a disease of our economic system" (Clark 1916, p. 212). "Unemployment is being traced partly to seasonal trades, as one of their unpaid costs of production" (Clark 1916, p. 218).

[5] "This changed attitude shows itself in economic matters in a hundred ways. The common law treated industrial accidents as matters of personal responsibility and attempted to fix a personal blame. The results were intolerable. Something was wrong. Contrast the attitude of a system of compulsory compensation which blames nobody, and seems almost to take away all responsibility, distributing it between the state and the employer and treating the employer impersonally, as the representative of the industry. This policy expresses a new idea of responsibility" (Clark 1916, pp. 210 f.).

clear that the laissez-faire notion of contract obligation is much too narrow a concept of individual responsibility since it ignores negative external effects. Regulating these market externalities (re-)establishes incentives for behaving more responsibly when doing business. Such regulation improves the integrity of business practice. It redirects value-creation processes in order to reduce social harm. Seen from this viewpoint, the examples elucidate the potential for *pro*-market regulation by the state.

((4)) After this clarification with regard to the (seeming) tradeoff between market and state, Clark comes back to the (equally seeming) tradeoff between individual and social responsibility. His argument in favor of an orthogonal position transcending this tradeoff works both ways. On the one hand, social responsibility in the sense of introducing incentives to reduce negative externalities helps individual market participants to behave more responsibly. On the other hand, for Clark it is part of the individual responsibility of business participants to take social responsibility. He holds them to be (partly) accountable for the rules of the game they play. Clark suggests that the social responsibility of business is to participate in regulating the market framework within which they operate.

Clark explicitly rejects the idea of a necessary tradeoff between individual and social responsibility:

> [A]nyone who thinks that individual responsibility is becoming less because collective responsibility is becoming greater is making a mistake ... For what is collective responsibility but personal responsibilities reflected in the social mirror? ... The scope of personal responsibility is broader than ever before, not narrower (ibid., pp. 216 f.).

From his perspective, there is no need for these two responsibilities to weaken each other. Instead, they can mutually reinforce each other. Properly understood, they are not substitutes but complements.

Furthermore, Clark criticizes the misunderstanding that leads to a tradeoff perception:

> It is a false notion of the meaning of determinism which interprets it in such a way as to undermine the responsibility of the individual for his own choices. ... [L]aying responsibility on the environment cannot take it off the shoulders of persons so long as the environment of each of us consists chiefly of the rest of us. The responsibility is harder to bring home to the subject, and the duties it imposes are harder to fulfil effectively, for »what is everybody's business is nobody's business.« But that simply means that our first obligation is to organize machinery by which these most difficult of obligations can be first effectively brought home and, second, effectively performed (ibid., p. 217).

This criticism leads him to two conclusions. On the one hand, he holds that a proper understanding of social responsibility makes it easier to take individual responsibility, while the latter would be neglected by following the narrow laissez-faire notion that equates moral obligation with fulfilling contract duties: "We are coming to see that our everyday business dealings have more far-reaching effects than we have ever realized, and that the system of free contract is by itself quite inadequate to bring home the responsibility for these effects" (ibid.). On the other hand, Clark holds the view that it has become an individual responsibility to take social responsibility. He explicitly writes: "[B]y making us jointly responsible for the general social environment ... our personal responsibilities are being broadened" (ibid.).

((5)) Summing up: Clark does not deny that (certain forms of) state action can destroy markets and that (certain forms of) social responsibility can destroy individual responsibility. But he insists that these insights do not tell the whole story. For him it is of utmost importance that the opposite is possible, too. He argues as follows: Through institutional reform, the state can help to create and improve markets, it can contribute to their flourishing. And in likewise fashion, social responsibility can pave the way for better taking individual responsibility: Improving, through institutional reform, the incentives for personal behavior, enables business people to take the right choices and to reduce the harm they may otherwise inflict on their fellow citizens.

2.4 The Strengths of Clark's Argumentation

John Maurice Clark wrote his seminal article during a conflict that became later known as the First World War. At the time of writing, he was still under the impression of the US Banking Panic of 1912. He therefore knew that laissez-faire policies might not be enough to prevent societal crises and that social reform might be necessary to bring individual incentives in line with the public interest.

Especially in this respect, Clark was a contemporary witness of fast and radical change. He thought of his time as the beginning of a new era. He had a sense that this era was problematic, and he therefore felt that orientation was needed to meet the challenges. He understood that many of his contemporary citizens were searching for a moral compass. And he was resolved to provide orientation for practice by re-orienting theory.

From an ordonomic point of view, three points deserve to be mentioned since they can be interpreted as strengths in Clark's line of argumentation that are inspiring even today:

- Clark had a special vision of the moral orientation that was needed. He thought that the central problem was not weakness of will but lack of information.
- Clark had a clear sense that a better economic theory was needed to provide the necessary orientation.
- The vanishing point of his vision was the democratic ideal of responsible self-governance.

This section documents and explains these three points and discusses their interrelatedness.

((1)) Moral problems can emerge from different sources. One source is weakness of will. Sometimes people know what is right, and they want to do what is right, but they lack the inner strength to behave accordingly. Modern economics discusses this problem under the rubric "time inconsistency" and recommends as a solution to build up the capacity for self-commitment (compare Schelling 1984, 1996).

Another source of moral problems is lack of orientation. Sometimes people want to do what is right and have the capacity to do what they want, but they do not know what is right. They are in doubt about how to behave properly. Here, a solution requires better information. Once people are convinced of what is the right thing to do, there is no further hindrance towards moral behavior.

From the start of his argumentation Clark makes clear that—as an economist—he wants to address a problem of moral orientation:

> The ideas of obligation which embody the actual relations of man to man in the twentieth century, and answer the needs of the twentieth century, are radically different from the ideas which dominated the nineteenth. ... [M]any men are honestly seeking to know what their obligations are in this new era, that they may meet them on their own initiative. More knowledge is wanted, that men may guide themselves. The modern prayer is not so much for strength as for wisdom (Clark 1916, pp. 209 f.).

((2)) As an economist, however, Clark has the impression that his own discipline is not ready to provide the solution, since it is part of the very problem. He holds that the laissez-faire tradition in economic thought, which had its heyday during the nineteenth century, is no longer appropriate to meet the challenges of the twentieth century. For him, it is not enough to fulfill one's contractual promises if business behavior exerts negative externalities. He criticizes a doctrine which recommends such a narrow understanding of moral obligation, in effect propagating immoral behavior:

> We have inherited an economics of irresponsibility. ... We need an economics of responsibility, developed and embodied in our working business ethics (ibid., p. 210).

This is why he thinks that a critique of laissez-faire—in the sense of a redirection of economic theory—can provide the information that is necessary for solving the problem of moral orientation: He hopes that once it becomes clear how social responsibility can enhance individual responsibility, people will understand that it is their individual responsibility to take social responsibility.

Clark is explicit about what he wants to accomplish as a theorist. He wants to fill a conceptual gap with regard to the relation between market and state, between the sphere of free exchange and the sphere of social reform.

> [U]ntil 'free exchange' and 'social reform' are both interpreted as governed by one consistent set of laws, they are not interpreted correctly. The crucial task of such a theory is to unify, to reveal those causes and consequences of things men do which transcend the scope of free exchange. These create responsibilities which, in turn, the policy of regulation is attempting to enforce. In a broad sense the great task of the theorist of our tremendously dynamic age is to substitute an economics of responsibility for the economics of irresponsible conflict. That is his part in furthering the growth of willing co-operation in the endless process of adapting our organization and industrial ways to the unforeseen needs and relationships which machinery and science are continually thrusting upon us (ibid., pp. 220 f.).

Clark holds the view that improved information about the causes and especially the consequences of individual behavior might create new responsibilities. Apart from economics, many sciences can contribute to societal learning processes that reduce avoidable harm, as his following example makes clear.

> [S]tatistics, together with the mass-phenomena they measure, have been the instrument of a surprising deal of altered thinking. When we are looking at John Smith alone, we cannot tell just what he will do in a given situation or what a change in environment will do to him. He is still an independent personality and a law unto himself. But we can tell in advance what such a change will do to a thousand John Smiths. It may kill so and so many, or save so and so many alive ... The environment has become responsible for John Smith.
>
> But at the same time John Smith has become responsible for the environment. A knowledge of bacteria makes criminal neglect out of what were once matters of purely private concern, and the outcome is to make medicine more and more a matter of maintaining a healthful environment and hence a matter of public prevention rather than of private cure.
>
> ... All these things have given us new ideas of causes and effects, and these have given us new ideas of responsibility. We are finding out that many things are not to be taken for granted as of old, because they are things over which someone can exercise control, and that means they are things for which someone is responsible (ibid., p. 213).

((3)) Instead of a top-down approach, Clark proposes a bottom-up approach to social reform. He wants citizens to understand "the changing basis of economic responsibility". In this sense, the title of his article is really programmatic. As a theorist, he wants to become practical by filling conceptual gaps with regard to both "social management and social interpretation" (ibid., p. 229).[6] He wants to convince his fellow citizens and especially the business community that it is their responsibility—and their prudent self-interest—to take care of the rules of the games they play.

For him "business men and theoretical economics alike are still shadowed by the fading penumbra of laissez-faire" (ibid.). They tend to regard market and state as substitutes, and they tend to favor a very narrow notion of individual responsibility. Against this background, Clark wants to improve the self-understanding of business actors. The numerous examples he discusses are meant to show that it is not enough to fulfill one's contractual promises (concerning individual moves in a game) if one wants to reduce avoidable harm, and they are meant to show that harm can be avoided by collective action, by politically (re-)forming the rules of the game. It is exactly this idea that makes him an early classic of "ordo" responsibility.

Furthermore, Clark argues that a business community which is blind to its responsibilities invites the state to take action. This might lead to reform from above, and such reform might be ill-designed. Against this background, Clark recommends a pro-active attitude towards taking responsibilities. With regard to negative externalities, he writes:

> If they are neglected, the result may be evils which will ultimately call forth legislation of an experimental sort, ill-informed and inept perhaps, and usually not calculated to improve the morale of our attitude toward government. But if these matters are treated as public obligations by those most directly responsible, much of this friction and waste motion can be avoided. The interested parties may ultimately want a law to help control them, for the sake of controlling also the bolters in their own ranks. But it will be a law asked for by the governed, not imposed on them from outside (ibid., p. 224).

((4)) Summing up, these three points belong closely together: Science provides new information about the non-intended consequences of individual behavior, some

[6] From an ordonomic perspective, this formulation comes close to distinguishing social structure (= institutions) and semantics (= ideas).

of which can be socially controlled. Knowledge about such control options creates new responsibilities, especially with regard to reducing avoidable harm that results from negative externalities. Understanding these new responsibilities changes the traditional attitude of laissez-faire. It helps people to realize that social responsibility can go hand in hand with individual responsibility, that these concepts are in fact complements, not substitutes. The culminating point of Clark's argumentation is therefore the democratic idea that proper government is self-government and that a proper regulation of markets can be perceived as self-regulation because citizens take responsibility for politically (re-)forming the rules of the games they play. His main message is that humankind is morally obliged to manage its own environment:

> One of the greatest things that the progress of science and industry has done for us is to give us responsible causes of a social and environmental sort. We used to think we could change men more easily than their environment, and we preached thrift, industry, and all the economic virtues, and let the rest stand as 'natural laws,' unchangeable. Now we are finding that to change the individual we must change his environment, and that preaching is not usually a big enough environmental change to get the desired results. We are coming to take a certain amount of human carelessness for granted and demanding safeguarded machinery and shortened hours with a view to securing an environment in which the natural weakness will be guarded against and the limited endurance not overtaxed (ibid., p. 215).

2.5 The Weaknesses of Clark's Argumentation

John Maurice Clark wrote his seminal article in a time of turmoil. The institutional arrangements of society were changing fast, and so were attitudes and semantics. The business sector had experienced unexpected crises, including banking panics. New policy options had to be invented. In this respect, many experiments were underway. Most of them did not follow economic textbook prescriptions. That is why Clark felt a strong pressure for learning processes in both practice and theory. The challenge he identified was not simply to apply an established theory to new problems. Rather, the challenge was to re-conceptualize theory such that it could be applied to new problems in a fruitful way.

The preceding section has shown that John Maurice Clark, aged 31 at the time his seminal article was published, was both extremely well-informed about the new nature of his contemporary societal problems and extremely far-sighted with regard to the deficits of laissez-faire economics and the theoretical options to overcome these deficits. In this respect, his argumentation contains many strengths.

However, especially in retrospect, it is possible to identify some weaknesses, too. From an ordonomic point of view, three points deserve to be mentioned:

- Though not a friend of moral appeals, Clark himself comes close to appealing morally when he argues for the need of a public spirit. However, this is a conceptual problem that could have been solved easily within his own framework of argumentation, which makes a strong case for a prudence basis of public-spirited behavior.

- Clark warns that the corporate firm might diffuse moral obligations and thus weaken individual responsibility. He therefore grossly misjudges the role of the firm and strongly underestimates the potential for corporate responsibility.
- When re-conceptualizing the seeming tradeoff between market and state, Clark has little or nothing to say about the free press or civil society organizations and their role for the "social interpretation" as well as for the "social management" of modern affairs. He is silent about the development that democracy converges towards a trilateral self-regulation involving public discussion and political negotiation among state actors, business actors and civil-society actors.

This section documents these three points. Furthermore, it shows that and *how* the concept of "ordo" responsibility can overcome these conceptual weaknesses.

((1)) Clark provides a clear rationale for (explaining) the existence of business associations. "[P]rivate individuals can act collectively where one alone is helpless and get results which would be impossible for the official machinery of government" (ibid., p. 227). For him, business associations set an example for taking social responsibility. "This is responsibility to a group, enforced by mutual interests. All that is needed is to make it cover a larger group—to make it general" (ibid.).

Clark hopes that business associations can serve as a role model. However, he identifies a hindrance that has to be overcome in order to accomplish this. In a business association, the relevant group is rather small. Therefore, group interest and public interest can—and often do—fall apart. Clark is fully aware of this hindrance. He exclaims:

> If only we could trust such bodies to act truly in the public interest, and not merely to eliminate competition for their own benefit or to fortify a wastefully numerous class of middlemen against the competition of more direct and efficient methods! (ibid.).

Against this background, Clark sets his hope on "public spirit" (ibid., p. 226) and especially on the gradual development of a "sense of general responsibility" (ibid., p. 227).

> In proportion as it grows in strength we can rely on it more and more to guide public policy. Perhaps in some future century we may even venture to ask business men's advice on proposed laws for the prevention of unfair competition without the uneasy feeling that their only purpose in giving of their wisdom is to make the laws ineffective and keep things as they are (ibid.).

This statement makes the conceptual weakness patently obvious. On the one hand, Clark calls for immediate action. He wants contemporary politics to change. On the other hand, a lot of patience will be needed if one has to wait for the emergence of public-mindedness among business associations in the sense that they would rank general welfare reliably higher than the individual welfare of their group members.

((2)) Clark is very critical of what was in his time a relatively new phenomenon—the modern corporation with limited liability and a multitude of shareholders.

He not only asks: "Has the principle of limited liability been carried too far?" (ibid., p. 228). He even asserts:

> [O]ne of the worst features of the internal organization of corporations is its wonderful aptitude for dividing responsibility, concealing it from outside observers and even from the members themselves, and making it thoroughly ineffective for other than »business« purposes. To an economics of irresponsibility this might appear as an incidental blemish; to an economics of responsibility it is one of the very roots of evil (ibid., p. 228).

This statement combines two masterful observations with two extremely one-sided—and highly dubious—value judgments. First, Clark identifies (correctly) that the division of responsibility is an important characteristic of the modern business firm. But he fails to ask himself whether the business division of responsibility is just an epiphenomenon of the business division of labor and whether both phenomena have to be judged as ambivalent, that is whether they provide both advantages and disadvantages. Second, Clark recognizes (again correctly) that, compared with an individual business person, the corporate business firm—as an organization—can have a much narrower focus on profit seeking. Natural persons have many interests, while judicial persons can be constitut(ionaliz)ed to follow one special interest only. But Clark seems to jump at conclusions when he equates this with a source of evil. Underlying his value judgment is the assumption of a tradeoff between business's self-interest in profit and the public interest in general welfare. However, assuming such a tradeoff grossly misjudges and strongly underestimates the potential of a business firm to assign instrumental value to other actors' interests, be they factor owners of capital or labor, clients, suppliers, competitors, local communities, regulation agencies or interest groups. Here, Clark seems to be blind to the fact that, although numerous conflicts of interest certainly do exist, a business firm can have market success only insofar as it wins partners in the creation of (added) value. In this sense, any profitable business firm "incorporates" numerous "orthogonal positions", in the sense that market success results from realizing business opportunities that prove to be mutually beneficial, both for the firm and for its value-creation partners, who cooperate on a strictly voluntary basis in competitive markets.

((3)) Judged in retrospect from an ordonomic perspective, Clark's analysis suffers from a blind spot with regard to the sector of civil-society organizations and their democratic role in controlling, guiding, criticizing and correcting both market and state (compare Valentinov et al. 2013). However, there is a paragraph in Clark's text that might have had the potential to serve as a starting point for conceptualizing democracy as a tri-sectoral cooperation between actors of market, state and civil society:

> With the idea generally accepted that »wealth is a trust« the next order of development is a gradually broadening revelation of how far the trusteeship extends. It most surely extends to the earning of the wealth as well as the spending of it. It extends to a sincere effort to make labor conditions as nearly right as possible in plants from which one draws dividends, and conditions of competition as fair and free from waste as they can be made (Clark 1916, pp. 227 f.).

Here, Clark uses the idea that "wealth is a trust" *normatively*. He wants to invoke the impression that there is a moral obligation on behalf of business actors to earn this trust. However, one could turn this idea upside down and use it as a *positive* argument. The idea that "wealth is a trust" can be translated to mean that business actors require a "license to operate". They need social acceptance—simply put: a good reputation—in order to be successful in finding partners for creating added value. This is why they are sensitive to public criticism. Since business activities require a societal mandate and since this mandate can be withdrawn—either formally, for example by regulation, or informally, for example by boycotts—business actors can rely on a calculus of prudence for taking social responsibility.

((4)) Finally, it might be helpful to point out that—and *why*—the notion of "ordo" responsibility rests on a self-referential multi-level distinction. To begin with, one has to distinguish three social arenas (Fig. 2.4a): (1) the basic game (BG), (2) the meta game (MG), and (3) the meta-meta game (MMG). It is convenient to think of these three arenas as business, politics, and the public. In ordonomic terms, the conceptual idea is that the "semantics" of discussion in the public arena (MMG) provide incentives for the political arena (MG), which defines the "social structure" for the basic games (BG) played in the business arena.

Take Clark's example of workplace safety as a case in point: Here, the basic game (BG) is the business practice of production that puts workers in a high-risk environment. This game results in (too) many accidents as long as safety is regarded solely as an individual responsibility of workers. The societal learning process that is reported by Clark starts on level 3—the meta-meta game (MMG)—with a public acknowledgement of statistical evidence and a political debate about the general desirability of reducing accidents in production. Then the learning process proceeds to level 2—the meta game (MG). Here, political negotiation leads to a new law that holds employers accountable for the workplace accidents of their employees. This dramatically changes the incentives for the basic game on level 1 and indeed contributes to decreasing the rate of accidents by influencing the behavior of employers

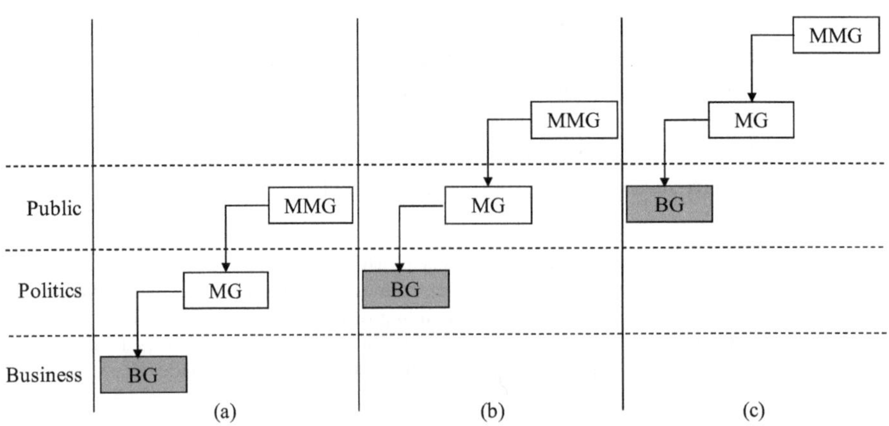

Fig. 2.4 The ordonomic three-level scheme of social arenas

and employees alike. Employers invest in reducing the risk of accidents in the first place and furthermore develop safety routines—like wearing helmets and observing other cautionary measures—that are made obligatory for employees in the basic game (BG).

Now assume that the societal learning process which, according to Clark's example, has functioned so perfectly well is somehow blocked. It may be blocked for two different reasons. On the one hand, it may not bring about the desired result because certain interest groups resist the new legislation. In this case, the problem is to be located on level 2—the political meta game (MG). On the other hand, the societal learning process may not work properly because public discussion does not converge towards a consensus on reasonable policy measures. In this case, the problem is to be located on level 3—the public meta-meta game (MMG).

For the first case, it makes sense to regard level 2—the meta game (MG) in Fig. 2.4a—as the relevant basic game (BG) of a new analysis, as is illustrated in Fig. 2.4b. If the political process does not work properly, the democratic public needs an open debate about the source of the problem and about possible changes in the institutional framework of the political process that align the self-interest of the relevant actors with the public interest of the citizens in their general welfare. Once appropriate options are identified, they can be implemented through constitutional reform, e.g. by urging more transparency about lobbying activities or by defining higher quality standards for the legislation process.

For the second case, however, it makes sense to regard level 3—the meta-meta game (MMG) in Fig. 2.4a—as the relevant basic game (BG) of a new analysis, as is illustrated in Fig. 2.4c. If the process of public discussion does not work properly, the democratic public needs an open debate about the source of the problem and about possible changes in the institutional framework within which the democratic public operates. Here, indeed many things can go wrong, thereby giving rise to *discourse failure*: On the one hand, marginalized interests may lack access (or resources) and are thus underrepresented in public discussion. On the other hand, some interest groups may be privileged and thus overrepresented. Furthermore, media may be biased, either for ideological reasons or simply because they (feel the need to) concentrate on personalized stories since it is much more difficult to sell information compared to entertainment. Once appropriate options for fighting discourse failure are identified, they can be implemented through institutional reform, e.g. by urging more competition in order to prevent a cartelization of the media market, by reforming liability law in order to provide stronger incentives for telling the truth, or by generally raising public awareness to the danger that interest groups might—willingly or unwillingly—misrepresent information that in effect manipulates public option.

((5)) Summing up, "ordo" responsibility means to enter meta games and meta-meta games—the social arenas of negotiating (MG) and discussing (MMG) the rules of the basic game—thus changing the players' incentives for choosing their moves in the basic game. For a manager, taking "ordo" responsibility may have two directions: a macro or a micro direction. Although thematically diverse, these two directions have the same structure.

In the macro direction, which is explicitly discussed by Clark (cf. cell I in Fig. 2.2), a manager might leave the business arena of the basic game and enter the two meta levels of public discussion and political negotiation, thus contributing to improving the institutional framework of markets through regulation. This is what Clark has in mind when he calls business actors to take social responsibility in the sense of a political self-governance of business.

In the micro direction, which is largely ignored by Clark (cf. cell II in Fig. 2.2), a manager takes responsibility for the rules that constitute the organization as a business actor—corporate governance in the strict sense—as well as for the rules the business firm negotiates with its diverse partners in creating added value—corporate governance in the broader sense. To make explicit that which is only implicit in Clark's argument, the following example will suffice (cf. Fig. 2.4a), since it makes clear how the ordonomic multi-level scheme can be applied to the internal structure of a firm: By deciding on safety routines (level 2, MG), by convincing employees to accept this decision as conducive to their own interest (level 3, MMG) and by incentivizing them to follow such routines (level 1, BG), managers enable their business organization to take corporate responsibility for reducing workplace accidents.

2.6 Conclusion: Lessons (to Be) Learnt

((1)) Reconstructing Clark's line of argumentation from an ordonomic perspective, the main message of his seminal article can be summarized in a single sentence: Taking *social* responsibility can provide an enabling environment for taking *individual* responsibility. With this message Clark offers a conceptual clarification of the seeming contradiction between individual and social responsibility. This is an important contribution to the *semantics* of responsibility.

Interestingly, this contribution to moral philosophy is at the same time an important contribution to economic theory, since it helps to better understand that institutions—the *social structure*—of the market and state are not substitutes but complements, especially in a world where business behavior leads to unintended effects, e.g. in the form of negative externalities.

((2)) Clark's seminal article provides further insights that are still interesting (and inspiring) today. As a case in point, he holds the view that theory should play an important *societal* role by (a) providing intellectual orientation and (b) by helping to solve conflicts. According to Clark, the first task for theory is to understand market and state—and especially the interplay between the business sphere and the political sphere—from a *unified perspective*. He writes: "[U]ntil 'free exchange' and 'social reform' are both interpreted as governed by one consistent set of laws, they are not interpreted correctly" (Clark 1916, p. 220). The second task which Clark identifies for theory is "to substitute an economics of responsibility for the economics of irresponsible conflict" (Clark 1916, p. 220). By this he means that economic theory should generate and teach the insight that the long-run self-interest of the business sector is ill-served by the traditional doctrine of laissez-faire and the consequent resistance to any (re-)form of political market regulation.

Although Clark himself takes first steps along the way towards the theoretical goal he has identified, he formulates a desideratum for future research. A century later, the following ordonomic conceptualization of a *unified perspective* can be offered:

- Society is a cooperative venture for mutual benefit.
- The constitutional state is an organization of society that produces law and order, thus overcoming the Hobbesian social dilemma. Once established, it can be used to finance a great variety of public goods. The state has a comparative advantage in solving free-rider problems.
- The market is a sphere of society where market participants produce and exchange private goods. Private contract law, provided and sanctioned by the state, is the institutional medium for stabilizing economic interaction, which otherwise would be endangered by opportunistic behavior. Market participants have a societal mandate to create added value and to improve value-creation through innovation.
- In a democracy, the constitutionalized state has a societal mandate to (re-)form the institutional order of markets, especially through the creation and protection of property rights.

In a nutshell, the *unified perspective* Clark asked for is provided by looking at market and state through the ordonomic lens of societal cooperation. Hence there is only one principle to guide democratic policy: the aim to foster mutual benefits. Social policy contributes to cooperation directly, economic policy indirectly: by employing competition as an instrument of furthering societal cooperation. While Clark was surely right in stressing the importance of reducing negative externalities, he seemed to underrate the importance of encouraging positive externalities from innovation.[7] Furthermore, the relation between market and state is not a one-way street. Market participants influence the state by paying taxes and by exerting political pressure.

((3)) Besides many strengths in Clark's analysis, there are some conceptual weaknesses, too. He sees the modern corporation as an institutional environment that dilutes individual responsibilities. His analysis tends to overlook the fact that individual responsibilities can be strengthened through business organizations, and it even seems to be blind for the fact that business organizations themselves can take (corporate) responsibility. Judged retrospectively from an ordonomic perspective, his analysis also suffers from a blind spot with regard to the sector of civil-society organizations and their democratic role in controlling, guiding, criticizing and correcting both market and state.

[7] This point is well taken by Baumol (2010), whose articles on social responsibility, written more than half a century after Clark (1916), are still another precursor of the ordonomic concept of "ordo" responsibility. Cf. Baumol (1970), (1975), and (1991).

These weaknesses can be overcome by employing the concept of "ordo" responsibility. While Clark seems to hope that in the course of time "a sense of general responsibility" (ibid., p. 227) will develop, it would be much more realistic—and much more in line with what Clark has to say about human nature and social environment (ibid., p. 215) —to think about *institutional* devices for creating and putting into practice such an attitude. The ordonomic logic of prudent self-commitments may help to clarify the central points:

- To establish a business organization requires collective action, which can be encouraged through the state by providing the legal form of a joint stock company.
- Once established, such an organization has an interest in qualifying as a credible und reliable interaction partner in processes of creating added value. In order to do so, it employs self-governance mechanisms at the micro level (and thus corrects the tendency to dilute individual responsibility within the business organization) —compare cell II in Fig. 2.2.
- However, not all problems can be solved this way. If a market exerts negative externalities, there is not much a business organization can do on its own. This problem is clearly identified by Clark. That is why he calls for collective action in this case, which makes him an early proponent of "ordo" responsibility at the macro level—compare cell I in Fig. 2.2.
- What he did not see is that (a) not only business people (private persons) but also business organizations (legal persons) can take "ordo" responsibility and that (b) business actors need an enabling environment to do so, that is an institutional framework that guides their political competition in lobbying quite analogous to their economic competition in market activities. Democratic society needs an institutional order that governs how both private citizens as well as corporate citizens (and civil-society organizations) can take "ordo" responsibility, e.g. by discouraging the strategic misinformation of public discourse and the rent-seeking search for privilege via irresponsible lobbying.

((4)) John Maurice Clark is an early classic of the concept of "ordo" responsibility. He saw very clearly that the self-interest of the business sector is ill-served if it resists any kind of state regulation. Faced with negative externalities (and even systems failures like bank panics), Clark strongly argued in favor of such regulation and called up the business sector to take "ordo" responsibility for the political (self-) governance of the rules of their market games. A century later, his call for "economic responsibility" can be extended into policies that promote "corporate citizenship" (see Pies et al. 2009, 2011, 2014).

Acknowledgements I would like to thank Michaela Haase, Stefan Hielscher, Matthias Georg Will, and Alexandra von Winning for critical comments.

References

Baumol, William J. 1970. Enlightened self-interest and corporate philanthropy. In *A new rationale for corporate social policy*, ed. William J. Baumol et al., 3–19. New York: Committee for Economic Development.

———. 1975. Business responsibility and economic behavior. In *Altruism, morality, and economic theory*, ed. Edmund S. Phelps, 45–56. New York: Russel Sage Foundation.

———. 1991. (Almost) perfect competition (contestability) and business ethics. In *Perfect markets and easy virtue. Business ethics and the invisible hand*, ed. William J. Baumol and Sue A.B. Blackman, 1–23. Cambridge, MA/Oxford: Wiley Blackwell.

———. 2010. *The microtheory of innovative entrepreneurship*. Princeton/Oxford: Princeton University Press.

Beckmann, Markus, and Ingo Pies. 2008. Ordo-responsibility – conceptual reflections towards a semantic innovation. In *Corporate citizenship, contractarianism and ethical theory*, ed. Jesús Conill, Christoph Lütge, and Tatjana Schönwälder-Kuntze, 87–115. Farnham/Burlington: Ashgate.

Beckmann, Markus, Stefan Hielscher, and Ingo Pies. 2014. Commitment strategies for sustainability: How business firms can transform trade-offs into win-win outcomes. *Business Strategy and the Environment* 23(1): 18–37.

Buchanan, James M. 1990. The domain of constitutional Economics. *Constitutional Political Economy* 1(1): 1–18.

Clark, John Maurice. 1916. The changing basis of economic responsibility. *Journal of Political Economy* 24(3): 209–229.

Hielscher, Stefan, Ingo Pies, and Vladislav Valentinov. 2012. How to foster social progress: An ordonomic perspective on progressive institutional change. *Journal of Economic Issues* XLVI(3)): 779–797.

Hielscher, Stefan, Markus Beckmann, and Ingo Pies. 2014. Participation versus consent: Should corporations be run according to democratic principles? *Business Ethics Quarterly* 24(4): 533–563. doi:10.5840/beq2014111919.

Olson, Mancur. 1965, 1971. *The logic of collective action: Public goods and the theory of groups*. Second Printing with New Preface and Appendix. Cambridge:Harvard University Press.

Pies, Ingo, Stefan Hielscher, and Markus Beckmann. 2009. Moral commitments and the societal role of business: An ordonomic approach to corporate citizenship. *Business Ethics Quarterly* 19(3): 375–401.

Pies, Ingo, Markus Beckmann, Stefan Hielscher. 2011. Competitive markets, corporate firms, and new governance – an ordonomic conceptualization. In *Corporate citizenship and new governance – The political role of corporations*, ed. Ingo Pies, and Peter Koslowski, 171–188. Dordrecht: Springer.

———. 2014. The political role of the business firm: An ordonomic concept of corporate citizenship developed in comparison with the Aristotelian idea of individual citizenship. *Business & Society* 53(2): 226–259.

Schelling, Thomas C. 1984, 2006. Self-command in practice, in policy, and in a theory of rational choice. In *Strategies of commitment and other essays*, ed. Thomas C. Schelling, 63–81. Cambridge, MA/London: Harvard University Press.

———. 1996, 2006. Coping rationally with lapses from rationality. In *Strategies of commitment and other essays*, ed. Thomas C. Schelling, 82–106. Cambridge, MA/London: Harvard University Press.

Valentinov, Vladislav, Stefan Hielscher, and Ingo Pies. 2013. The meaning of nonprofit advocacy: An ordonomic perspective. *The Social Science Journal* 50(3): 367–373.

Chapter 3
Externalities, Complexity and Justice: Exploring the New Paradigm of 'Deliberative Trade Policy'

Carsten Herrmann-Pillath

Abstract The current stalemate of the Doha round clearly reveals the severe institutional deficiencies of the design of the WTO and international trade policy. This reflects economic and socio-political developments which stay in the focus of Clark's seminal treatment of economic responsibility, namely increasing complexity and interdependence. The reality of the WTO stays in stark tension with the constitutionalist claims that have been made after its establishment. I argue that these problems partly result from adopting a wrong conceptual framework going back to Kant, coined 'transcendental institutionalism' by Amartya Sen. In the context of economics, this amounts to highlighting 'efficiency' as the ultimate beacon to evaluate institutions of international trade, against the background of general equilibrium models of 'free trade'. The alternative approach is 'realization-focused-comparisons' which entail procedural justice in including diverse values and perspectives in a deliberative process judging institutional changes and their outcomes. However, I show that the existing rules and practices of the WTO already implement realization-focused-comparisons, though incompletely and messy. My example is the TRIPS: On the one hand, the implementation of the TRIPS and recently related 'TRIPS plus' initiatives in bilateral and plurilateral trade policy initiatives clearly aim at harmonization and hence reflect the 'transcendental institutionalism' stance. On the other hand, many TRIPS rules, even the basic ones, already allow for the inclusion of diverse values and conditions. What is problematic is the fact that the interpretation of these rules is only left to the dispute settlement process, thus becomes strongly path-dependent, without allowing for systematic and comprehensive deliberative processes among all affected parties beyond their representation by member governments. I propose to move from Kant to Hegel in designing the institutional setting of 'deliberative trade policy'. Hegel offers a systematic solution to the puzzle how to reconcile the idea of national sovereignty in trade policy with the notion of a global civil society as a constitutive element of the international trade order.

C. Herrmann-Pillath (✉)
Max Weber Centre for Advanced Cultural and Social Studies, Erfurt, Germany
e-mail: cahepil@online.de

M. Haase (ed.), *Economic Responsibility*, Ethical Economy 53,
DOI 10.1007/978-3-319-52099-5_3

3.1 Complexity and Interdependence: Challenges to Global Trade Policy

From the viewpoint of many observers, the creation of the WTO[1] in 1995 was seen as the transition towards a constitution of world trade, even a first, small step towards world government.[2] Today, widespread pessimism regarding the future of this international organization reigns, and countries have re-focused their efforts in trade liberalization on concluding a rapidly growing number of regional agreements.

If we ask for the reasons of this development, a single driving force looms large which stands at the centre of attention in J. M. Clark's (1916) seminal article: complexity and interdependence. This is salient in the length and convoluted dynamics of the ongoing Doha round and shows that these problems of complexity and interdependence cannot be solved in the existing institutional setting.[3] This applies for trade policy in the narrow sense, as well as in the larger context, such as climate change policies. In this paper, I will explore the relevance of this experience in developing a new approach to trade liberalization which I coin 'deliberative trade policy'.[4] Methodologically, this approach is based on institutional economics and thus follows a long-standing tradition in international political economy research utilizing insights from economics. However, I add a substantial input from philosophy, recognizing the fact that in foundational debates over the nature of the WTO, Kant plays a towering role. I argue that the real-world experience with the WTO can

---

[1] This paper uses a number of acronyms: ACTA: Anti-Counterfeiting trade agreement; DSB: Dispute Settlement Body; GATS: General Agreement on Trade in Services; GATT: General Agreement on Tariffs and Trade; GMO: genetically modified organism; IPR: Intellectual property rights; NAFTA: North American Free Trade Agreement; TTIP: Transatlantic trade and investment partnership; TRIPS: Agreement on trade-related aspects of intellectual property rights; WTO: World Trade Organization.

[2] See, for example, Jackson (1997, pp. 339 ff.); for an overview of the debates, see Dunoff (2009).

[3] I notice that not every trade economist will agree. Bagwell and Staiger (2011) argue that the problems with the Doha round result from the fact that so far an approach is chosen for developing countries that deviates from the fundamental principle of reciprocity in trade negotiations ('special and differential treatment'). In their view, reinstating the basic GATT negotiation principles would resolve the stalemate. This follows from their general equilibrium analysis of terms of trade effects in trade policy (see below Sect. 3.2).

[4] The original statement of this is Herrmann-Pillath (2007). In that paper, I analyse trade policy as a communication process using speech act theory. The point is that communication is not only working via negotiations but also via the trade policy measures themselves, which are 'signals' of their own kind used by the different parties as communication devices. That means, 'deliberation' is not only taking place during the negotiations, but, for example, anti-dumping measures can be also seen as elements of a deliberative interaction between the parties because information is communicated and responses are sent. I use the term 'deliberation' in the standard sense of political philosophy, referring to a rational, rule-based discourse about alternative options in a community that aims at achieving a shared understanding of the issues at stake, though not necessarily resulting into consensus, but enabling coordinated action that avoids violent conflicts and impositions of power. Deliberation differs fundamentally from mere aggregation of individual preferences via voting, but includes voting as one possible way to conclude the process of deliberation. For related views on deliberation and the WTO, see Nanz and Steffens (2004) or McGrew (2011).

be better understood from a Hegelian point of view, in both positive and normative terms. My Hegelian argument reinforces the relevance of Clark's reasoning for designing international trade policy, because I interpret the notion of responsible action in terms of the radical shift from efficiency to justice as the benchmark for policy evaluation. In this shift the pivotal institutional economics idea is that efficient institutions achieve a proper level of internalization of externalities; I show that this is tantamount to claiming that the institutions are just or fair.[5]

The conceptual bridge between these two notions is built by Amartya Sen's recent distinction between 'transcendental institutionalism' and 'realization-focused-comparisons': The former presents the Kantian approach to trade policy and the analytical stance of standard economics which adopts an external standpoint in evaluating the efficiency of certain policies. The latter invokes Hegel's Kant critique (a step that I do, but which Sen overlooks) and argues that standards of evaluation can only be identified in deliberative processes in which the different affected parties are involved.[6] These processes establish evaluations in terms of justice, which at the same time also reflect endogenous criteria of efficiency, if we recognize

[5] For reasons of space I cannot discuss definitional issues in detail. My understanding of the terms 'fairness' and 'justice' is mainly grounded in economic interpretations of classical philosophical debates, which refer to 'ordinary' or 'everyday life' conceptions of fairness, aiming at pragmatic relevance. This is the intellectual tradition of Smith's 'Theory of Moral Sentiments', as received in modern economic interpretations as forwarded by Sen (2009) or, with an explicit critique of Kant, by Binmore (1994, 2005). The basic idea is that in sequences of social interactions, standards of impartiality will emerge that build on the mutual recognition of interests. In philosophical ethics, my use of the terms would amount to establishing 'thick evaluative concepts'. This includes, as we shall see, the claim that certain real world institutions such as the WTO embody certain conceptions of fairness and justice, thus reflecting major ethical concerns of the members. That corresponds to the standard economic approach that assumes that those institutions would (or, should) reflect 'efficiency', in the common sense of minimizing costs with maximal performance and output, with 'efficiency' also having both a descriptive and a normative content. The Pareto criterion of efficiency ties up with the notion of fairness used in the paper, if we consider whether in a Pareto-inefficient change of state the person who suffers a loss has the opportunity to take action against this change, thus being able to prevent it from occurring. Having to accept a Pareto-inferior change of state involuntarily would constitute a violation of fairness principles.

[6] In Boldyrev and Herrmann-Pillath (2013) we argue that Hegel is the missing link connecting Sen's combination between economics and ethics with the original contribution of Smith in the 'Theory of Moral Sentiments', which is significant in our context because Smith can be duly regarded as one of the fathers of the notion of 'free trade'. Sen (2009) refers extensively to Smith in developing his cosmopolitan vision of evaluating institutions. However, Smith clearly fails to establish a clear and concise argument why his ethics can move from particularism to universalism, see, for example, the detailed discussion in Forman-Barzilai (2010). This bridge can only be provided by Hegel, whose relationship to Smith, however, is somewhat obscure. We discuss the pertinent evidence extensively also in our book Herrmann-Pillath and Boldyrev (2014, pp. 149 ff.). Relating Sen to Hegel cannot be supported by Sen's writings directly, but in spirit. Sen (2009: 124 ff.) relates Kant's view on impartiality to Smith, but I think that there is a tension here with Sen's reference to reasoned public debate as the ultimate anchor for achieving impartiality. This is because in the public debate, impartiality emerges from the specific contributions of the different participants having different perspectives, and not from a universal principle, which is Kant's categorical imperative. Whether Smith's notion of impartiality converges with Kant's categorical imperative is a bone of contention in the philosophical literature.

analytically that externalities cannot be evaluated from the viewpoint of external observers using an allegedly objective benchmark. This Hegelian and Senian approach to deliberative trade policy entails many implications for implementing trade institutions and trade policies, in particular with regard to the inclusion of civil society in policy design processes.

This way of reasoning questions the common interpretation of 'freedom' in the notion of 'free trade', which is notoriously seen as the retreat of government from interfering with international markets by means of border-related measures, such as the classical case of tariffs. If we focus on externalities, standard economics routinely recognizes the possibility of market failure. In the context of international trade, however, this analysis becomes much more complicated because governments that intervene into domestic markets in order to cope with externalities might create new externalities in the international domain and other countries. I argue that these 'regulatory externalities' play a crucial role in the future development of the institutions of international trade.[7] One important aspect is the transfer or extension of national regulations on the international level. Since the establishment of the WTO, this has become a central feature of international trade policy, thus clearly revealing the insufficiency of the standard notion of 'freedom' in international trade, since the globalization of regulations directly impacts on the degrees of freedom of domestic policies. Whereas in the 'good old days' of the GATT 'freeing up' trade, hence trade liberalization, just meant to reduce border interventions, today the core issue is how domestic regulations affect international trade and how global trade institutions affect different countries, possibly also creating additional externalities in terms of asymmetric impacts.

In order to substantiate this analysis empirically, in this paper I will look at one of the central WTO agreements, the TRIPS (Agreement on trade-related aspects of intellectual property rights), in some more detail. On the one hand, the TRIPS aims at internalizing externalities that may result from regulatory differences in IPR institutions across countries, but at the same time the global convergence of institutions might impose asymmetric costs across different affected groups in different countries which cannot adequately take part in the design of those international institutions.

In terms of Clark's reasoning, this raises the question how responsible action is possible in designing trade policies. As is already transpiring in the previous brief discussion, this question needs to be considered on two levels. One is the level of domestic political economy, where domestic interests groups may represent their concerns to their domestic governments, yet without taking the international effects, viz. externalities, into consideration. The other is the international level, where governments need to adopt responsible attitudes in both representing their domestic constituencies and heeding attention to the legitimate interests of other governments and the domestic interests which they represent. Evidently, a core issue in this is how the WTO can mediate between highly diverse and complex domestic political economies and the governments involved in the negotiation process. On first sight,

[7] This is a view seminally deployed in Gerhart (2003).

this is manifest in the fact that the WTO is lacking a direct democratic legitimization beyond the participation and representation of member governments. But this description is too coarse, as a particularly difficult issue emerges in recognizing that all governments represent only those domestic interests that manage to get their voice recognized in the respective domestic political economy. As a result, international constellations might emerge in which groups that are affected significantly by trade policies across different countries might nevertheless lack representation on the truly relevant global level. This is what I identify as a possible failure of international trade policy in achieving both 'efficiency' and 'justice': Deficits of internalizing externalities create inefficiencies, but also imply that the lack of inclusiveness towards affected interests violates principles of justice. This raises the important question what role the WTO could play in making up for this deficiency of representation.

Thus, we can conclude that a direction for further reforms of the WTO is to eschew the traditional view of seeing the WTO as a mere mediator in international trade negotiations.[8] In the approach of deliberative trade policy, the WTO would assume a pivotal role in collectively establishing certain global standards of justice in different domains of trade policy, thus harmonizing with other institutions of the United Nations, and in developing measures to remedy the 'representation gap' in domestic political economies. In fact, using my workhorse TRIPS, I argue that actual WTO institutions and practices already have prepared the ground for this transition. One major obstacle in achieving this is the deeply ingrained normative approach to trade liberalization in standard economics. If we reconsider the idea of trade liberalization against the background of the previous reasoning, this might mean, most generally, improving and enhancing the institutional mechanisms of 'socially embedding markets'. In Ruggie's (1982) famous concept of 'embedded liberalism' this notion referred to the Bretton Woods system in toto. It applied also for the GATT and means specifically, that the GATT is not simply an institutional mechanism aiming at the liberalization of international trade, but that it leaves systematic room for governments to pursue public policy aims related to employment and social welfare. Thus, it remains the task of the national governments 'to embed' markets. The so-called 'neoliberal' shift to 'disembed' markets therefore defined itself mainly in terms of curtailing this role of governments. In this paper, I will claim that there is an alternative way to socially embed markets which breaks through the simple-minded 'state vs. market' dualism which continues to shape public debates in this area. Clark already was aware of the limitations of both polar conceptions, the 'business is business' perspective and the call for public intervention and regulation. Considering the WTO framework, this dualism is enshrined in the institutional structure because only governments are members and decide consensually about the regulation of international trade. The question is how far the institutional structure can be changed in order to overcome this dualism. In practice, that points towards enhancing the inclusion of various responsible actors in the trade policy process and incentivizing responsible action.

---

[8] This position is shared by many others, such as Charnowitz (2002, 2011) or Wilkinson (2011).

This institutional metamorphosis was firstly pushed by the Seattle events in 1999, after which the drive to include civil society in the WTO process has been gaining considerable momentum.[9] There is, however, a considerable difference between UN organizations in general and the WTO in particular. Whereas the UN is relatively flexible in creating channels of communication, inclusion and participation of civil society organizations in the policy process, the role of the WTO is more constrained because of its clearly defined procedural principles and design. These principles reflect certain basic assumptions about the nature of international trade as developed by economics, and a close orientation of economics and economic criteria in defining what interests are those that can and should be articulated in the trade policy process. Therefore, engaging in foundational philosophical and ethical reflections is of utmost importance also for practical policies. This is where Clark's legacy is alive today.

3.2 The Central Role of Externalities in Understanding the Impact of Trade Policy Institutions

Clark's early emphasis on complexity and interdependence provides the empirical starting point for my foundational reasoning. In the context of trade policy, the complexity of trade negotiations has increased tremendously in the past decades for two reasons:

- First, the number and nature of trade issues has changed substantially, today including such diverse topics such as environmental policies, food safety, labour laws or the entire field of trade in services. In the early GATT rounds, countries negotiated over lowering tariffs in trade in goods; in the 1970s, non-tariff trade restrictions came to the fore and leveraged complexity considerably. But with the creation of the WTO and the adoption of the 'single undertaking' approach as a negotiation framework, the scope and interdependence of economic and social issues in trade has increased by the order of magnitudes.[10]
- The second cause of growing complexity results from the issue-dependent formation of country interests and country coalitions. Gone are the days when just a so-called 'Third World' met with the industrialized countries. Today, we have emerging economies, transitional economies, energy exporting countries and so forth, and in areas such as agriculture the dividing lines are criss-crossing the old distinctions.[11]

[9] For a vivid 'insider' perspective, see Moore (2003).

[10] Actually, even the modest Bali agreement was only possible because the parties agreed to suspend the 'single undertaking' approach. The 'single undertaking' approach means that all possible externalities across different trade policy dimensions might be included into the negotiation agenda, which must lead to consensus. So, complexity is not just a 'given' but is also shaped by the design of the negotiation process. However, this approach also undergirded the aforementioned constitutionalist interpretations of the WTO.

[11] Costantini et al. (2007) distinguish between three different kinds of groups in contemporary trade policy: 'structural groups' such as free trade areas (e.g. NAFTA), 'Representative groups' where

Further, issues of interdependence have become much more salient. The old GATT was about border issues, and what happened within a country was plainly irrelevant for agreeing on lowering tariffs. This is fundamentally different for trade in services, where domestic regulations are an essential determinant of trade barriers, and for which therefore the separate agreement GATS was created. But beyond its pertinent scope, interdependence is driving the inclusion of environmental and social issues into regional trade agreements, among many others. However, 'interdependence' means two different things here. One is interdependence which is exogenous to trade negotiations in the first place, such as environmental issues, and which is ultimately rooted in global public goods where a wedge is driven between the individual countries' interests and global welfare. For example, if a country prohibits the import of certain products which appear to damage the environment, these damages may not even directly affect this country, but only indirectly in changing the future availability of global public goods (such as killing dolphins by certain technologies of fishing tuna). However, this trade restriction may directly harm poor workers in the exporting country. The other kind of interdependence is emerging endogenously in the trade negotiations. A foremost example is the workhorse in this paper, the TRIPS agreement which aims at creating convergence across countries regarding the protection of intellectual property rights. Then, for example, the availability of cheap pharmaceuticals for poor groups in developing countries may be affected directly in a negative way, if a certain standard for IPR protection is created that increases local prices of pharmaceuticals. Finally, interdependence is also intentionally created if, for example, as in the case of the TRIPS, different policy issues or even domains are connected in the trade negotiations, particularly against the background of the 'single undertaking' approach. So, the TRIPS was tied up with industrial countries' concessions in agricultural trade, among other linkages, which constrained the institutional choices of the developing economies with regard to detailed regulations of the TRIPS.

If we adopt an institutional economics perspective, we can approach the Clarkian theme of interdependence in terms of the notion of 'externalities'. However, I propose to extend this notion considerably beyond the common usage in economics, which focuses on consequences of economic actions that are not reflected in pricing, along Coasean lines. Beyond that, if we approach the WTO as a constitutional arrangement, we also need to consider the externalities that emerge in the trade policy negotiation process. In more detail, we have to distinguish between the level where certain general rules of international trade policy are set (the constitutional level), the level of the negotiations that are conducted under that regime and which result into trade policy institutions, and the level of trade transactions under these institutions. Then, we can directly interpret those negotiations as a 'market' of its

important players team up to push certain policy initiatives, (such as the 'Quad' of Canada, EU, Japan and the US), and the 'bargaining coalitions' which gather countries with shared interests (such as the 'Cairns group' of agricultural exporters). This diversity of groupings only emerged in the aftermath of the Uruguay round, which had been still dominated by a much smaller number of big players, in particular the US and the EU.

own kind because trade negotiations between countries are done by governments who represent their exporters' interests and which result in agreements about the exchange of rights to market access under which the trade transactions take place.[12] This is a market-like arrangement, though lacking certain features such as a medium of exchange. So, we can also apply the standard notion of externalities on this level: The exchange of market access may fail to internalize the impact of trade policy on third parties. This prepares the ground for an integrative approach to efficiency and justice by looking at trade policy institutions through the lenses of a Hegelian approach to institutions, since Hegel's theory of civil society is substantially influenced by his understanding of market exchange.[13]

I distinguish between four different kinds of externalities, which are influenced by or even directly determined by institutions and regulations, and which emerge on the two levels of markets for goods and services and markets for market access.

- The first kind is technological externalities across countries such as global warming being triggered by Chinese CO_2 emissions which are partly driven by industrial relocations from Western countries. These are externalities of economic processes that are caused by market actors, but that are also determined by the prevailing institutional setting: For example, domestic environmental regulations might fail to contain cross-border pollution, or low levels of environmental protection might trigger an international 'race to the bottom' in creating pollution havens.
- The second kind of externalities are regulatory externalities which, for instance, loom large in the context of standardization, food safety issues and other technology related policy domains, where, for example, imposing certain safety standards

[12] For an excellent survey of the negotiation principles, see Hoekman and Kostecki (2001, pp. 25 ff.). My approach adopts the perspective of constitutional economics and of certain schools of thought in Public Choice theory originating in Buchanan and Tullock's application of economic calculus on institutional arrangements for taking political decisions, such as voting systems; for an overview, see Hamlin (2013). I outline the three level structure in Herrmann-Pillath (2004, p. 465). The market-type arrangement emerges on the intermediate level because, for example, a tariff is negotiated between the governments explicitly considering the value and volume of trade transactions that would take place under this institution, and aiming at achieving reciprocity (even in the marginal sense, not in terms of absolute values). Yet, these transactions are undertaken by the market actors independently, responding to the incentives created by the new institution. So, a market access right differs fundamentally from the rights that are traded under its regime, yet it is also valued in terms of the prices and quantities that are transacted.

[13] I have developed this market paradigm of international trade policy in a number of contributions, such as Herrmann-Pillath (2006a, b; 2008). For related views which inspired my more comprehensive analysis, see Hillman and Moser (1996) or Bagwell and Staiger (2001). In Herrmann-Pillath and Boldyrev (2014, pp. 195 ff.) we establish the connection to our interpretation of Hegel's thinking about institutions. On the role of the market as a paradigm for Hegel's analysis of the civil society in his 'Grundlinien der Philosophie des Rechts', for example, as far as his notion of 'recognition' is concerned, see Neschen (2008: 178ff). So, Hegel anticipated the recent debates about Sandel's critique of markets, in which more sophisticated responses of economists aimed at highlighting the ethical foundations of market relations, see Sandel (2013) vs. Bruni and Sugden (2013).

internationally might leave domestic politics with no alternative than to impose the standard also for all domestic production and consumption.[14]

- The third kind is externalities that are directly caused by trade policy institutions of particular countries, and which are mediated via international trade. In trade theory, the narrow and classical case is terms of trade externalities. If a country is large relative to the world market and sets tariffs autonomously, this will also affect world market prices and hence the welfare of countries which do not export to this country directly. Therefore, this is a form of 'market failure' in a system which would only be based on unilateral liberalization without any mutual commitment of countries in a shared trade policy framework.[15] In this view, markets for market access are the institutional means to internalize these externalities, since the exchange of rights creates mechanisms of commitment und mutual enforcement.
- The fourth kind of externalities results on the level of markets for market access, such as when the interests of certain affected groups are not adequately reflected in the negotiation process. We need to distinguish between contingent and systematic externalities here. Contingent externalities result from certain contextual factors that impede this inclusion, such as lacking negotiation power or capacities to participate. Systematic externalities are caused by the rules of negotiations, as is typically emphasized in constitutional economics, such as when voting rules lead to disadvantages for minority positions. In international trade, we observe a new additional effect in which domestic voting can impose costs on minorities in other countries which cannot be internalized because those positions are not represented by their respective governments and the underlying majorities.[16]

In case of our empirical workhorse, we can specify the following externalities. If standards of IPR protection differ, countries with low level protection can exploit IPR of countries with high level protection. In the common view, this means that

[14]This is a big issue, for example, in the case of GMO, which are seen by many as panacea for solving the future bottlenecks in feeding the world. For example, European regulations on GMO, if being recognized by the international system, may affect purely domestic uses in developing countries' agriculture, because those countries lack the capacities for risk management in monitoring exports to the EU (for example, clearly separating GMO and non-GMO production and distribution tracks); see Stewart (2009).

[15]In Bagwell and Staiger's (2002) theory of the international trade system and the WTO, terms of trade externalities play a pivotal role. The institutions are being geared towards the purpose of internalizing these externalities. However, in this strictly economic approach only a limited number of options are considered how to achieve this internalization, which run via the channels of prices and quantities, such as tariff policies. In the Hegelian approach, as we shall see, these mechanisms are enlarged to include mechanisms of deliberation, mutual recognition and so forth. The Bagwell and Staiger approach meets substantial criticism in the literature, though being one of the leading paradigmatic approaches in contemporary trade policy theory, see, for example, Ethier (2004) or Regan (2006).

[16]This is a special twist in the standard 'taxation without representation' argument and substantiates the widespread argument that the WTO is suffering from a lack of democratic legitimization; for an overview, see WTO (2007, pp. 83 ff.).

they can benefit from innovations that are incentivized by the high-level regime, while shifting costs to these countries and producers. The globalization of an IPR regime is a way to internalize these externalities and hence may raise global efficiency of IPR, since beneficiaries of innovations pay for patents directly or indirectly via higher product prices. However, there are two fundamentally different ways to achieve this aim, harmonization and mutual recognition. This relates to the specific rules that are implemented in the trade negotiations. The TRIPS in practice so far imposes harmonization (i.e. convergence of institutions), but in fact, as we shall see, would also enable mutual recognition. Mutual recognition would mean that countries accept regulatory divergences between them under the condition that there is a policy process which resolves tensions and conflicts in particular cases. For example, if India allows much leeway for local producers of generic pharmaceuticals in its judicial procedures, this creates uncertainty for global pharmaceutical companies; this could be accommodated by implementing a more systematic, transparent and predictable process of compulsory licensing. Then, IPR standards would certainly differ across countries, but would be mutually recognized in the framework of TRIPS, because the TRIPS allows for the recognition of diverse conceptions of public interest and general welfare. So, in the mutual recognition regime a supporting institutional framework for internalization via conflict resolution is required. In case of harmonization, internalization would build on certain internalization mechanisms that alleviate the asymmetric costs of adapting to the harmonized institutions.

Finally, there are externalities that emerge on the level of the rules that govern the negotiation process. As I already mentioned, in the case of the TRIPS, combining it with the issue of market access to agriculture in developed countries was intended to serve as an internalization mechanism, taken as a mutually advantageous exchange of market access rights. Obviously, as interests and impact must differ considerably between countries, this lump sum approach of the 'single undertaking' obviously leads to internalization failures on the level of single countries which were not able to match their specific interests and costs of adapting to the TRIPS with their commitments and gains. Other relevant aspects of rules concern the regulations of dispute resolution, as we shall see later.

I will now develop my argument on the convergence between efficiency and justice in designing international trade institutions, once we follow the general idea that internalization of externalities is a central concern of institutional design. Clearly, this requires firstly, an adequate inclusion of all possibly affected parties in the process of designing the trade policy institutions, and secondly, that these institutions incorporate mechanisms that allow affected parties to resolve conflicts that result from perceived asymmetries in the distribution of the costs of trade policy and its impacts. Interestingly, we can connect this idea with Sen's distinction between two fundamentally different ways how to evaluate institutions.[17] 'Transcendental institutionalism' presupposes a convergence towards what is chosen as the transcendental reference point. Obviously, if we consider externalities we cannot assume

[17] See Sen (2009).

that such a reference point exists because the very definition of externalities implies that there is no common benchmark for valuations, especially in terms of market prices. In addition, we cannot even assume that all parties share the perceptions of the nature and type of the externalities. Therefore, the only way to reach a valuation which can also possibly be shared among different parties is via realization-focused-comparisons, which directly involve the different value-based perspectives of affected individuals and groups. What is the medium of realization-focused-comparisons? As in the original Coasian approach, this is a negotiation process, but more fundamentally, negotiations are embedded in deliberation. In the context of our topic, I refer to this process with the new notion of 'deliberative trade policy'.

The paradigm of deliberative trade policy differs fundamentally from standard views in several respects:

- Firstly, there is no conception of 'free trade' as an ideal-typical reference for trade policy in the sense of institutionally unconstrained market access. The prevailing view in trade theory approaches institutions mostly as 'trade restricting', and less as 'trade enabling'. Thus, I introduce the Hegelian notion of 'freedom' as a generic reference in considering the meaning of 'free': Freedom is a state which can only be enabled by institutions, and which includes not only rights, but also capabilities to trade and participation in trade governance.
- Secondly, I correspondingly criticize the standard thinking as being geared towards 'transcendental institutionalism'. This has important implications for interpreting the current shape of trade negotiations. Most economists think that this is mostly inefficient haggling over special interests of countries and industries.[18] I argue that in fact the institutional evolution of the trade regime already reflects and partially implements what Sen calls 'realization-focused-comparisons'.
- Thirdly, deliberative trade policy is inclusive in the sense of explicitly heeding respect for consumers' and hence citizens' interests in the negotiation process, beyond their representation by the governments that are the principal actors of trade policy up to date. This is what is actually increasingly relevant in practice, but cannot yet fully be reflected in the legal framework of the WTO which is based on the standard model.

As we see, my approach builds on theoretical and philosophical conceptions that have been worked out by Amartya Sen, but have been rarely applied on international trade policy so far, if at all. I think that this notion of deliberation is also a hallmark of Clark's approach, who does not use the term, of course, but effectively roots his

[18] A much cited critique of real-world trade negotiations is Krugman (1997) who exposes of what he sees as implicit mercantilism in trade negotiations. Indeed, in the simplest model of 'free trade', this idea is just an application of the general principle of division of labour and market exchange; against this background all institutional constraints for market exchange must appear as 'inefficiencies' and hence 'irrational'. Once one considers the question of whether and how institutions of free trade can be sustained, apparently 'mercantilist' policies and negotiation frameworks may make sense, as has been shown in a stream of literature originating in seminal contributions such as Bagwell and Staiger (1990).

idea of responsible action in a deliberative discourse. On a more fundamental level, I go back to Hegel's practical ethics and theory of civil society.

3.3 From Kant to Hegel: Rethinking 'Free' Trade

3.3.1 Limits to Kantian Constitutionalism in the International Domain

In foundational thinking about the international trade regime, Kant is the towering referent. This reference suggests the idea of an increasing constitutionalisation of the trade regime via the gradual transition to a global federal structure in which the rights and obligations of states are enshrined. The Kantian legacy implies that only in such an institutional framework rights to free trade would be recognized as cosmopolitan *individual* rights, like human rights (and not just as rights of governments). This view is not only cosmopolitan in outlook, but is also based on the notion of legal monism, that means, ultimately the international trade system must be based on one single and coherent legal framework.[19]

There are two difficult problems with this view. The first is empirical. Although one can certainly envision constitutionalisation, the current WTO regime does not manifest corresponding traits, and in fact, the failure of the Doha round reveals these constitutional weaknesses. The second problem is the tension between the notion of a constitution and the lack of democratic legitimization of the WTO: In the WTO process, national governments represent sovereign interests, which in turn are not constitutionally rooted in democratic procedures, and there is no direct democratic mechanism which mediates a potential trade constitution with policies. Obviously, the idea of a democratic legitimization of the WTO is an utopian idea and stays in deep tension with the concurrent idea of legal monism: The WTO aims at unifying the legal order for the trade system, implying that countries become members without any conditioning with regard to the domestic political system or human rights performance.[20]

[19] One leading protagonist of the Kantian approach is Petersmann (1997, pp. 23 ff.). However, Petersmann also points out that Kant originally envisaged an evolutionary process of 'republics' establishing those structures, that is, he took a peculiar domestic political constitution as the precondition. As I will discuss below, this already presupposes a high degree of institutional convergence across those countries, whereas the WTO system today includes all kinds of political systems, apart from a few rogue or failed states. On the issue of legal monism see Kumm (2009) who argues that this connection between constitutionalism and legal monism is misplaced as constitutionalism can be also seen as a framework of legal pluralism.

[20] For an extensive overview of empirical evidence against the constitutionalist interpretations of the WTO see Dunoff (2009). According to Dunoff, the constitutionalist reasoning seems to be fashionable among trade economists and trade lawyers because this is seen as a venue to depoliticize international trade policy in the sense of the strong impact of interest groups on institu-

In a nutshell, the problem with the constitutionalist claims is that we cannot yet identify a global 'demos' that is the ultimate reference of the constitutionalist 'we, the people', if only because of the simple fact that the members of the WTO are governments, not individuals. Does this mean that the idea of a constitutionalisation is doomed to fail? I think, not, if we radically change our basic conceptual framework. This is possible if we move from Kant to Hegel and thereby eschew the idea of legal and institutional monism. Granted, Hegel is certainly a very surprising reference in discussing international trade policy. However, recently we observe an upsurge of interest in Hegel's practical philosophy in general, but also in the context of international relations theory, especially with regard to questions of how a sustainable and just international order can be maintained in the face of the diversity of cultures and political systems in the world.[21]

Hegel is mostly cited as a 'realist' in international relations theory.[22] He criticised Kant's approach to cosmopolitanism in arguing that legal institutions need to be anchored in certain more fundamental notions of 'ethical life' ('Sittlichkeit') which are peculiar to different ethnic groups and nations and which evolve in a historical process. In Hegel's view, national sovereignty is paramount and represented in political institutions, in his original writings, literally the monarch as the sovereign. Countries stay in a competitive relationship with each other, and the dynamics of this competition, which often turns to military means, is driving 'world history' ('Weltgeschichte'). World history is the ultimate arbiter of the fate of single countries and manifests increasing realization of freedom as conceptualized in Hegel's theory of civil society. Although this dynamics appeared to culminate in protestant Prussian enlightened absolutism of Hegel's times, Hegel himself was open towards further developments, for instance, like his contemporaries such as Goethe, regarding America as the country of the future. World history is not seen as a Hobbesian

tional design. However, as he rightly states, in fact it was the 'trade diplomacy' approach of the former GATT which was less politicized than the WTO, though being less inclusive.

[21] On the ongoing revival of Hegel in the Anglo-Saxon world, see Beiser (2008), with leading contributions such as Pippin (2008). As far as his practical and social philosophy is concerned, this relates to the much-misunderstood analysis of Fukuyama (1992) who emphasized that Hegel presents a systematic and comprehensive alternative approach to a liberal political order compared with the Anglo-Saxon contractarian one. Indeed, the latter view cements the simple dualism of state versus individual (market) that has driven the evolution of the design of the international economic order after World War II. For a survey of the current debate on Hegel in the context of international relations, see Buchwalter (2012b).

[22] A fundamental difference between economics and certain influential schools of thought in international political economy (cf. Gilpin 2001) is that economics follows the methodological principle of 'methodological individualism', whereas 'realism' supposes that states are autonomous actors pursuing independent interests, mainly defined in terms of relative power. This implies that economics necessarily adopts an interest-group based analytical approach to trade policy. For an overview of these different methodological approaches in analysing international trade, see WTO (2007: Part B). Quante (2011, chapter 12) discusses Hegel's philosophy against the background of those methodological distinctions and concludes that Hegel's approach is 'vertically holistic', that is, Hegel posits higher-level social entities such as the state, however, emphasizing causal interdependencies and relations of mutual recognition.

state without order, but states develop relations of mutual recognition out of which norms of inter-state behaviour emerge which, however, fall short of the Kantian ideal of 'perpetual peace'.[23]

Hegel was deeply sceptical about cosmopolitan legal monism because different nations represent different cultural traditions and historical legacies. For him, however, shared culture was a necessary condition for sustainable and workable legal and political institutions of the 'civil society'.[24] This idea is helpful if we consider the perceived deficit of democracy in global institutions such as the WTO today. From the Hegelian view, the question is of secondary importance as to whether there are formal institutions of democratic participation in a global organization, because what matters in the first place is whether there are values shared across the different nations which would only make those institutions work successfully. We can draw a positive insight from this argument: Evidently, if we think about the possibility of global democracy, what counts is whether deliberative processes are enabled in the first place, and only in the next step whether we can establish formal democratic procedures in the global policy process. Here, the notion of deliberation refers to a public sphere in which different groups participate and conduct a discourse that aims at creating shared values or preferences, and which enables mutual understanding and recognition of diverse values and opinions. From this perspective, the constitutionalist interpretations of the WTO may only fail if they manifest a bias towards electoral mechanisms of democracy, or, more fundamentally, argue in a contractarian framework, and overlook the deliberative dimension.[25]

[23] For a seminal clarification of Hegel's approach to international relations, see Vincent (1983), for the comparison with Kant see Mertens (1995) and for a systematic overview in the context of Hegel's philosophy see Hicks (2012). It is important that Hegel sees philosophy as a 'science', hence a descriptive and analytical endeavour. So, his approach to international relations refers to the conditions of his times. That affects, for example, his conception of war, which is certainly problematic from a contemporary point of view, and envisages rule-based and limited warfare which expresses the emotional commitments of citizens to the fundamental values of civil society, see Smith (1983). Browning (2012) shows how Hegel's views on war relate to his famous analysis of the 'struggle for recognition' on the level of the individual in the 'Phenomenology of Spirit'.

[24] Already at this point, following Stillman (2012) among others, it is important to notice that although civil society is rooted in the ethical life of particular communities and societies, some of its principles are cosmopolitan, since they relate to the organization of economic activity in a universal fashion, which in turn allows also for the acceptance of cultural diversity in civil society (such as non-discrimination on the marketplace). This is why Hegel also believed that international trade can be a mediator of the universalization of values, thus reflecting earlier notions of 'doux commerce'. Buchwalter (2012a) describes the interaction between universal values and local ethical life as 'glocalized cosmopolitanism'. In this respect. Hegel seems to closely follow up with Adam Smith's related ideas, compare the analysis in Forman-Barzilai (2010).

[25] This exactly matches with contemporary debates over the WTO beyond the framework established by economics. For example, Nanz and Steffek (2004) criticize views that simply assess the WTO against the backdrop of existing models of national democratic systems, and also propose the perspective of deliberative democracy which includes many more channels and mechanisms of citizens' participation. These academic viewpoints fit well into post-Seattle thinking of leading

The most straightforward way to explore the Hegelian perspective on international trade is to reflect upon the foundational notion of 'freedom' in the free trade doctrine, which basically also underlies the intuitive understanding of trade liberalization, namely in the sense of approaching the ideal state of 'free trade'.

3.3.2 The Hegelian View on 'Sovereignty' in Trade Liberalization

What is the meaning of 'freedom' in the context of liberalizing trade by means of TRIPS and related institutions? Clearly, the IPR system is a means to balance freedoms of action of different groups, producers of knowledge, competing producers, users and consumers. The existing framework emphasizes the individual freedom of producers of knowledge in safeguarding their interests as 'owners' of knowledge, thus apparently adopting the Kantian approach towards seeing the international trade order as a constitutional means to protect individual rights in the economic domain. However, even in this respect the freedom of other producers might be curtailed, also in the sense of impairing their capacities to generate competing new knowledge, such as in case of the current business practice of accumulating patent rights in order to block other companies entering these tracks of innovation, even if the owner does not use the patents.

This observation leads us to reconsider the notion of free trade in a threefold way, receiving and adapting the three Hegelian dimensions of personal, moral and social freedom.[26] In doing this, I abstract from the primary reference to persons, but generalise over the abstract notion of agency, which can also be ascribed to political organisations such as governments. Personal autonomy can be conceived as 'sovereignty' in this context. Indeed, in the original Hegelian notion, personal freedom does not mean to do what one wants but refers to the sovereignty of the individual mind over desires, that is, the capacity to take purely autonomous actions without being pushed by inner drives, desires, and other natural determinants of action in the sense of causal forces. This understanding of personal freedom builds on Hegel's theory of the will, and Hegel also applied this on the role of the sovereign, thus exactly implementing this transition from natural persons to abstract agency in other domains, such as governments.

---

trade diplomats, such as in Pascal Lamy's (2001) notion of 'cosmopolitics' as a new agenda for the WTO.

[26] This distinction follows Neuhouser (2008). In Herrmann-Pillath and Boldyrev (2014, pp. 155 ff.) we show that this interpretation can be matched with Sen's capability approach, which I cannot further detail here but provides the background of the subsequent reasoning. The starting point is to recognize that Hegel's most fundamental notion of freedom of the will matches with Sen's critique of the economic notion of rationality in his famous argument about 'rational fools'. Sen argues that the traditional economic agent cannot be considered as free because she cannot choose her preferences. In contrast, a free and rational person is able to choose simultaneously means and ends of actions.

If we transfer this thinking to trade policy, we reach a first intriguing insight: Freedom in international trade would be interpreted as sovereign freedom in participating in or constraining trade, hence giving ultimate priority to the national actors, and not to the individual actors, as in the aforementioned modern Kantian interpretations.[27] On first sight, this seems to concur with the realist position in international relations, and indeed underlies the WTO framework as well: In the WTO, only governments are recognized as actors, and individuals or interest groups can only influence the WTO process if they act via the representation of their governments. But the notion of sovereignty in the Hegelian sense also means that trade policy, in direct correspondence with the Hegelian analysis of the individual, should be isolated from the impact of domestic interest groups, in analogy to personal autonomy from inner drives.[28] Taking TRIPS as an example, the US position was clearly driven by powerful industry lobbies and did not even include the interests of domestic consumers of knowledge (being affected by many forms of impact, reaching from very high costs of pharmaceuticals to very restrictive applications of copyrights in the cultural industries). Thus, Hegelian 'free trade' would insulate trade policy from these influences, interpreting sovereignty in *both* the contexts of international relations *and* domestic political economy.[29]

This idea is by no means new in the context of game theoretic analyses of trade policy, especially regarding so-called 'two level games'.[30] Here, the question is whether governments can commit themselves to policies that are conducive to

[27] For reasons of limited space, I cannot discuss the systematic reasons of why governments emerged as primary carriers of agency in international trade policy, for an extensive discussion see Herrmann-Pillath (2004, 2008). We can just take it as a current fact, but if we look at the problem of externalities and legal ordering in general, it is straightforward to show that governments necessarily have to act as representatives of their national constituencies, as long as they are universally recognized as the primary source and enforcer of law. Indeed, as Teubner (1997) discusses in detail, the role of individual actors might only come to the fore once we consider a wholesale dissolution of international law in a complex network of non-governmental legal orderings.

[28] This understanding of sovereignty is unusual, of course. For example, Bagwell and Staiger (2004) adopt the current understanding in political science which is the 'Westphalian' notion: Sovereignty means insulation of domestic policies from external influences. So, an externality caused by other governments' policy choices impairs sovereignty, or any international agreement that shifts purely domestic policy considerations away from the original optimum.

[29] Consider well-established models of the policy process in economics, going back to seminal papers such as Grossman and Helpman (1994, 1996). In these models, governments have preferences, in particular incumbents aim at re-election, and they might weigh general welfare partially. This allows defining 'political support functions'. Then, the actions of governments are strictly determined causally by the preferences and the givens. The governments cannot 'free' themselves from this causation, like the Hegelian animal which is just driven by its natural instincts. This assumption is fundamental for understanding the peculiar theoretical developments in modern theorizing about trade policy and international institutions; compare Regan (2006).

[30] For an overview, see Snidal and Thompson (2004). They emphasize the role of internal state structure for determining the nature of international agreements. Interestingly, in a highly centralized state, international agreements solve the problem that this apparently powerful actor nevertheless cannot credibly commit itself to a certain policy. This is exactly the Hegelian problem of will. For an interesting case study that highlights this reasoning, see Young (2011).

sovereign interests reflecting some notion of general welfare, though confined to their constituencies. Then, international agreements might be necessary to achieve this commitment, countervailing the impact of domestic special interests. So, considering the IPR issue in the US today, many observers agree that the IPR system has evolved into a dysfunctional state because domestic industries abuse the system in order to protect market positions and to generate rents, even if they are not active in innovation. This might be a case of sovereign weakness facing the actions of special interest groups. Then, an international agreement can provide commitment mechanisms which stabilize institutions that are also in the sovereign interest.

I conclude that it is the international system that provides for sovereign autonomy, so that we cannot start out from assuming this as a given on which the analysis of the international system might be based. This is a Hegelian turn in the notion of 'free trade': Governments do not enter the trade policy process as autonomous and sovereign actors, but it is the trade policy process that only enables them to *become* this kind of actors. Certainly, even though this statement does not match with the formal and legal definition of sovereignty in international law, it is by no means perverting the facts. Even the WTO officially pronounces as one of its functions that, via the help of the WTO, governments can become more independent from the impact of domestic interest groups.[31]

This is a Hegelian claim: Free trade presupposes sovereign autonomy, and is only jeopardized if this autonomy is undermined by special interest groups, and it is the international system of states which actually creates the conditions for sovereign autonomy, and not the other way round. The WTO enshrines the idea that the international system constitutes the capability of national governments to represent the idea of 'general welfare' vis à vis individual actors in their constituencies.

3.3.3 Recognition and the Democratic Deficiency of International Trade Policy

Achieving the Hegelian autonomy of national policies is close to impossible in current democratic systems, and probably only partially possible in certain authoritarian settings, such as purportedly during the heyday of the 'East Asian miracle'.[32] In this view, the dilemma of democratic trade policy in a national context is that it cannot possibly maintain a political equilibrium in which free trade emerges as a

[31] "The WTO system helps governments take a more balanced view of trade policy. They are better-placed to defend themselves against lobbying from narrow interest groups by focusing on trade-offs that are made in the interests of everyone in the economy" (http://www.wto.org/english/thewto_e/whatis_e/10thi_e/10thi05_e.htm).

[32] A classical statement is Amsden (1991). In explaining the transition to an export-oriented development strategy in a number of East Asian countries such as Taiwan and South Korea, political scientists emphasized the relative autonomy of authoritarian governments which at that time, for example, were able to implement and enforce performance based subsidy schemes for exporters.

solution.[33] However, perspectives change when we consider Hegelian 'moral freedom'. Moral freedom means to be able to rationally decide upon the rules that would govern one's behaviour. Evidently it is impossible to take this decision independent from others who also follow those rules, unless one party can unilaterally impose rules on all others. This is the point where Hegelian dialectics introduces radically new perspectives, because now 'recognition' ('Anerkennung') comes into play. On the individual level, recognition is essential to create individual freedom because only then rule-based behaviour is possible at all. The moral freedom of the individual can only be realized in the interaction with others, including mutual recognition.

If we apply these ideas to trade policy, and consider the democratic setting, an intricate problem emerges. As I mentioned earlier, conventional trade policy can be best understood in a market paradigm, namely as mutual exchange of market access rights. Lacking a medium of exchange and valuation, this means that in trade negotiations, the different parties need to mutually assess and compare the costs and benefits of certain agreements. Considering democratic systems, that amounts to comparing the valuations and the weighting of different interest groups across different countries.[34] For example, regarding IPR, there is an interest group in the industrial countries, which represents producers, and another one in developing countries, which presents producers and consumers. In the standard GATT negotiation framework, an agreement can only be reached when the different governments also recognize the valuations of other governments, and then compare these with their own valuations. This problem is well known in social contract theory under the heading of 'empathy': Mutual understanding and recognition is necessary not only to reach the agreement but also for implementing it in a uniform way.[35]

[33] In the aforementioned economic models of trade policy lobbyism (Grossman and Helpman 1994 and others), free trade emerges if the policy process is fully inclusive, thus balancing out the diverse interests. However, as I detail in Herrmann-Pillath (2004), building on seminal contributions such as Magee et al. (1989) or Furubotn (1998), this overlooks the political transaction costs and dissipation of rents in rent-seeking activities. Either asymmetric political transaction costs such as of the Olson type would always result in interest-biased deviations from free trade, or the resource costs of expanding inclusiveness would finally consume the gains from trade (which Magee et al. call a 'black hole').

[34] This argument follows the seminal approach by Sykes (1996) and Schwartz and Sykes (1996). These authors show how the many exceptions in the rules of the WTO (such as anti-dumping) actually imply that governments indirectly weigh and compare the costs and benefits of certain actions across countries. Interestingly, as Gerhart (2003) points out, this relates to a serious constitutional issue in the international order: Sovereign actions create externalities across countries, without offering a channel for affected parties in other countries to influence the pertinent decisions. For example, a tariff that affects world prices via Terms-of-Trade externalities is a case of 'taxation without representation'.

[35] For the general role of empathy in social contract theory see Binmore (1994) which Binmore extends to the theory of justice in Binmore (2005). In political science, and even in the literature on trade policy, this is taken into account in theories of 'integrative leadership', see Deese (2008, p. 18). An integrative leader in trade policy negotiations is an actor who is able to understand valuations of others and can strike a balance across these different valuations in submitting proposals that could finally be accepted by all parties.

If we interpret 'free trade' in Hegel's terms of moral freedom, an ongoing process of mutual recognition is absolutely necessary, which we can see as the pivotal element of deliberative trade policy. This has immense consequences for the evaluation of trade policies. Take, for example, the current wave of concluding regional trading agreements, which is mostly seen as a negative development from the vantage point of transcendental institutionalism of standard trade theory. Mutual recognition is more easily to achieve if countries share a historical legacy, culture or are bound together by closely aligned interests: All this amounts to the enhanced capacity for mutually understanding the costs and benefits of a certain trade policy measure.[36] However, in the transcendental-institutionalist perspective, regionalism directly violates criteria of allocative efficiency and leads to redistribution between members and non-members which might lead to global welfare losses in the aggregate. If we take a process-based perspective and, hence the realization-focused-comparisons view, we would argue that regionalism is a process which at the same time changes the valuations and interests of the different partners and groupings such that in the end the goal of multilateralism might be achieved. In our context, therefore, we might interpret regionalism as being part and parcel of a deliberative trade policy regime: Regionalism would obtain a systematic role in the multilateral WTO process, hence could be seen as an important constitutional element.[37]

So, we can summarize the discussion of the 'moral freedom' aspect of free trade that this defines free trade in terms of the mutual recognition of institutional and regulatory divergence reflecting the diversity of interests and valuations across countries.[38] This is clearly very different from the 'level playing field' approach that emphasizes institutional convergence and harmonization. Mutual recognition is the pivotal element in internalizing cross-border externalities and hence making up for the fundamental deficiency of democratic mechanisms in expressing domestic interests in other countries whose governments nevertheless affect those interests via the impact of their decisions channeled through international trade. This even applies for unilateral liberalization: This creates market access for exporters of other countries, but there is a negative externality for importers, because the stronger demand

[36] For a theoretical approach based on my 'market exchange' paradigm, see Herrmann-Pillath (2006a, b). This has been well-established empirically, see, for example, WTO (2013, p. 206), where it is shown that there is a positive correlation between a measure of cultural closeness and the prevalence of so-called 'deep' preferential trading agreements.

[37] For an excellent survey of these different interpretations, see WTO (2011: part C). These different viewpoints often directly reflect different disciplinary backgrounds, such as economics vs. political science or trade law. The debate is often moulded in the opposition between regional agreements as 'stumbling stones' vs. 'building blocks'. In economics, the 'building block' view has been most vocally supported by Baldwin (e.g. 1997). His approach comes very close to a deliberative framework because he emphasizes the endogeneity of trade policy preferences in evolving regional structures. For the constitutional interpretation of regionalism, see Herrmann-Pillath (2006b).

[38] I want to emphasize that this view does not necessarily contradict some established positions in economics. One of the leading trade economists, Jagdish Bhagwati, has always been highly critical of harmonization claims in international trade policy, see Bhagwati (1996).

for the exporting countries currency may induce an appreciation.[39] Hence, even in this ideal-typical case of transcendental institutionalism flowing out from self-interested 'enlightened' policies, there remains an efficiency gap in terms of externalities; closing the gap requires internalization, which is only viable via a deliberative process in which a shared view on diverse valuations of trade policy outcomes is achieved.

3.3.4 Capabilities and Inclusiveness of the International Trade Policy Process

Mutual recognition, however, does not suffice for completing the picture of deliberative trade policy, because in complex processes of deliberation involving many actors, the question arises as to who can actually participate and adequately articulate their concerns. Turning to the Hegelian 'social freedom' aspect, we include the Senian capability perspective which clearly has been anticipated in Hegel's conception of rights in emphasizing not only the formal rights dimension, but also the capabilities of individuals to understand, claim and enforce rights. This directly translates into the trade policy dimension on different levels. On the more specific level, we ask whether countries are included in the policy process, and whether they have the capacity to activate trade policy institutions in their own interest. It has been recognized in the trade policy literature for long that the current process is lacking full inclusiveness, and that capabilities differ a lot across countries. This applies both for the negotiations in general and for using instruments such as dispute settlement in particular. Even when joining and using the institutional means, capacities in terms of personnel and expertise may be limited. Indeed, critics of the TRIPS agreement had argued that one reason why developing countries agreed was that their trade negotiators simply did not overlook all the consequences.[40]

This discussion pinpoints the capabilities of countries. If we look at the individuals, the problems are more complex and again relate to the notion of externalities. The WTO system does not provide any institutional means for affected groups directly participating in the trade policy process, which is an essential determinant of their capacities to influence the policy process: affected interests can only influence trade policy via their governments. So, their capabilities in participating in trade policy are determined by the capabilities to raise political support in the

[39] On this argument, see in detail Coates and Ludema (2001).

[40] Leading trade economists criticised the results of the Uruguay round for these reasons, see, for example, Panagariya (2000) or Finger and Nogués (2002). For an overview on the capacity issue in trade policy, see Hoekman and Kostecki (2001, pp. 391 ff.). In applying Sen's notion of 'capability' here, I skip the complex issue how individual and collective capabilities connect. Sen's approach originally focuses on individual capabilities, but my reasoning refers to collective capabilities. Sen (2009: 244 ff.) is aware of this dimension and clearly recognizes the role of collective capabilities, yet also is sceptical about conflating individual and group identities.

domestic political scene. This creates a considerable tension with the cosmopolitan interpretation of the alleged 'constitutional' character of the WTO. There is no guarantee that the political constellations of the highly diverse national scenes will result in a proper representation of interests in the global context. Here, again, TRIPS is an excellent example: Powerful domestic lobbies in the US influence a powerful government which is able to shape global trade policies, but affected groups in other countries may not be able to influence their government accordingly. Even within the US, similar groups might fail to impact on trade policy decisions of the US government. In particular, sovereign interests in other domains such as security might filter this domestic impact in an even more biased fashion.

We see that against the background of the Hegelian notion of social freedom, the current world trade system manifests a highly distorted and constrained distribution of social capabilities in participating in trade policy. Again, we observe a clash between the ideational foundations and real-world practice. In fact, the WTO is active in expanding the scope of groups that might participate in trade policy in some way, just as the UN system in general has been opening up in the recent two decades. But certainly this process is much slower in case of the WTO, because of its origin in trade diplomacy and its principle of being a member-driven organization, with only governments being acceptable in the club.[41] But there is also a fundamental issue, even paradox here: As we have seen, the WTO perceives itself as a bulwark against special interest groups. So, opening up channels of influence for affected groups would mean to open up the WTO to interest group politics. Indeed, I have previously argued that the WTO actually creates the conditions for sovereignty in the domestic political economy, hence the capability to pursue general welfare goals. How can we resolve this paradox?[42]

Can the Hegelian perspective help? One aspect of Hegel's practical philosophy looms large: This is the role of the public and of civil society. Here, we can envisage enlargements and modifications of his position which, however, still keep his original basics. In spite of his idea that sovereignty also needs to be embodied in a sovereign who is not democratically elected, he nevertheless assigned a very important role to public opinion and to consultative mechanisms. The latter emerge out of civil society which Hegel perceived as a 'market society': That means, civil society would be structured according to occupational distinctions, hence economic

[41] On the role of diplomatic procedures and norms in the GATT and the WTO, see Weiler (2001). These principles still loom large, for example, in negotiations over regional trade agreements and therefore lead to clashes with public demands about transparency, as recently in the TTIP case.

[42] Van den Bossche (2008) offers a detailed and comprehensive overview about the engagement of the WTO with NGOs. Comparing this analysis with the current status as reflected on the WTO website, there has been not much progress (see http://www.wto.org/english/forums_e/ngo_e/ngo_e.htm). Basically, even accredited NGOs only have special access to certain information, but mainly it is the WTO that targets NGOs in its public relations activities (such as the 'public forum'), and refrains from creating a direct participatory role, such as by granting certain NGOs observer status, as it is practice at other UN organizations. This can be partly explained by the resistance of member countries, as in the case of including amicus curiae briefs in the dispute settlement process.

functions, and the resulting associations would have the task and the right to regulate economic activities in their domain. What would that imply for trade policy?

This depends on whether one views civil society as being constrained to the national domain. This was certainly Hegel's original viewpoint, but is not a systematically necessary assumption. In a global economy markets and functional roles transcend the nation state, for example, with companies operating transnationally. Indeed, Hegel's original view appears to result into what I have identified above as the standard interest group approach in trade policy. In this approach, if extended to including the global interactions, trade policy measures would actually operate like a substitute for democratic consultations, as we have seen above. That points towards an alternative which is actually already operative in many domains, such as technological standards: Apart from the sovereign model of nations negotiating over institutions, one can imagine a global civil society where global associations of industries would participate in the policy process. This would result into an internalization of disputes over regulations. For example, if there were a global federation of national associations of pharmaceutical industries, issues of IPR could be negotiated within that framework with implicating the national governments.[43]

In this context, it is important to notice that in the WTO setting, different from other areas of UN organizations, member governments appear to be extremely reluctant to open up the WTO to civil society. So far the dispute resolution process, apart from the negotiation rounds, is almost the only audience where realization-focused-comparisons can take place. Civil society could participate by way of the amicus curiae practice (i.e. inviting opinions of concerned, but non-litigant parties in Common Law regimes), which is not systematically defined in the WTO agreements, but has been launched as a new practice by Appellate Body decisions. However, member countries mostly oppose this practice, such that the role of amici curiae is highly circumscribed until today. Clearly, one way of reforming the system is to acknowledge the pivotal role of the dispute resolution process as a forum of realization-focused-comparisons, and not just as a means of conflict resolution, given the fact that the Panels and the Appellate Body actually create case law that interprets and often only gives operational meaning to what is frequently a very vague wording of the agreements. Then, establishing a systematic and regular rule for civil society participation would be a Hegelian reform of the system. This step would need to be linked up with an approach to foster the capabilities of governments in dealing with such an enlarged and more complex judicial process.[44]

---

[43] Teubner (1997) therefore argues that one possible direction of the evolution of global law might be its 'de-etatization' in the sense of becoming embedded into networks of private or para-governmental organizations, along the lines of international commercial law. My Hegelian view does not concur, because national governments retain an essential constitutional role as an intermediate level where domestic and global valuations of legal rules are negotiated, thus mediating between a national view on general welfare and a global one.

[44] For an overview of the amicus curiae practice in the WTO, see Squatrito (2012). Squatrito investigates into the factors that drive governments' willingness to include amici curiae in dispute resolution procedures. Interestingly, it does not play a role whether these governments are themselves

The Hegelian approach also allows for a broadening the concept of civil society. In practice, this often means that NGOs are involved which are both non-governmental and not-for-profit even in the stronger sense that they are not part of the global trade and business systems, such as humanitarian organizations, human rights initiatives or environmental groups. This definition is by far too narrow. As we have seen, Hegel's notion of civil society was very different because he lived in an historical period in which markets and business themselves where driving the emergence of a civil society separate from the 'old order'. Yet, this role of market-based civil society is actually also evident in global trade policy. One area that I mentioned already is standardization, and most conspicuously in the context of what has been emerging as a core phenomenon in twenty first century trade, namely global supply chains. Here we observe what has been coined 'non-state market-driven governance systems' which do no longer only affect narrow economic topics such as technological standards but increasingly issues that are also characteristic for civil society in the previous sense, such as standards on eco-labelling, fair trade or sustainable forestry. These standards are managed by global organizations that have been established on business initiative, hence are 'market driven', yet we can say that these are civil society initiatives in the Hegelian vein.[45]

What is important here is the fact that such standards are not directly covered by WTO agreements, though they can be accommodated, for example, in the context of the Agreement on Technical Barriers to Trade. As long as governments do not legally subscribe to the standards, it would be impossible to involve the Dispute Settlement Body even in case that a private standard would result into trade barriers, for example between a developed and a developing country, because the latter is lacking capacities to meet the standard. Then, the limitations of the existing WTO system spring to the eye: One the one hand, we observe the emergence of trade governance structures which are entirely out of the scope of the WTO, but if the WTO were to include these standards in its jurisdiction, the WTO would assume responsibilities and tasks that go far beyond its original mission and are currently, if at all, covered by other UN organizations. That means, again, only via a fundamental reform of the WTO in the direction of growing inclusiveness would help to resolve this contradiction.

liberal democracies. The single most important determinant is legal capacity; that means whether the governments can rely on pertinent expertise to deal with the procedure. This matches with my 'social freedom' perspective.

[45] For a detailed analysis of this phenomenon and its analytical assessment relative the established conceptions of trade policy, see the excellent contribution by Bernstein and Hannah (2008). Interestingly, since 2002 there is an umbrella organization of different organizations in the area of sustainability standards, ISEAL (http://www.isealalliance.org/). This differs significantly from the largest and very comprehensive ISO organization in being a multi-stakeholder initiative in which members also participate in governing business practices via ongoing policy decisions. Therefore, ISO is being criticised as showing similar biases as the WTO, for example regarding capabilities of developing countries to participate. ISO has observer status at three WTO committees.

3.3.5 *Interim Conclusion*

To summarize the 'Hegelian turn' in understanding the WTO and international trade policy, I propose a radical rethinking of the idea of trade liberalization which is based on Hegel's analysis of freedom. However, this is not merely a normative position, but I also claim that the Hegelian view makes better sense of what WTO negotiators are really doing and what they achieve. In the standard view, these negotiations often are portrayed as haggling over special interests that are represented by self-interested governments. In my view, they appear to be an example of realization-focused-comparisons that would aim at identifying, evaluating and ultimately internalizing externalities that result from international trade policies. Then, the WTO would be conceived as an element of an evolving constitution of international trade that makes up for the deficiencies of purely domestic political processes that fail to internalize those externalities. The fundamental Hegelian prerequisite for this to happen is that the international interactions constitute the domestic governments as autonomous actors vis à vis domestic special interests, thereby creating the conditions for identifying and pursuing the national and global common interest. This is what I regard resulting into a transition from efficiency to justice as the benchmark for evaluating trade policies.

3.4 Disentangling TRIPS: Misplaced Transcendental Institutionalism and the Potential for Realization-Focused-Comparisons

3.4.1 *Global Political Economy and Value-Based Imposition of IPR Regimes*

Let us now substantiate the Hegelian analysis by looking at the TRIPS agreement and intellectual property rights in some more detail. On first sight, the TRIPS agreement clearly is a case of applied transcendental institutionalism and hence, the Kantian view. There is widespread agreement among certain intellectual circles that the protection of intellectual property rights is a precondition of innovation and sustainable growth. If national IPR systems differ, regulatory arbitrage is possible and a race to the bottom. Systems with low protection can exploit knowledge created in systems with high protection. Therefore, runs the argument, it is necessary to unify the global IPR legal regime. TRIPS imposed this in parts. Via regional trading agreements, industrialized countries push this process of institutional convergence further on: So, we also observe a sort of linear progression towards the 'transcendental' institutional reference point.[46] As we have seen, the TRIPS creates

[46] There is no room for a more detailed empirical analysis in this paper. Suffice to mention that both the US and the EU are very active in including extensions of the TRIPS into diverse regional trade

a number of externalities on its own, which we can take as a starting point for a Hegelian reconsideration.

IPR are of special interest from a Hegelian perspective, as they are purely artificial means of creating an economic asset beyond the material goods that are mainly the object of international trade. In creating them, it is already necessary to apply a weighting procedure that compares the interests of different affected parties. Indeed, even though there seems to be general agreement that IPR are necessary to foster technological change and cultural creativity, there is almost no foundation for any other 'transcendental' claims regarding the specific design of IPR, such as the appropriate length of IPR protection via the legal validity of rights (duration of patents), or the scope of rights (for example, regarding the inclusion of software). However, one can also take a more negative attitude and approach IPR from a pure political economy perspective which would highlight that IPR always serve the interests of knowledge producers in gaining monopoly rents from excluding others.[47]

Therefore, it seems that the current view on IPR is reflecting a certain set of ethical and political values which cannot be posited as a transcendental reference point a priori, but is itself embedded into an historical pattern. This is especially true if we consider the context of the TRIPS agreement which was dominated by the US initiatives which in turn go back on the growing consensus in the US that knowledge is an economic asset that needs to be evaluated in financial terms, such as in accounting statements. The expansion of the IPR ideological framework happened in parallel with the 'financialization' process that affected global accounting practices.[48]

---

and investment initiatives. This has attracted much public attention, because those negotiations follow trade diplomacy principles, that is remain secretive until the latest stage. There are also initiatives only focusing on IPR, such as the (in)famous ACTA agreement, which was also pushed by the EU commission, only to fail receiving the consent of the European Parliament. Many lawyers agree with civil society activists that these agreements push the IPR protection agenda to a level by which other human rights on personal integrity, freedom of expression or privacy may be violated. Further, given this fact, the lack of democratic legitimization via the standard construct of negotiations between governments becomes particularly salient and worrying. For a detailed analysis of the EU case, see Araujo (2013).

[47] There is a clear lack of empirical and theoretical support for the standard thesis that further strengthening of IPR protection regimes is conducive to and even necessary for economic growth and innovation. Historically, there is no clear correlation between the level and the quality of IPR across nations and their respective industrial developments, see, for example, Moser (2005) or Mokyr (2009). This literature is surveyed by Boldrin and Levine (2008) who add thorough theoretical analysis showing that in a dynamic competitive market, even with very low IPR protection innovators will receive sufficient first-mover rents and can apply other methods of profit generation (e.g. offering services connected with product innovations) in order to create sustainable business conditions. After all, the modern ITC and software revolution was launched without software being protected as intellectual property in the beginning; only after the industry had established itself, the drive for extending software related IPR speeded up, and significantly, firstly and most intensively in the US, the lead country in these industries.

[48] I have put the pertinent literature in the context of a comprehensive approach to performativity of institutions in Herrmann-Pillath (2013). The financialization paradigm was established by Krippner (2005) and refers to the observation that companies are increasingly governed by finance-

It must be stated in very clear terms that this is by no means a necessary outcome of institutional evolution. As I said, there are no reliable external criteria to fix institutional details of the IPR regime. But beyond that, even the very idea of IPR can be put into doubt by economic reasoning. Therefore, we can conclude that, in fact, TRIPS imposed certain value judgments on the global economic system. This applies for both functional and historical perspectives: On the one hand, TRIPS clearly reflects values and interests of producers of knowledge, and on the other hand, as we have seen, TRIPS reflects historical developments especially in the US, which were readily also received in the EU in the context of global competition over technological and business leadership.

Therefore, the values and ideas undergirding this institutional reference are not necessarily shared across all groups who are affected by those institutions. If the IPR argument takes the producer perspective, this matches with the theory of international trade policy in general: The purpose of IPR is to protect the interests of the producer of new knowledge, and the assumption is made that the interests of the consumers are included automatically here and in most generic terms, namely as welfare gains resulting from new knowledge and the economic growth generated. So, specific interests and opinions of consumers of knowledge do not count. The same applies for international trade in general: The entire system is geared towards producers' interests in gaining specific opportunities to market access, and consumer welfare is assumed to be automatically respected via the effects of trade liberalization on general welfare.

However, if we look at the situation that was created by TRIPS, there are many problems with this perspective, because it appears to be necessary that consumer interests have to be included and weighted in a specific way. A well-known fact is that in pharmaceutical industry, the system creates incentives for pharmaceutical companies to neglect the needs of poor consumers living in developing countries in the process of research and development. Other issues involve the costs of establishing the organizations and institutions of IPR protection in countries on a different level of development. Compared with the earlier logic of GATT negotiations, the WTO and the TRIPS agreement broke with an implicit norm of bargaining, namely that institutional changes should proceed not on the same absolute level, but with the same degree of induced country-specific costs of adaptation. The TRIPS agreement, in exporting the existing framework of industrialized countries, imposed heavy asymmetric costs on the developing countries, thus generating an unequal distribution of costs of implementing the agreement. This approach is substantially leveraged in negotiations over regional agreements, especially bilateral trade and investment agreements, where often the legislation of the more powerful partner

related business strategies that take the financial investors' perspective, thus, among other phenomena, resulting into the fact that a growing share of corporate profits even of 'main street' corporations is generated by financial operations. On the corresponding changes in accounting practices in general, see Perry and Noelke (2006). On the evolution of the patent regime towards the commodification of knowledge, see Coriat and Weinstein (2005).

(typically, the US or the EU) is even simply copied into the text of the agreement.[49]

From the viewpoint of the established theory, all this should be not a problem as all partners of the WTO agreement agreed to sign the treaty. Further, TRIPS also included transition periods for developing countries and contains specific regulations for sensitive areas such as pharmaceuticals. However, this is the outcome of negotiations between governments, so that, for example, consumers of pharmaceuticals in poor countries even did not know what was agreed upon. In practice, for example, the possibility of compulsory licensing provided by TRIPS is rarely used by developing countries.[50]

We can directly apply the Hegelian framework here and generate meaningful questions. Firstly, considering the stalemate in further developing the WTO, one issue appears to be the tension between its transcendental institutionalism and the reality of the policy and negotiation process. Secondly, apparently the stalemate results from the fact that increasingly diverging values of different groups within and across countries impact on the governments' negotiation strategies, and that the resulting complexity cannot be managed within the standard negotiation framework. Thirdly, could this problem be solved by moving towards a realization-focused-comparison approach?

In contrast, deliberative trade policy would amount to a process in which a convergence of values and perspectives is negotiated, which is the precondition for any further formal negotiation procedure. In Hegelian terms, that would imply that the process itself is conceived as a historical one in which a global form of ethical life would emerge. That sounds like a great vision which itself were nothing else as transcendental. But in fact I think that the deliberative trade policy framework is not just a vision, but actually describes real-world aspects of the trade policy process. This even applies to the TRIPS, as we shall see now. So, my claim is not simply that the WTO should move to a deliberative trade policy framework, but that this framework is already enshrined in that organization, and that it is this fact that creates the uneasiness of trade economists in dealing with apparent 'irrationalities' of the WTO. Once one recognizes the deliberative nature of many existing WTO practices, the way towards reforms points in another direction than 'transcendental institutionalists' normally show.

[49] For a detailed overview of this approach to exporting IPR norms by the different multilateral, plurilateral or bilateral channels, see Yu (2014) and on the EU case Araujo (2013). Even if these agreements are apparently based on reciprocity, Bhagwati (1996, 2002) has always emphasized that the old GATT was based on what he calls 'first difference reciprocity', that is, the relative comparative costs of adjusting to an agreement should be equal on a reciprocal basis. This, as in the principle of comparative advantage, would not result into the harmonization and convergence of institutions, which is imposed via the TRIPS.

[50] For example, India's recent adoption of a more aggressive approach towards pharmaceutical industry has therefore attracted much international attention, see http://www.theguardian.com/sustainable-business/patent-wars-india-takes-on-big-pharma. However, even India only issued the first compulsory license in March 2013, and between 2005 and 2011 only 12 compulsory licences were issued worldwide.

3.4.2 Reconsidering TRIPS as a Framework for Deliberative Trade Policy

Looking at the TRIPS agreement in more detail, we notice that in fact it gives much leeway to including diverse valuations into the policy process. This shows a general phenomenon that is especially salient in the discourse about constitutionalisation: There is a gap between the ideas that are maintained about trade policy, especially in certain epistemic communities such as experts and diplomats trained in economics, and the reality of trade policy and what is being enshrined in the agreements.[51] This gap results into serious issues of intellectual legitimacy of the WTO, as long as the so-called scientific foundations are generated by standard economics maintaining its transcendental-institutionalist perspective. In other words, I think that there is a deep contradiction between the intellectual edifice of trade theory and the way how global institutions such as the WTO actually operate which can only be resolved in eschewing the transcendental institutionalism of the theory. In a nutshell, trade economists approach the WTO in terms of 'efficiency', whereas in fact the WTO pursues 'justice', albeit imperfectly, and should do so. As I have detailed previously, the two notions converge if we adopt the realization-focused-comparisons perspective.

Taking the TRIPS as an example, firstly, article 1(1) clearly defines a minimum standard, which is the reason why especially the US wants to introduce 'TRIPS plus' clauses in new regional trading agreements, and why there are new pluri-lateral initiatives such as ACTA. Secondly, this is also the first time that a trade-related agreement includes the protection of private rights directly, yet further implying that an activity claiming those rights is a civil law case: That means, private claimants cannot use the WTO system in order to enforce their rights but have to go via the national courts. That means, only violations of the TRIPS by government action in establishing and enforcing the national laws according to the TRIPS can be subject to WTO complaints. For example, when Chinese companies violate domestic IPR laws, affected companies of other countries have to go through the Chinese judicial system, but other governments can complain about the way how the Chinese authorities deal with IPR violations and implement the TRIPS locally.[52]

Further, Articles 7 and 8 explicitly provide room for considering national conditions and valuations of particular IPR issues and, most importantly, do not only protect producers but also consumer interests in terms of very general obligations of

[51] This gap is highlighted in the analysis by Dunoff (2009), who, however, concludes that therefore the constitutionalisation rhetoric is erroneous. However, as I detail in Herrmann-Pillath (2006b), following the general approach of Voigt (1999), there is a difference between normative and positive analysis of constitutions which also applies for the WTO, but which is confused in the debate. In the current section, I also argue in the positive analytical stance, trying to show that the WTO institutions do have constitutional functions, yet without pursuing transcendental institutionalism.

[52] On a pertinent analysis of the Chinese case and the pertinent dispute settlement procedure documented in http://www.wto.org/english/tratop_e/dispu_e/cases_e/ds362_e.htm, see Yu (2011) who also discusses the implications for the TRIPS in general. Yu also points out that the panel avoided statements about the more fundamental aspects of the agreement, even though they were clearly relevant.

rights owners ("balance of rights and obligations", "prevent abuse"). Even more pronouncedly, article 7 clearly states that IPR should be used in a way "conducive to social and economic welfare". In more detail, for example, § 41(5) introduces the notion that the enforcement of TRIPS should not entail a disproportionate shift of resources in the legal and administrative system towards the protection of IPR. This amounts to a relative assessment of enforcement capacities and would imply that developing countries do not need to establish the same actual level of implementation and protection as industrialized countries. Further, there are explicit regulations on compulsory licensing, and many other details.

Taking these observations together, the TRIPS agreement actually allows governments to adapt their legal conditions and their practice of enforcement to their own policy priorities and national conditions. But this process happens outside the scope of the WTO and might only be subject to trade policy reviews and some other procedures in the context of specialized committees. The only place where such local practices are systematically evaluated and, in particular, where different evaluations of certain policies really meet and are being weighted and possibly reconciled, is the Dispute Settlement Body DSB. Against the background of the aforementioned general reflections, only the DSB allows for systematic deliberative processes beyond the setting of negotiations. Given the fact that many WTO agreements remain very open and await for substantial interpretation, such as in the case of the TRIPS, this means that the DSB takes a pivotal role in further developing the legal framework of international trade, even in the sense of assuming constitutional functions. However, this fact alone is one forceful reason why the formal constitutionalism of the WTO is highly deficient, since legislative and judicial functions are enmeshed in one single institution with only very limited scope of action, at the same time. In other words, only the DSB embodies deliberative trade policy in constitutional terms, which is highly circumscribed.

The dispute resolution process only allows for specific forms of interaction, including affected groups in a very limited way. To begin with, the process only starts if there is a complaint with a specific content. This creates strong path-dependent effects of the ensuing process of interpreting the WTO legal norms. Next, decisions are taken by an expert body, the composition of which is determined by negotiations among the affected parties.[53] That means, even if a case is of general importance for other groups, there are only limited ways how they can participate. The most important and formally established one is that other governments sign up as supporters of a claim or as observers. Other affected groups can only be included via the so-called amicus curiae briefs, which are, however, non-binding for the panels and just constitute an opinion and advice, if at all. All this leads to the fact that

[53] Controversial issues of international trade have always been highly technical, but in the context of modern technology this legal complexity is leveraged by technological complexity, such as in the context of modern biotechnology. At least in the Agreement on Sanitary and Phyto-sanitary Measures, the WTO directly refers to science as a benchmark for evaluating trade measures. Therefore, the composition of panels and the invitation of expert statements influence even most fundamental issues in defining the ontology of modern technology, for example, the legal status of genetically modified organisms; see Bonneuil and Levidow (2011).

the actual meaning of the TRIPS is only slowly explored in a deliberative fashion, even though, as we have seen, the TRIPS is in fact manifesting strong potential for being adapted to diverse perspectives and valuations. In this highly fragmented and punctuated process mainly driven by litigation, there is a high probability that panels only focus on specific formal aspects of an issue, and therefore do not touch upon the more fundamental conceptual issues of valuation. This means, that certain basic assumptions are not changed, resulting into the aforementioned gap between the ideational and ideological foundations and the actual content and potential interpretations of the institution and its textual embodiment.

Thus, what the DSB actually does is to implement realization-focused-comparisons. Matching with its role as a trade court, it is a place where justice comes to the fore in place of efficiency. However, this is not necessarily what drives the dynamics of the actual processes and the final decisions by the panels, as these are shaped by the epistemic communities from which the members are chosen. So, in this particular case a proposal for reform is easily at hand and has been demanded by many scholarly observers, trade lawyers and civil society for long: Strengthening the voice of affected parties in the DSB. I have already mentioned the 'amicus curiae briefs' which were even instituted as a channel of enhancing the legitimacy and improving the decisions by the Appellate Body. However, in this particular case a strong tension emerged between this 'quasi-constitutional action' by the Appellate Body and the opinion of what appears to be the constitutional assembly in the case of the WTO, namely the member governments, who voiced serious concern about this decision. So, until today the role of amicus curiae briefs remains weak and did not assume a formalized and mandatory status in the adjudicative process.[54]

However, the question is of course whether including other affected parties in the DSB is the right way to amend the constitutional weaknesses of the WTO. This could again reflect the strong path-dependencies of institutional developments in the WTO context which might lead to suboptimal solutions. Therefore, I raise the question whether we might better adopt a comprehensive approach for reform along Hegelian lines. The example of the TRIPS shows that the WTO already features institutional properties that enable realization-focused-comparisons, albeit in a highly circumscribed and partial way. The economist's dismay about the WTO is reflecting her misplaced transcendental institutionalism in interpreting what is actually a process of realization-focused-comparisons. The solution can neither be containing these processes in highly contextualized and contingent legal procedures of international dispute resolution, nor supplementing the WTO regulations by regional agreements outside the scope of multilateralism. The only way is to strengthen the existing potential of TRIPS regulations in enhancing the capacities of countries and

[54] It is important to realize that this question is already reflecting a clash between different legal cultures and hence values among the members of the WTO, since the 'amicus curiae' is a common law institution. So, we have a specific example how the Hegelian perspective helps to analyse what appears to be a highly technical legal issue in the first place. For a concise summary of the legal and political issues here, see Umbricht (2001). Interestingly, whereas many member countries voiced concerns about this development, the US emerged as a strong supporter. Charnowitz (2002) presents arguments putting this special legal institution in the larger context of redefining the 'cosmopolitan' nature of the WTO. I return to this point in the next section.

affected parties for furthering institutional evolution of IPR in internalizing affected interests to a maximum degree possible, decidedly widening the scope of the inclusiveness of the WTO procedures, and to conduct any further extensions and amendments of the international IPR regime within the framework of the WTO and the respective specialized committees.

3.5 Conclusion: Rethinking the WTO as a Constitutional Body for Deliberative Trade Policy

I summarize my argument, which necessarily remains incomplete. On the one hand, the Hegelian approach to international trade policy reinstates the role of national sovereignty in trade policy, but on the other hand it argues that the system of negotiations between countries must be embedded into a global and institutionalized civil society. This is the 'embedded liberalism' 2.0. This might appear as old wine in new bottles, as this clearly reflects post-Seattle trends in changing WTO practices towards greater transparency and inclusiveness. However, these developments are so far lacking a concise theoretical underpinning that ties up with economics. As a result, the process is meandering, often inconclusive, and obviously ineffective, as the sad state of the Doha round shows.

In the Hegelian view, the 'wisdom of history' has already put the WTO on the track of becoming a constitutional setting of realization-focused-comparisons which implies that justice is the paramount value implicit in its various practices. What is needed is a fully-fledged institutional elaboration of these developments. That means, among other things[55]:

- Vastly enhancing the role of the WTO in developing and establishing rules of international trade policy, thus becoming a truly cosmopolitan autonomous actor in this policy domain, and overcoming the severe limitations of its role as a mere coordinator of negotiations among member countries;
- Formally including civil society in the different committees, bodies and assemblies of the WTO, and giving an independent role to civil society in participating in all processes of rule development and dispute settlement;
- Broadening the scope of civil society in including non-business *and* business actors, especially in fostering the emergence of cross-domain and cross-sector international NGOs (as in the aforementioned context of supply chains) – this would tie up with Kofi Annan's 'Global Compact' approach for the UN in the context of the WTO;
- Highlighting and activating the deliberative nature of all WTO decision-making and operational tasks, especially in the sense of enabling cross-national valuations of policy consequences, far beyond the actual limitations of the dispute settlement process;

[55] This list ties up with earlier contributions, in particular the approach of 'WTO cosmopolitics' as proposed by Charnovitz (2002), or the ideas ventilated by McGrew (2011).

- Actively promoting and institutionalizing policy networks across different international organizations beyond the scope which has been established in current agreements.

Deliberative trade policy differs fundamentally from the standard economic approach to trade policy in emphasizing justice versus efficiency. However, this notion of 'justice' is in turn based on sound economic reasoning, albeit with a methodological twist. This results from turning to the economic analysis of externalities and interdependencies in the modern world economy and approaching the trade policy process in terms of institutional economics. 'Justice' is specified here especially in procedural terms. That means, firstly, the question is how the interests and preferences of different affected groups are recognized in the trade policy process, secondly, how and to which extent they can participate in the process, and finally, whether all affected parties are satisfied with the outcome such that the resulting institutional regime is sustainable. According to these criteria, the current WTO system fails to realize justice. I do not claim that this notion of justice also covers general aspects of global development and welfare, such as distributional justice of opportunities for growth and development, since these topics are extremely difficult to assess regarding the question whether international trade in the narrow sense is the most important determinant of those outcomes.

Following Clark's perspective, the notion of externalities is essential for deriving my analysis and also my policy recommendations. The fundamental problem in the existing system is the fact that the system itself creates a lot of externalities, because representation of interests is only working through the intermediation of governments, even though the effects of trade policy directly affect the different groups across countries. That means, the domestic political economy is the filter that determines inclusion of interests in the global trade policy negotiations, thus creating a strong path-dependency in institutional change, as is most evident in the case of TRIPS. This biases representation in two respects: Firstly, some domestic interests may not be represented in the negotiations for purely domestic reasons, in spite of being highly relevant for the trade policy issue at stake, and secondly, shared interests of different groups across different countries, though possibly adding up to a very high weight in considering trade policy outcomes, may not even be expressed in the assembly of governments as WTO members. This means, the institutional structure of the system itself creates externalities which could be internalized via reforming the system. This is an institutional economics reasoning, which directly ties up with the deliberative approach. It gives an institutional economics rationale for the extension and deepening of civil society representation in global trade policy. Clearly, this does not automatically imply that, for example, distributional justice would result. But we would approach justice in the sense of the Senian notion of realization-focused-comparisons.

In the end of the day, 'efficiency' and 'justice' are no longer concepts staying in tension. If we approach justice in terms of enhancing the inclusiveness of the system both formally and substantially (in the sense of strengthening the capabilities of individuals and groups to take part in it), this is also increasing efficiency in terms of internalizing externalities in what I see as a 'market for exchange of markets access rights', which is the standard conceptualization of international trade negotiations. In this sense, reforming the WTO starts with changing our way of thinking about it by unearthing the potential of rules and practices that already exist.

References

Amsden, Alice. 1991. Diffusion of development: The late-industrializing model and Greater East Asia. *American Economic Review* 81: 282–286.

Araujo, B.A. Melo. 2013. Intellectual property and the EU's deep trade agenda. *Journal of International Economic Law* 16(2): 439–474.

Bagwell, Kyle, and Robert W. Staiger. 1990. A theory of managed trade. *American Economic Review* 80(4): 779–795.

———. 2001. The WTO as a mechanism for securing market access property rights: Implications for global labor and environmental issues. *Journal of Economic Perspectives* 15: 69–88.

———. 2002. *The economics of the world trading system*. Cambridge, MA/London: MIT Press.

———. 2004. National sovereignty in an interdependent world. *NBER Working Paper* 10249.

———. 2011. Can the Doha Round be a development round? Setting a place at the table. *NBER Working Paper* 17650.

Baldwin, Richard E. 1997. The causes of regionalism. *The World Economy* 20(7): 865–888.

Beiser, Frederick C. 2008. Introduction: The puzzling Hegel renaissance. In *The Cambridge companion to Hegel and nineteenth-century philosophy*, ed. Frederick C. Beiser, 1–14. Cambridge: Cambridge University Press.

Bernstein, Steven, and Erin Hannah. 2008. Non-state global standards setting and the WTO: Legitimacy and the need for regulatory space. *Journal of International Economic Law* 11(3): 575–608.

Bhagwati, Jagdish. 1996. The demands to reduce domestic diversity among trading nations. In *Fair trade and harmonization. Prerequisites for free trade?* ed. Jagdish Bhagwati and Robert E. Hudec, Vol. I, 9–39. Cambridge: MIT Press.

———. 2002. Introduction: The unilateral freeing of trade versus reciprocity. In *Going alone: The case for relaxed reciprocity in freeing trade*, ed. Jagdish Bhagwati, 1–30. Cambridge/London: MIT Press.

Binmore, Ken. 1994. *Game theory and the social contract I: Playing Fair*. Cambridge, MA: MIT Press.

———. 2005. *Natural Justice*. New York: Oxford University Press.

Boldrin, Michelle, and David K. Levine. 2008. *Against intellectual monopoly*. Cambridge: Cambridge University Press.

Boldyrev, Ivan, and Carsten Herrmann-Pillath. 2013. Moral sentiments, institutions, and civil society: What can Hegel contribute to Sen's Theory of Justice? *Review of Social Economy* LXXI(4): 502–525.

Bonneuil, Christophe, and Les Levidow. 2011. How does the World Trade Organization know? The mobilization and staging of scientific expertise in the GMO trade dispute. *Social Studies of Science* 42: 75–100.

Browning, Gary. 2012. Hegel on war, recognition and justice. In *Hegel and global justice*, ed. Andrew Buchwalter, 193–210. Dordrecht/ Heidelberg/New York/London: Springer.

Bruni, Luigino, and Robert Sugden. 2013. Reclaiming virtue ethics for economics. *Journal of Economic Perspectives* 27(4): 141–164.

Buchwalter, Andrew. 2012a. Hegel, global justice, and mutual recognition. In *Hegel and global justice*, ed. Andrew Buchwalter, 211–232. Dordrecht/Heidelberg/New York/London: Springer.

———, ed. 2012b. *Hegel and global justice*. Dordrecht/Heidelberg/New York/London: Springer.

Charnowitz, Steve. 2002. WTO cosmopolitics. *New York University Journal of International Law and Politics* 34: 299–354.
———. 2011. A post-Montesqiueu analysis of the WTO. In *Governing the world trade organization: Past, present and beyond Doha*, ed. Thomas Cottier and Manfred Elsig, 265–288. Cambridge: Cambridge University Press.
Clark, John M. 1916. The changing basis of economic responsibility. *Journal of Political Economy* 24(3): 209–229.
Coates, Daniel E., and Rodney D. Ludema. 2001. A theory of trade policy leadership. *Journal of Development Economics* 65: 1–29.
Coriat, Benjamin, and Olivier Weinstein. 2005. Patent regimes, firms and the commodification of knowledge. *Socio-Economic Review* 10: 267–292.
Costantini, Valeria, Riccardo Crescenzi, Fabrizio De Filippis, and Luca Salvatici. 2007. Bargaining coalitions in the WTO agricultural negotiations. *The World Economy* 30(5): 863–891.
Deese, David A. 2008. *World trade politics: Power, principles, and leadership*. London/New York: Routledge.
Dunoff, Jeffrey L. 2009. The politics of international constitutions: The curious case of the World Trade Organization. In *Ruling the world? Constitutionalism, international law, and global governance*, ed. Jeffrey L. Dunoff and Joel P. Trachtman, 178–205. Cambridge: Cambridge University Press.
Ethier, Wilfred J. 2004. Political externalities, nondiscrimination, and a multilateral world. *Review of International Economics* 12: 303–320.
Finger, J. Michael, and Julio J. Nogués. 2002. The unbalanced Uruguay round outcome: The new areas in future WTO negotiations. *The World Economy* 25(3): 321–340.
Forman-Barzilai, Fonna. 2010. *Adam Smith and the circles of sympathy: Cosmopolitanism and moral theory*. Cambridge: Cambridge University Press.
Fukuyama, Francis. 1992. *The end of history and the last man*. New York: Free Press.
Furubotn, Eirik. 1998. *Economic efficiency in a world of frictions*. Jena: Max Planck Institut zur Erforschung von Wirtschaftssystemen, Diskussionsbeitrag 09–98.
Gerhart, Peter M. 2003. The two constitutional visions of the World Trade Organization. *University of Pennsylvania Journal of International Law* 24(1): 1–75.
Gilpin, Robert. 2001. *Global political economy. Understanding the international political order*. Princeton/Oxford: Princeton University Press.
Grossman, Gene M., and Elhanan Helpman. 1994. Protection for sale. *American Economic Review* 84(4): 833–850.
———. 1996. Electoral competition and special interest politics. *Review of Economic Studies* 61: 265–286.
Hamlin, Alan. 2013. Constitutional political economy. In *The Elgar companion to public choice*, 2nd ed., ed. Michael Retsulak, Laura Razzaloni, and William F. Shugart II, 72–82. Cheltenham/Northampton: Edward Elgar.
Herrmann-Pillath, Carsten. 2004. *Kritik der reinen Theorie des internationalen Handels, Band 2: Evolutionäre Politische Ökonomie*. Marburg: Metropolis.
———. 2006a. Endogenous regionalism. *Journal of Institutional Economics* 2(3): 297–318.
———. 2006b. Reciprocity and the hidden constitution of world trade. *Constitutional Political Economy* 17(3): 133–163.
———. 2007. Deliberative trade policy. *Evolutionary and Institutional Economics Review* 3(2): 209–238.
———. 2008. International market access rights and the evolution of the international trade system. *Journal of Theoretical and Institutional Economics* 164(2): 302–326.
———. 2013. Performativity of economic systems: Approaches and implications for taxonomy. *Journal of Economic Methodology* 20(2): 139–163.
Herrmann-Pillath, Carsten, and Ivan Boldyrev. 2014. *Hegel, institutions, and economics: Performing the social*. Abingdon/New York: Routledge.
Hicks, Steven V. 2012. Hegel on cosmopolitanism, international relations, and the challenges of globalization. In *Hegel and global justice*, ed. Andrew Buchwalter, 21–48. Dordrecht/Heidelberg/New York/London: Springer.

Hillman, Arye L., and Peter Moser. 1996. Trade liberalization as politically optimal exchange of markets. In *The new transatlantic economy*, ed. Matthew Canzoneri, Wilfred Ethier, and Vittorio Grilli, 295–316. Cambridge: Cambridge University Press.

Hoekman, Bernhard M., and Michel M. Kostecki. 2001. *The political economy of the world trading system. The WTO and beyond*. Oxford: Oxford University Press.

Jackson, John H. 1997. *The world trading system. Law and policy of international economic relations*. MIT: Cambridge/London.

Krippner, Greta. 2005. The financialization of the American economy. *Socio-Economic Review* 3: 173–208.

Krugman, Paul R. 1997. What should trade negotiators negotiate about? *Journal of Economic Literature* XXXV: 113–120.

Kumm, Martin. 2009. The cosmopolitan turn in constitutionalism: On the relationship between constitutionalism in and beyond the state. In *Ruling the world? Constitutionalism, international law, and global governance*, ed. Jeffrey L. Dunoff and Joel P. Trachtman, 178–205. Cambridge: Cambridge University Press.

Lamy, Pascal. 2001. Harnessing globalisation. Do we need cosmopolitics? Public lecture at the Centre for the Study of Global Governance, London.

Magee, Stephen P., William A. Brock, and Leslie Young. 1989. *Black hole tariffs and endogenous policy theory. Political economy in general equilibrium*. Cambridge: Cambridge University Press.

McGrew, Tony. 2011. After globalization? WTO reform and the new global political economy. In *Governing the World Trade Organization: Past, present and beyond*, ed. Thomas Cottier and Manfred Elsig, 20–46. Cambridge: Cambridge University Press.

Mertens, Thomas. 1995. Hegel's homage to Kant's perpetual peace: An analysis of Hegel's philosophy of right §§ 321–340. *The Review of Politics* 57(4): 665–692.

Mokyr, Joel. 2009. Intellectual property rights, the industrial revolution, and the beginnings of modern economic growth. *American Economic Review: Papers and Proceedings* 99(2): 349–355.

Moore, Michael. 2003. *A world without walls. Freedom, development and global governance*. Cambridge: Cambridge University Press.

Moser, Petra. 2005. How do patent laws influence innovation? *American Economic Review* 94(4): 1214–1236.

Nanz, Patrizia, and Jens Steffek. 2004. Global governance, participation and the public sphere. In *Global Governance and Public Accountability*. Government and Opposition, special issue 2: 314–334.

Neschen, Albena. 2008. *Ethik und Ökonomie in Hegels Philosophie und in modernen wirtschaftsethischen Entwürfen*. Hamburg: Meiner.

Neuhouser, Frederick. 2008. Hegel's social philosophy. In *The Cambridge companion to Hegel and nineteenth-century philosophy*, ed. Frederick C. Beiser, 204–229. Cambridge: Cambridge University Press.

Panagariya, Arvind. 2000. T*he millenium round and developing countries: Negotiating strategies and areas of benefit* (G-24 Discussion Paper No.1), UNCTAD and Harvard University Centre for International Development.

Perry, James, and Andreas Nölke. 2006. The political economy of international accounting standards. *Review of International Political Economy* 13(4): 559–586.

Petersmann, Ernst-Ulrich. 1997. *The GATT/WTO dispute settlement system. International law, international organizations and dispute settlement*. London/Boston: The Hague, Kluwer Law International.

Pippin, R.B. 2008. *Hegel's practical philosophy. Rational agency as ethical life*. Cambridge: Cambridge University Press.

Quante, Michael. 2011. *Die Wirklichkeit des Geistes – Studien zu Hegel*. Suhrkamp: Frankfurt am Main.

Regan, Donald H. 2006. What are trade agreements for? – Two conflicting stories told by economists, with a lesson for lawyers. *Journal of International Economic Law* 9(4): 951–988.
Ruggie, James G. 1982. International regimes, transactions, and change: Embedded liberalism in the postwar economic order. *International Organization* 36(2).
Sandel, Michael J. 2013. Market reasoning as moral reasoning: Why economists should re-engage with political philosophy. *Journal of Economic Perspectives* 27(4): 121–140.
Schwartz, Warren F., and Alan O. Sykes. 1996. Toward a positive theory of the most favored nation obligation and its exceptions in the WTO/GATT system. *International Review of Law and Economics* 16: 27–51.
Sen, Amartya. 2009. *The Idea of Justice*. London/Cambridge, MA: Allen Lane/Harvard University Press.
Smith, Steven B. 1983. Hegel's views on war, the state, and international relations. *American Political Science Review* 77: 624–632.
Snidal, Duncan, and Alexander Thompson. 2004. International commitments and domestic politics: Institutions and actors at two levels. In *Locating the proper authorities: The interaction of domestic and international institution*, ed. Daniel W. Drezner, 197–233. Ann Arbor: University of Michigan Press.
Squatrito, Theresa. 2012. Opening the doors to the WTO dispute settlement: State preferences on NGO access as Amici. *Swiss Political Science Review* 18(2): 175–198.
Stewart, Richard B. 2009. *GMO trade regulation and developing countries* (New York University Public Law and Legal Theory Working Papers No. 165). http://lsr.nellco.org/nyu_plltwp/165.
Stillman, Peter G. 2012. Hegel, civil society, and globalization. In *Hegel and global justice*, ed. Andrew Buchwalter, 111–130. Dordrecht/Heidelberg/New York/London: Springer.
Sykes, Alan O. 1996. The economics of injury in antidumping and countervailing duty cases. *International Review of Law and Economics* 16: 5–26.
Teubner, Gunther. 1997. Legal pluralism in the world society. In *Global law without a state*, ed. G. Gunther Teubner, 3–28. Brookfield: Dartmouth.
Umbricht, Georg C. 2001. An 'Amicus Curiae Brief' on Amicus Curiae briefs at the WTO. *Journal of International Economic Law* 2001: 773–794.
Van den Bossche, Pieter. 2008. NGO involvement in the WTO: A comparative perspective. *Journal of International Economic Law* 11(4): 717–749.
Vincent, Andrew. 1983. The Hegelian state and international politics. *Review of International Studies* 9: 191–205.
Voigt, Stefan. 1999. *Explaining constitutional change: A positive economics approach*. Cheltenham: Edward Elgar.
Weiler, Joseph H.H. 2001. The rule of lawyers and the ethos of diplomats. Reflections on the internal and the external legitimacy of WTO dispute settlement. *Journal of World Trade* 35(2): 191–207.
Wilkinson, Rorden. 2011. Barriers to WTO reforms: Intellectual narrowness and the production of path-dependent thinking. In *Governing the World Trade Organization: Past, present and beyond Doha*, ed. Thomas Cottier and Manfred Elsig, 313–336. Cambridge: Cambridge University Press.
WTO. 2007. *World trade report 2007: Six decades of multilateral trade cooperation: What have we learnt?* Geneva: WTO.
———. 2011. *World trade report 2011: The WTO and preferential trade agreements: From co-existence to coherence*. Geneva: WTO.
———. 2013. World Trade Report 2013: Factors Shaping the Future of World Trade, Geneva: WTO.
Young, Alasdair R. 2011. Of executive preferences and societal constraints: The domestic politics of the transatlantic GMO dispute. *Review of International Political Economy* 18: 506–529.
Yu, Peter K. 2011. TRIPS enforcement and developing countries. *American University International Law Review* 26(3): 727–782.
———. 2014. The non-multilateral approach to international intellectual property normsetting. In *International intellectual property: A handbook of contemporary research*, ed. Daniel J. Gervais, 83–120. Cheltenham/Northampton: Edward Elgar.

Chapter 4
The Regulative Idea of Recursive Operations: A Second-Order Cybernetic Approach to Responsibility

Stefan Hielscher and Helge Löbler

Abstract Drawing on a cybernetic understanding of systems, this paper introduces the broader notion of "second order responsibility" and distinguishes it from a traditional model of responsibility, which, in terms of cybernetics, can be described as "first order responsibility." We regard this concept as being capable of addressing major shortcomings related to the standard concept of individual responsibility without retreating to a rejectionist position, which dismisses the concept of responsibility in modern society at all. Instead of ascribing responsibility to actors, and analyzing it in terms of actors, actions and consequences—which is becoming more and more difficult in light of interdependent and increasingly competitive interactions in modern societies—we propose a perspective that applies responsibility to responsibility itself, i.e. to the process of negotiating the norm of ascribing responsibilities, which, a priori, cannot be taken as universally given in a pluralistic, modern society.

4.1 Introduction: Responsibility in Modern Societies

Modern societies are characterized by complex structures of interdependent social interaction. People are intertwined in personal relationships such as family, with friends or in local communities, but they are also integrated in a variety of different ways into the anonymous societal structures in the modern global society. These structures are increasingly complex and interdependent. They encompass long chains of interactions that bind together a cascade and networks of social actors, organizations and institutions, which have long since transcended the traditional boundaries of the nation state and reached a global level. The striking feature of

S. Hielscher
University of Bath, Bath, UK
e-mail: s.hielscher@bath.ac.uk

H. Löbler (✉)
University of Leipzig, Leipzig, Germany
e-mail: loebler@wifa.uni-leipzig.de

M. Haase (ed.), *Economic Responsibility*, Ethical Economy 53,
DOI 10.1007/978-3-319-52099-5_4

interdependence is that many consequences of social action cannot be attributed to single individual causation.

The challenge of global climate change provides an illustrative case in point. In negotiations to provide a Post-Kyoto architecture for a common global climate policy, decision-makers have become increasingly aware that climate change is caused by multiple interdependent factors. As a result, negotiation partners do not try to assign the causes of climate change to single factors or single actors, such as individuals, organizations, states or institutions.

As in the example of climate change, though actors fuel the process of social interaction that creates the result, their individual contribution remains small, dispersed and difficult to trace back to individual causation. In light of these challenges in an interdependent and complex modern society, many contemporary observers see the traditional concept of individual responsibility that requires an evaluation of intentions, motives and the consequences of actions (Young 2005) threatened with erosion, diffusion or rejection (Nunner-Winkler 1993, p. 1191; Bierhoff and Neumann 2006; Luhmann 1984, pp. 528 ff.).

In a sense, John Maurice Clark's groundbreaking 1916 paper can be seen as an early anticipation of this situation. Almost a hundred years ago, John Maurice Clark (1916, p. 210) reacted to the consequences of industrialization, which came along with an increasing interdependence of actors demanding a new understanding of responsibility: an "economics of responsibility." According to his view, responsibility in an age of modernization and industrialization required going beyond the individual "to cover a larger group—to make it [responsibility] general" (Clark 1916, p. 227). However, in his paper it remains an open question what this generalization would mean.

In the present paper, we share John Maurice Clark's analysis of complex structures of interdependent social interaction and their challenges to the traditional concept of responsibility. Instead of extending the concept of individual responsibility to "cover a larger group" in an effort to generalize it, we rethink the concept of responsibility by approaching it from a second-order cybernetic perspective. Drawing on a cybernetic understanding of systems, we introduce the broader notion of "second order responsibility" and distinguish it from a traditional model of responsibility, which, in terms of cybernetics, can be described as "first order responsibility." We believe this concept capable of addressing major shortcomings related to the standard concept of individual responsibility without retreating to a rejectionist position, which dismisses the concept of responsibility in modern society at all (Luhmann 1984, pp. 528 ff.). Instead of ascribing responsibility prima facie to actors, and analyzing it in terms of actors, actions and consequences—which is becoming more and more difficult in light of interdependent and increasingly competitive interactions in modern societies—we propose a perspective of responsibility that applies responsibility to responsibility itself, i.e. to the process of negotiating the norm of ascribing responsibilities, which cannot be taken as universally given in a pluralistic, modern society. In this paper, we interpret this process as an ongoing recursive operation, and we describe it in detail. Using the regulative idea of recursive operations, the cybernetic concept of responsibility emphasizes the role of negotiations and stable agreements as "Eigenforms" to overcome an unsatisfying state of affairs. In line with Bayertz (1995, p. 65), we agree that identifying causal links between subjects and objects of responsibility is not sufficient. In contrast, it may be important to identify a consensually and positively evaluated state of affairs to be established or maintained. We conjecture that a second-order type of responsibility is open and forward-looking: It includes actors with diverse moral or normative orientations and focuses on creating options for future negotiations.

We proceed with our argument in three sections: Section 4.2 reviews the responsibility literature, identifies a standard model of individual responsibility and shows why some critics view this concept to be threatened with erosion. Section 4.3 introduces the perspective of second order cybernetics and applies it to the concept of responsibility. Section 4.4 concludes with some implications and limitations of our argument.

4.2 The Threat of Erosion in the Standard Model of Responsibility

4.2.1 The Standard Model of Responsibility

Traditionally, philosophical discussions on responsibility have addressed the relationship between the individual, his/her actions and the actions' consequences. Frequently, the perspective of individual responsibility is used to judge individuals for being responsible for what happened as a result of their failing or neglecting to perform certain actions (Mellema 1985, p. 57 and 1988, p. 1). Given the overwhelming focus on the negative consequences of individual behavior, responsibility scholars use the term "blame responsibility" (Ladd 1992) or "liability model" (Young 2005, p. 717) as a reference point for the standard model of individual responsibility. This standard model of responsibility requires identifying and evaluating the desirable or undesirable consequences of individual action for which an individual then can be praised or blamed. According to Ladd (1992), this standard model of responsibility is both "closed" and "backward looking:" It is closed in the sense that it ascribes responsibility to *one* individual or *one* actor, and it is backward looking in the sense that it builds on hindsight knowledge about the consequences, the acting individual and an entity to identify the results' desirability.

In reference to the notions of "blame" or "liability" responsibility, Fig. 4.1 illustrates what we refer to in this paper as the standard model of individual responsibility. Depicted in a triangular relationship, the standard model of responsibility creates at least a four-digit relationship between a subject (actor, responsibility "of", 1) an object (action, responsibility "for", 2) and a third party (addressee, responsibility "to", 3) with respect to a norm (4). Typically, responsibility is defined as an actor

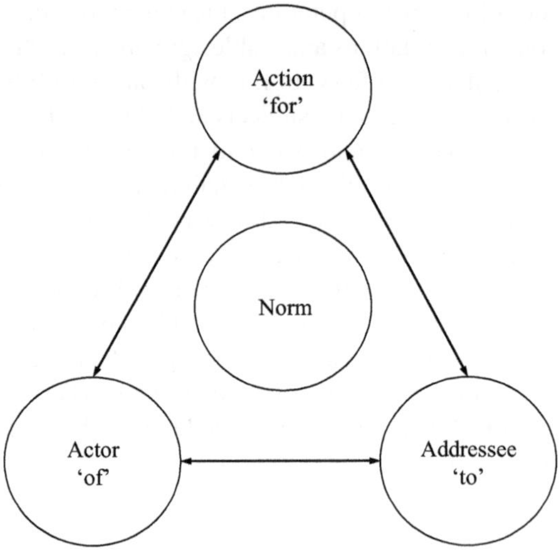

Fig. 4.1 The standard model of responsibility as a four-digit relationship ascription of responsibility and relationships in four dimensions

being responsible for something towards an addressee or a normative standard (Düwell et al. 2011, pp. 541 ff.; Zimmerli 1987).

4.2.2 Adaptations in the Standard Model of Responsibility

In the last decades, philosophical discussions on moral responsibility have shifted focus. In addition to analyzing individual moral responsibility, scholars have also begun elucidating the super-individual responsibility of agents who are acting within the context of larger groups, group collectives or even whole systems. It is perhaps not an overestimation to argue that the interest of scholars with "collective responsibility" (Feinberg 1968; French 1971; Cooper 1972), "group responsibility" (Mellema 1988) or "system responsibility" (Bühl 1990) is sparked by the empirical observation that many individual *actions* are embedded in a larger context of *interactions* in social groups or systems. In turn, this behavioral pattern in modern societies also prompts a widening of focus within the concept of responsibility, as Mellema (1988, p. 2) observes:

> As contemporary societies become more complex, there seems to be more occasion to judge the moral status of group actions. … [T]hose responsible for harms to society are often groups, and these are frequently groups operating in institutional settings. It is less likely in the contemporary scene that harms to society are found to be caused by persons acting alone.

Social scientists use different concepts to describe the consequences of the complex social interactions in modern societies. As societies are becoming not only more complex, but also interdependent and systemic in the sense of functional differentiation (Luhmann 1977), aggregate social results are the results of loosely coordinated action of a multiplicity of interdependent actors. The central problem, which arises, is that the aggregate social results are almost impossible to assign to the level of the individual. This is also the reason why economists refer to, for example, the results of market competition as a system's effect. For instance, it becomes more and more obvious not to hold companies 'individually' responsible for negative environmental degradation. For sure, some companies or their managers do not seem to care much about the environmental pollution caused by their production activities. Yet it is questionable whether environmental degradation such as climate change can be traced back to the individual action of companies and their managers. On the contrary, it seems much more appropriate to interpret climate change as an aggregate effect caused by many interdependent actions of a multiplicity of polluters.

These intertwined features of many spheres in modern societies present themselves as challenges for the standard model of individual moral responsibility: In this context, it is difficult to unequivocally single out those individuals whose actions caused either societal harms or benefits, let alone the sheer quantity of involved actors. As a reaction, responsibility scholars have made multiple attempts to refocus the concept of responsibility on the challenges of widespread complexity and interdependency in modern society (for an overview, cf. Nunner-Winkler 1993 or Lenk and Maring 2001). Without making any claim to be exhaustive, we shortly review those attempts we interpret as being archetypically important for the general discussion of responsibility in modern societies:

- A prominent approach in ethics is to supplement the standard model's focus on individuals by introducing the notion of a collective, non-distributive responsibility of groups (Feinberg 1968; Cooper 1972). Its conceptual strategy is to extend the concept of individual responsibility to a multiplicity of individuals. A typical question that arises in the course of such endeavors is whether it is possible to identify forms of collective responsibility that are non-distributive in the sense that they cannot be fully described by or reduced to the sum of all individual responsibilities within a group. As a consequence, the literature intensively discusses the relationship between individual and collective responsibility. While some authors tend to accept that the existence of a collective responsibility also diminishes the weight of individual responsibility (diminishing approach), others invoke an "ethical anti-dilutionism" to work against the subtle erosion of individual responsibility in the face of collective responsibility (invariant approach) (compare Mellema 1988, pp. 83–102).
- Another important attempt to deal with the complex and systemic nature of modern societal interaction is to interpret a conglomerate of more or less hierarchically organized individuals as a super-individual entity capable of moral action. This attempt's strategy is to extend the concept of individual responsibility not to a multiplicity of individuals, but to a newly created moral agent—a *corporate* actor. The wide range of positions promoted in the discussion shows how the literature struggles with the idea of introducing a new, super-individual moral actor: While the so-called corporatist approach goes so far as to claim that the

"the actual moral subject is the corporate actor" (Ropohl 1992), others defend an ethical individualism and argue that there is no such thing as a responsibility of corporate actors independent of a moral responsibility of individuals (Lenk 1998).

The extension of responsibility to a wider range of actors (groups or systems) and or even to new actors (corporate actors) prompts different reactions, and there is no doubt that many scholars are skeptical about such attempts. Perhaps, this unease does not come as a surprise if the prime strategy is to extend the *standard model* of individual responsibility and to apply it to complex and interdependent societal phenomena. Mellema's (1988, p. 3) central question figuratively shows that the extension of the model is still a proposed strategy: "According to what criteria should individuals be held responsible for the harm brought about by group action?" Thus, it is possible to argue that the implicit fear of scholars crystalizes in the explicit potential of individual responsibility to diffuse if applied in the context of larger group settings in complex and interdependent modern societies (Bierhoff and Neumann 2006).

4.2.3 The Aporia of the Standard Model of Responsibility

A moment's reflection reveals that the interdependent and complex character of interactions in modern societies is difficult to reconcile with the standard model, even if scholars try to extend the concept to a wider range of individuals and actors. For example, influential economists have long been emphasizing that individual responsibility is difficult to reconcile with the behavioral patterns of modern societies:

- As Cooper (1972) argues, Karl Marx can bc seen as one of the first proponents of the view that individuals are difficult to hold responsible for the *systems* effects their actions unintentionally provoke. In his seminal piece, *Capital,* Marx claims that "[i]nasmuch as I consider the development of the economic structure of society to be a natural process, I should be the last to hold the individual responsible for conditions whose creation he is" (Marx 1964, p. 864, cited from Cooper 1972, p. 85).
- In modern societies, however, ascribing responsibilities might not only be difficult in large group settings, but even in the seemingly much more simple case of bilateral interaction, as Coase's seminal (1960) paper, *The problem of social cost*, prominently illustrates. Coase (1960) argues that deciding upon how society should deal with the harmful effects actors inflict on others (ibid, p. 1), assigning responsibilities according to predetermined principles might go astray if it follows a traditional victim-perpetrator-scheme. Coase puts it the following way: "The question is commonly thought of as one in which A inflicts harm on B and what has to be decided is: how should we restrain A? But this is wrong. We are dealing with a problem of reciprocal nature. To avoid the harm on B would inflict

harm on A. The real question that has to be decided is: should A be allowed to harm B or should B be allowed to harm A? The problem is to avoid the more serious harm" (ibid, p. 2). Our point in invoking Coase here is not to discuss his frequently contested (and also misinterpreted) governance solution to this problem (for a discussion, compare Pies 2000). For us, Coase is rather pointing the way towards the provocative observation that the assignment of responsibilities in reciprocal interactions is not independent of transaction costs. In a situation of positive transaction costs, taking into account merely the initial causation of harm turns a blind eye on the possibility that the very assignment of responsibility can inflict further harm on both interaction partners, resulting in adverse moral consequences. From our point of view, Coase can be interpreted as calling attention to the fact that a closed and merely backward-looking assignment of responsibilities can itself cause serious problems if it restricts the problem-solving mode to the polluter-pays-principle and, thus, reduces options in the future.

Against this backdrop, many critics see the standard model to be threatened if it is applied to social interactions in complex and interdependent modern societies. In essence, interactions in modern societies *result* in interdependence, which means that the strategic actions of individuals are dependent on the strategic choices made by other individuals and vice versa. To the extent that individuals act in interdependent contexts, actors are deprived of their power to determine the consequences of their actions.

In other words, applying the standard model of responsibility in the complex context of interdependence in modern societies and extending it to more and more subjects may result in a concept too broad to be meaningful. This is particularly true if actors face difficulties to determine the uncontrollable chains of consequences, which renders it difficult to assign responsibility to the level of the individual at all. Thus, many scholars are highly critical of these attempts. For example, Nunner-Winkler (1993, p. 1191, cited in Beckmann and Pies 2008, pp. 87–88) views the concept of responsibility "threatened with erosion." Niklas Luhmann is even more critical. In a functionally differentiated modern society, he refuses responsibility point-blank as a pre-modern and, thus, outdated concept (Luhmann 1984, pp. 528 ff.).

Yet the question remains how to deal with the problem of diffusion, erosion or overextension of responsibility. Looking at the standard definition of the concept of responsibility, we believe there is an implicit door opener for a different perspective on responsibility. The definitions used in the standard models of responsibility are implicitly self-referential insofar as they define "responsibility" as an actor being responsible for someone or something. Yet, most surprisingly, this self-referentiality is by no means substantially reflected. The approach presented in this paper is an attempt to explicitly do so by using second-order cybernetics, which has been specifically developed for a substantial analysis of self-referentiality. Drawing on a cybernetic understanding of systems, we introduce the broader notion of "second order responsibility," which we present in the next section as a concept capable of addressing the threat of erosion of responsibility without retreating to a rejectionist position, such as seemingly presented by Niklas Luhmann.

4.3 A Second-Order Cybernetic Approach to Responsibility

In reflecting on the notion of responsibility, we start with the question whether it is possible to apply the regulative idea of recursive operations as introduced by second order cybernetics to the concept of responsibility. In doing so, we distinguish between a first-order and a second-order type of responsibility.

4.3.1 Second-Order Cybernetics

In second order cybernetics, the regulative idea of recursive operations can be traced back to the perspective of second order cybernetics and the idea of Eigenforms as introduced by von Foerster (Foerster 1981a, b, c) and extended by Kauffman (2003, 2005) and Füllsack (2012).

The regulative idea of recursive operations usually presents itself in the form of "cybernetics of cybernetics" (Kauffman 2005). According to this perspective, one considers the possibility of applying a field of intellectual endeavor to itself and the way in which it can support the endeavor. Kauffman mentions the following possibilities: "Cybernetics of Cybernetics, Mathematics of Mathematics, Computation of Computation, Linguistics of Linguistics, Magic of Magic, Logic of Logic, Geometry of Geometry, Pattern of Pattern, Will of Will, Teaching of Teaching, Learning of Learning and Meaning of Meaning." (2005, p. 130). Thus, it should be clear from the outset that, in the first instance, the process of recursive operations is intellectually separated from the actors performing the operation. This intellectual disconnection is also a major benefit when applied to the concept of responsibility in modern societies. Due to the interdependence of increasingly complex interactions, we face the problem that social results cannot be easily attributed to single causations and, thus, to single individuals. A regulative idea that enables us to separate the process from the actors involved is, thus, felicitous to conceptually structure the problem in a meaningful way.

To illustrate the underlying logic of this recursive process, we use an example from Löbler and Wloka who applied the regulative idea of recursive operations to the translation of translation and description of description (Löbler and Wloka 2015). This example also helps understanding the role of Eigenforms, which are, according to von Foerster (1981a, b, c), stable states of such processes of recursive operations. Let us assume you use a digital translator such as Google translator. If one types in the German sentence "Sag mir, wo Gefühle sind, "you get the English version "Tell me where emotions are." If one now translates this English sentence through Google translator back into German, you receive the version "Sag mir, wo Emotionen sind." The word "Gefühle" was changed into "Emotionen." If one repeats this process with the new German sentence "Sag mir, wo Emotionen sind," one gets back the English sentence "Tell me where emotions are." Now the recursive translation has reached a stable state, which can be called an Eigenform of the recursive process according to second-order cybernetics. Due to the stability of the recursive operation (the translation of the translation), the user tends to accept this translation although he is neither able to proof it nor may know what "Gefühle" or "emotions" really means (Löbler and Wloka 2015).

Against this backdrop, we identify three aspects important for the regulative idea of recursive operations:

(a) First order operation: translation of sentences
(b) Second order operation: translation of the translation of sentences
(c) Stability as reference point based on acceptance. This stability is called Eigenforms.

4.3.2 *Distinguishing Between First-Order-Responsibility and Second-Order Responsibility*

Now, we apply the regulative idea of recursive operations to the realm of responsibility in interdependent and complex modern societies. In doing so, we follow the three above-mentioned steps (a) – (c):

(a) In the standard model, responsibility refers to an actor and her action as well as to the consequences these actions have for others. As a result, the standard model of individual responsibility can be illustrated as possessing three different kinds of references as indicated in Fig. 4.2.

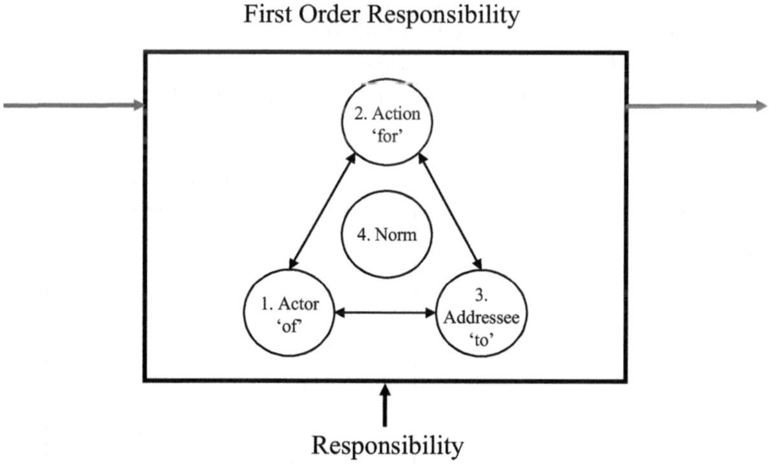

Fig. 4.2 The standard model of responsibility as first order responsibility (FOR)

Responsibility 'of' refers to the people or organizations ("the actor") that are held 'responsible' for performing a specific form of action for something or to someone (people or institutions). Responsibility 'for' refers to the norm in question, the thing or the activity mentioned above. This duty is mainly performed by an action. Finally, responsibility 'to' refers to the person to which responsibility is performed. It refers to the consequences the action may exert on others. Thus, responsibility can be seen as a concept that connects three different entities—actor, action and addressees—, which are important for assigning of "responsibilities to act" in specific contexts. We refer to this relationship as first order responsibility illustrated in a four-digit relationship (FOR). Note that all potential issues over the assignment of responsibility are connected to these three kinds of references in relation to a specific normative standard. They can appear in different forms:

- Who (actor) is responsible for what (action) to whom (actor) with regard to which normative standard?
- Is a specific (actor) actor responsible for specific activities (action) to specific institutions or people with respect to a normative standard?

If during negotiations individuals refer to the above FOR, it is difficult to escape the temptation to dealing with and answering the two questions. Yet, as argued above, doing so involves the difficulty to allocate and assign responsibility, which is particularly true when individuals find themselves in interdependent and complex interactions. Such situations are characterized by the very fact that their results are system effects of multiple intertwined interactions that cannot readily be assigned cannot be attributed to single causations, as Clark (1916) already pointed out.

(b) Using the idea of recursive operations means thinking about the consequences of applying responsibility to responsibility itself. According to this perspective, applying responsibility to itself and not directly to actor/action/consequences means stepping out of the FOR-logic, thus overcoming the principle to assign responsibilities in situations of interdependence. Instead, responsibility of responsibility looks at the process of negotiations as a recursive operation. In essence, this calls for finding a new viewpoint for the perspective of responsibility, which can be referred to as a second-order responsibility process (SOR).

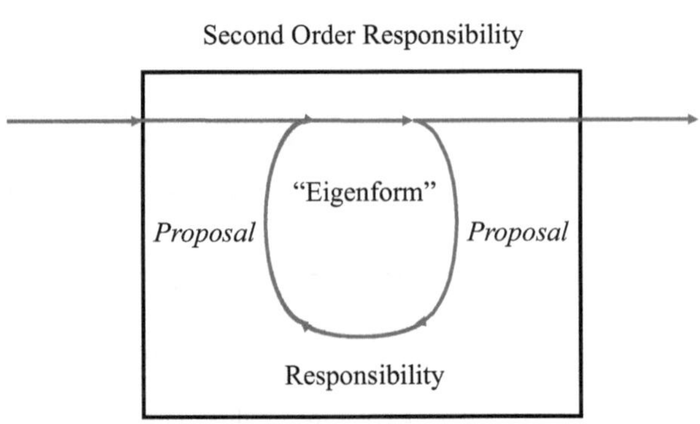

Fig. 4.3 Responsibility as a process: the perspective of second order responsibility (SOR)

What distinguishes first order responsibility from second order responsibility is illustrated in Fig. 4.3, which is based on an idea introduced by George Bateson and Margret Mead in 1976 (Brand 1976). In Bateson and Mead's example, the second order perspective applies the model building process to the model builder herself. In the case of responsibility, a second order perspective means applying responsibility to the process of assigning responsibility itself. Second order responsibility is a type of responsibility that takes into account that although in situations of interdependence all parties are involved in the process of creating outcomes, it may not be helpful to quarrel about the amounts and assignments of responsibility in the sense of the FOR. Against this backdrop, second order responsibility tries taking responsibility for responsibility seriously and looks for Eigenforms in recursive processes, which are negotiations in essence.

(c) Originally, the idea of Eigenforms was introduced by von Foerster (Foerster 1981a, b, c) and extended by Kauffman (2003, 2005) and Füllsack (2012). The underlying idea can be explained by using a simple mathematical recursion (taken from Löbler and Wloka 2015): If we take the simple operation 4 + 5/x and use it in a recursive way, starting with x = 10, we get: 4.5; 5.111..; and finally 5. The number 5 solves the eq. 4 + 5/x = x and is thus a stable state of the recursion. Since this is a stable state it is an Eigenform. In the next example, the stable state is not in the realm of recursive operation, but again we get an Eigenform. If we change the operation to 4–5/x, we cannot find a stable state in real numbers. However, we find a stable state in complex numbers, which is 2 ± 1i. We can now operate with this complex number as if it was real (but not claiming that it is a real number). Thus, Eigenforms are possible not only in within a given framework of thought, but also by going beyond a given framework of thought. In essence, this means that Eigenforms allow finding solutions not only in a given set of options, but also new and unusual set of options which may appear "unreal" in the first view.

In a similar way, we apply the idea of Eigenforms to the recursive process of offering proposals during negotiations. What we suggest is that an agreement emerging from an ongoing recursive operation is an Eigenform in the sense of second order cybernetics. Even if participants agree not to start with cause-and-effect discussions, the negotiating parties need to start with any kind of proposal for transforming the unsatisfying situation. If the other party does not agree, it will propose a counter-proposal to the initial proposal. Then the other party will react to that proposal again. Hence, the parties will offer proposals to proposals and so on. This process is a recursive operation of offering proposals to proposals as indicated in Fig. 4.3. Finally, if all parties agree to a proposal, the recursive operation has reached stability in the sense that there is no need for further change. This can be called an Eigenvalue or an Eigenform.

However, whether a particular agreement solves an underlying problem may still be an open question. It may be open either because the problem was not stated clearly enough at the outset or because the consequences are unclear as participants deal with future concerns. It is important to note that the negotiating parties do not and powerful heuristic, we are fully aware of the need for further elaboration on this concept in future research.

References

Bayertz, Kurt. 1995. *Verantwortung: Prinzip oder Problem?* Stuttgart: Wissenschaftliche Buchgesellschaft.

Beckmann, Markus, and Ingo Pies. 2008. Ordo-responsibility – Conceptual reflections towards a semantic innovation. In *Corporate citizenship, contractarianism and ethical theory on philosophical foundations of business ethics*, ed. Jesús Conill, Christoph Lütge, and Tatjana Schönwälder-Kuntze, 87–115. Aldershot/London: Ashgate.

Bierhoff, Hans-Werner, and Eva Neumann. 2006. Soziale Verantwortung und Diffusion der Verantwortung. In *Handbuch der Sozialpsychologie und Kommunikationspsychologie*, ed. Hans-Werner Bierhoff and Eva Neumann, 174–179. Göttingen: Hogrefe.

Brand, Steward. 1976. Conversation with Gregory Bateson and Margaret Mead. *CoEvolutionary Quarterly* 10(21): 32–44. doi:10.4472/9783037342695.0016.

Bühl, Daniel. 1990. *Verantwortung für soziale Systeme. Grundzüge einer globalen Gesellschaftsethik*. Stuttgart: Klett-Cotta.

Clark, John M. 1916. The changing basis of economic responsibility. *Journal of Political Economy* 24(3): 209–229. doi:10.1086/252799.

Coase, Ronald Harry. 1960. The problem of social cost. *Journal of Law and Economics* 3(1): 1–44.

Cooper, David E. 1972. Responsibility and the system. In *Individual and collective responsibility: The massacre at My Lai*, ed. Peter French, 81–100. Cambridge, MA: Schenkman Publishing Company.

Düwell, Markus, Christoph Hübenthal, and Micha H. Werner. 2011. *Handbuch Ethik*. Stuttgart: Metzler.

Feinberg, Joel. 1968. Collective responsibility. *Journal of Philosophy* 65(21): 674–688.

Foerster, Heinz von. 1981a. Notes on an epistemology for living things. In *Observing systems*, ed. Heinz von Foerster, 258–271. Seaside: Intersystems Publications.

———. 1981b. Objects: Tokens for (eigen-) behaviors. In *Observing systems*, ed. Heinz von Foerster, 274–285. Seaside: Intersystems Publications.

———. 1981c. On constructing a reality. In *Observing systems*, ed. Heinz von Foerster, 288–309. Seaside: Intersystems Publications.

———. 2003. Ethics and second-order cybernetics. In *Understanding understanding: Essays on cybernetics and cognition*, ed. Heinz von Foerster, 287–304. New York: Springer.

French, Peter A. 1971. *Individual and collective responsibility: The massacre at My Lai*. Cambridge, MA: Schenkman Publishing Company.

Füllsack, Manfred. 2012. Information, meaning and eigenforms: In the light of sociology, agent-based modeling and AI. *Information* 3(3): 331–343. doi:10.3390/info3030331.

Hayek, Friedrich August von. 1976. *Individualismus und wirtschaftliche Ordnung*. Salzburg: Neugebauer.

Kauffman, Louis Hirsch. 2003. Eigenforms – Objects as tokens of eigenbehaviour. *Cybernetics and human knowing* 10(3–4): 73–89.

———. 2005. EigenForm. *Kybernetes* 34(1–2): 129–150. doi:10.1108/03684920510575780.

Ladd, John. 1992. Bhopal: Moralische Verantwortung, normale Katastrophen und Bürgertugend. In *Wirtschaft und Ethik*, ed. Hans Lenk and Matthias Maring, 285–300. Stuttgart: Reclam.

Lenk, Hans. 1998. *Konkrete Humanität. Vorlesungen über Verantwortung und Menschlichkeit*. Suhrkamp: Frankfurt am Main.

Lenk, Hans, and Matthias Maring. 2001. Verantwortung. In *Historisches Wörterbuch der Philosophie*, ed. Joachim Ritter and Karlfried Gründer, Vol. 11, 569–575. Basel/Stuttgart: Schwabe.

Löbler, Helge, and Michelle Wloka. 2015. 'Loyalty' between talk and action – Meaning as eigenforms of recursive operations. In *Always ahead: Ideen für das Marketing*, ed. Silke Bartsch and Christian Blümelhuber, 449–458. Wiesbaden: Springer Gabler.

Luhmann, Niklas. 1977. Differentiation of society. *Canadian Journal of Sociology* 2(1): 29–53. doi:10.1086/227995.

———. 1984. *Soziale Systeme – Grundriss einer allgemeinen Theorie*. Frankfurt am Main: Suhrkamp.

Marx, Karl. 1964. *Capital*. London: J. M. Dent & Sons.

Mellema, Gregory. 1985. Groups, responsibility and the failure to act. *International Journal of Applied Philosophy* 2(3): 57–66. doi:10.5840/ijap1985232.

———. 1988. *Individuals, groups and shared moral responsibility*. New York: P. Lang.

Nunner-Winkler, Gertrud. 1993. Verantwortung. In *Lexikon der Wirtschaftsethik*, ed. Georges Enderle, Karl Homann, and Martin Honecker, 1185–1192. Freiburg: Herder.

Pies, Ingo. 2000. Theoretische Grundlagen demokratischer Wirtschaftspolitik – Der Beitrag von Ronald Coase. In *Ronald Coase' Transaktionskosten-Ansatz*, ed. Ingo Pies and Martin Leschke, 1–29. Tübingen: Mohr Siebeck.

Pies, Ingo, Stefan Hielscher, and Markus Beckmann. 2009. Moral commitments and the societal role of business: An ordonomic approach to corporate citizenship. *Business Ethics Quarterly* 19(3): 375–401. doi:10.5840/beq200919322.

Rawls, John. 1993. *Political liberalism*. New York: Columbia University Press.

Ropohl, Günter. 1992. Ob man die Ambivalenz des technischen Fortschritts mit einer neuen Ethik meistern kann? In *Wirtschaft und Ethik*, ed. Hans Lenk and Matthias Maring, 47–78. Stuttgart: Reclam.

Valentinov, Vladislav, and Lioudmila Chatalova. 2014. Transaction costs, social costs, and open systems: Some common threads. *Systems Research and Behavioral Science* 31(2): 316–326.

Young, Iris M. 2005. Responsibility and global justice: A social connection model. *Anales de la Cátedra Francisco Suárez* 39: 709–726.

Zimmerli, Walther C. 1987. Wandelt sich die Verantwortung mit dem technischen Wandel? In *Technik und Ethik*, ed. Hans Lenk and Günter Ropohl, 92–111. Stuttgart: Reclam.

Part II
Topics: Problematic Online Advertising and Female Homeworkers in a Global Supply Chain

Chapter 5
Who Is Responsible? Institutions for Self-Control and the Spread of Problematic Online Advertising

Jutta Krautter, Markus Feiks, Uta Müller, and Guido Zurstiege

Abstract This article focuses on the "changing basis" of advertisings' "responsibility" in the wake of new media and digitalization. The ethical concept of responsibility is usually defined as a four digit-relation: (1) Who is responsible (2) for what (3) toward whom or what – and (4) on the basis of which norm of judgment. Each of these relations will be shortly clarified and then related to or marked as changing circumstances in the advertising business. One of the main aspects of this article will be the question of *who is responsible* for potentially unethical advertisements and their circulation. It will be shown that the circle of responsible agents has extended as it not only includes the advertisers, the advertising agencies or their self-regulatory institutions, but also the everyday internet user. Hence internet users have to take more responsibility for their actions because they are not only users but also "produsers": they communicate, exchange data, and spread advertisements.

5.1 Changing Media

In our paper we argue that new digital media give rise to new ethical[1] problems in advertising.[2] These problems especially concern the question of *who is responsible*, who and which groups could be responsible for ethically problematic advertisements on the internet that have taken on "...a life of their own, meaning that it is no

The project 'Ethics of Advertisement in Times of Media Change' (project-number 249557738), by which the article was created, was funded by the German Research Foundation (DFG).

[1] The concepts "ethics" and "moral" are closely related but mean different things in German. While "moral" refers to rules, norms, values of actions and practices of the daily life, "ethics" is the reflection, evaluation and justification of those rules, norms and values, of "morals".

[2] This paper relates mainly to advertising in western developed countries.

J. Krautter (✉) • M. Feiks • U. Müller • G. Zurstiege
University of Tübingen, Tübingen, Germany
e-mail: jutta.krautter@uni-tuebingen.de; markus.feiks@uni-tuebingen.de; uta.mueller@uni-tuebingen.de; guido.zurstiege@uni-tuebingen.de

M. Haase (ed.), *Economic Responsibility*, Ethical Economy 53,
DOI 10.1007/978-3-319-52099-5_5

as morally wrong or right"[4] (Smith et al. 2015, p. 721; translation by authors). On the individual level, there are reflections about values and conflicts of marketing managers, about decision-making processes or concepts of professional education (cp. Smith et al. 2015). On the organizational level, there are questions of how to develop appropriate corporate and business/professional ethics. The differentiation between the individual and the organizational levels acknowledges different spheres of influence, different roles of organizations or individuals, and allows the consideration not only of the agencies and their personnel themselves but every group of people that are involved in broadcasting advertisement, e.g. the internet user as a "spreader" (Jenkins et al. 2013). It also recognizes diverse demands and constraints with which a person can be confronted in different areas of life and roles, such as in his or her role as an advertising professional or as a parent.

Moreover advertising is connected to another important field of ethics: As advertising needs media and new media always lead – amongst other things – to new forms of advertising (McFall 2008), many aspects about advertising ethics can be seen as a part of media ethics in general. On the basis of new media-options and possibilities to implement their message, advertising practitioners develop new, adapted strategies and ways to reach and persuade the prospective customers as target groups. It was, for example, an entirely new commercial experience for advertising-creators to show a watch on TV that was placed on a map of the USA together with a gentle voice that spoke the words "America runs on Bulova time" (for one example of the many sources, see: TheBdscraps 2012), or in Britain to display a "tingling" toothpaste in the midst of a purling brook (for one example of the many sources, see: AdvertJury 2013). It was also an entirely new experience to perceive such an advertisement: The pictures seemed more real, and the more real images seem, the higher is their credibility and therefore persuasiveness. And not only the visual and cinematic quality of advertisements and ways of their perception and influence changed and grew, but also the range of coverage, which could be significantly increased by the new transmitting technology at that time.

With the increasing influence of advertising *and* its bad image, it was thus all the more important to create a more reliable and responsible image of the advertising field, an advertising of responsibility so to say, which is "developed and embodied in [their] working business ethics" (Clark 1916, p. 210). Self-regulatory institutions have been established equally to respond to public complaints about questionable commercials, to prevent the development of further legal regulations that may result from such complaints, and to generally improve the image of the advertising business. Most regulations are founded, as Clark has emphasized, on "a well-developed basis of agreement as to what in general the mutual obligations of the parties are" (Clark 1916, p. 210). Clark understood self-regulation as the preferred way to regulate business economics: "[I]t becomes well-nigh impossible when the rules are

[4]The original reads: "[...] mit der systematischen Evaluation von Marketingentscheidungen, Marketingpraktiken und Marketinginstitutionen beschäftigt. Darüber hinaus werden [...] Normen und Standards entwickelt, welche Marketingentscheidungen als moralisch richtig oder falsch kategorisieren."

passed by out-siders, themselves unfamiliar with the details of the situation, who are forced to interpret all advice from the interested parties in the light of those parties' interests and to suspect it of subtly aiming to thwart the ends of public policy" (Clark 1916, p. 210). As a consequence, today almost every country has an advertising self-regulatory system, an advertising standards authority with ethical codices. These authorities try to reduce discriminatory or misleading advertisements – for example by banning unethical advertisement.

Some short remarks should be made about the procedure of "banning", which is important in order to understand how this paper proceeds. Self-regulatory institutions in different countries follow a comparable path: First, for example the Deutsche Werberat, the UK's Advertising Standards Authority (ASA), the European Advertising Standards Alliance (EASA) and so forth register complaints about ads from the public and react to them. Eventually, if they consider these complaints valid, they judge these advertisements. What are the consequences of a judging from, for example, ASA? "If we judge an ad to be in breach of the UK Advertising Codes, it must be withdrawn or amended and the advertiser must not use the approach again." (ASA n.d.a) So, if the ASA judges a commercial in such a way, it is not tolerable to show the commercial on TV or anywhere else. "The vast majority of advertisers and broadcasters comply with ASA rulings, however for the small minority who don't, there are consequences" (ASA n.d.b) as there especially is "adverse publicity" for marketers which will not withdraw the ad on their own websites (ASA n.d.c). The procedure for Germany is similar but much less restrictive and powerful: When the Deutsche Werberat approves public complaints about a commercial, they call upon the advertising company or their clients to change or withdraw the particular ad. If they are not compliant and will not follow their order, which is not often the case, all they get is a public reprimand (Deutscher Werberat n.d.a). Accordingly, self-regulatory institutions appear to have a say in distributing or banning advertisements – but things have changed, we "have gone through a revolution of late in many realms of thought" (Clark 1916, p. 210). Policy – and especially technology – which has consequences for the influence of self-regulatory institutions has changed too.[5]

5.3 Digitalization – Developments and Challenges

Over the last three decades, one can witness a massive change in media usage: the increasing importance of the internet, the digitalization of every type of data, which includes personal information. This seems to be exaggerated, but at a closer look it is indeed the case that almost any information appears to be somewhere in the digital world, and therefore in "the world". This has consequences for both our lives in general, which will be clarified in the next section firstly, and, secondly, also for the advertising sector.

[5] See Sect. 5.4.4.2.

5.3.1 Some General Developments and Challenges Regarding Digitalization

The internet plays a more and more important role in our daily lives (van Eimeren and Frees 2013). Many people today spend a great amount of time, if not most of their day on the internet (see www.internetworldstats.com). We work online, communicate, exchange data, order things, organize our lives, watch series, play games. Another important change of how people share data and communicate is the mobile phone. People do not have to be at home to be connected and to communicate anymore: "Most of the time, we carry that technology with us" (Turkle 2011) so it is possible to interact with each other and get and spread any information at any time and at any place – even anonymously and about our most private topics.

Internet and mobile phone users participate more actively in the media environment than users did and could with "traditional" forms of media such as TV, radio or print: First, internet users can choose and decide when and where to watch a TV series, listen to their favorite music and so on. New media technologies are not just one-directional anymore – it is the user, too, who decides. Then again, this is just one of the central aspects of the media change. The second and almost more substantial transformation refers to the new options and possibilities of the internet users' actual involvement and *actions* in the media arena. They are no longer just recipients, that is to say, they do not just absorb and receive information, news, music, shows or advertisements. They are now *able* to participate in the media scene and environment, they can gain a voice in political life and discussions, produce their own and new content like texts, "wikis", pictures, videos, writings, comments, and blogs, comment in networking-platforms or evaluate restaurants, physicians – and products. Or they can just reconfigure, rearrange and redesign already existing content, pass it on and share it with friends or visitors of their own webpages. Internet users are not only passive consumers and users of information and data anymore, they are *prosumers* (Toffler 1980) or *produsers* (Bruns 2008): They consume, use *and* produce information and data. This aspect has a substantial impact on questions about responsibility, which will be discussed later in the Sect. 5.4.4.4. Moreover, their *prodused* internet content can actually acquire quite a bit of (not just local) publicity and popularity. *Produsers* of internet content can gain fame within a very short period of time – or, if things take a sharp turn for the worse, an unsavory reputation. They can act as their own PR management. In this regard, *Time Magazine* crowned "You" to be the most important "TIME's person of the year 2006" (Grossman 2006). "You" are producing information not only for yourself but also for others, to connect, communicate, exchange not only pictures and films, but also opinions, values etc.

The internet with its possibilities and structures to communicate, connect, and share data, brings both benefits and problems that affect society in general, as well as journalism, other media professions, and also advertising. There are countless new fields of possibilities, actions and their consequences to discover, and because they are new there are still but few regulations, rules, and ideas of what could go in the wrong direction. To approach the concerns about digitalization and advertising, it is helpful to correspondingly show different developments, benefits and problems that arose with the digital development in general.

The first and much-discussed issue recurs on the digitalization of data, which is especially crucial regarding personal information. People tend to reveal much of themselves in the net, they expose their feelings, reveal their innermost thoughts, make fun of people or criticize others – always supposing the anonymity and control over their personal data. That supposition has been changed with Snowden's revelations: People have to acknowledge that their data, their own and private information are not so much "private" anymore – but rather quite public. They feel a loss of privacy as a consequence of the loss of their own data.

Besides this possible loss or harm of privacy there is yet another challenge. The new ways and qualities of interaction, interactive *produsing*, have several consequences: Content of all kind can develop a life of its own as soon as it has found its way into the net. It can be forwarded and shared by anyone in the easiest and most simple way possible – just by a few clicks, content can be replicated, exchanged, modified by anyone, and just like that it wanders from computer to computer, from internet user to internet user.[6] No one knows what happens to the content fed into the net or which ways the images, videos, texts could take. As soon as that content is online, everybody else can access it and, if acknowledged as worthy, interesting, or extreme enough, download, potentially alter and upload it again into the net. The so called "memes" have already gone viral[7] which means they have been replicated and distributed all over the world. They are well known by uncountable people and contribute to cultural life – they spread and mutate like a virus. And even if this phenomenon of sharing, spreading, imitation is not utterly new, the *dimension* of distribution, the immediacy and speed such memes can achieve *is*. In short, the internet is uncontrollable when it comes to any kind of data and information, and whatever goes public becomes uncontrollable.

The uncontrollability of the internet is not a problem *in general*. Every technology provides its advantages and disadvantages, and most of the developments and changes have ambivalent sides: The uncontrollability of the net can be understood as the basis of the freedom of media and speech – which in itself is ambivalent. For example, the interactive evaluation can be seen as an important emancipatory aspect of the uncontrollable internet. Everybody is able to inform "the world" about unfair production-processes or unhealthy ingredients of food; while no one, no company, no organization can control these kinds of evaluations.

---

[6] A good term for this kind of independent content existences are the so-called memes (Becker et al. 2003). They can be interpreted as an "image, video, piece of text, typically humorous in nature that is copied and spread rapidly by internet users, often with slight variations" (Meme n.d.). Memes can be seen as a *pars pro toto* for a new user conduct, for new practices in the web. The three video examples described and discussed in this text are in a way such memes: They were rapidly copied and spread, and despite their old age (2004 and 2006) a lot of people know them.

[7] It is called "viral" because information or data is getting spread from person to person in a very short time – just like a virus.

But – why and for whom can it be a challenge, when content-like evaluations, information, develop a life of their own? The challenge and problem begins when this evaluation is unfair or untruthful. Since the data is in the world, it is very difficult to get it out of the web. This is all the more problematic when it comes to news and other possibly important information, as noted by Stephen J. A. Ward: "…the emergence of a 'mixed news media.' News media is 'mixed' because many types of practitioners use many types of technology to create many types of content. […] Mixed media puts pressure on a mainstream ethics designed for a different era…" (Ward 2014, pp. 45 f.). It is difficult to attribute responsibilities, when some news platforms on the internet, "Reddit" for example, are seen as "contained spaces of speculation" (Ward 2014, p. 47). In these "spaces of speculation" everybody is able and allowed to write anything, to "speculate", to put information, whether it is true or not, honest or not. "The nature of their platforms means that no one is responsible to verify what is shared or 'voted up' on a site" (Ward 2014, p. 47) – responsibility appears to be more than diffuse.

The uncontrollable internet is also challenging and problematic when discriminating or otherwise unethical (or even illegal) content gets into the internet, even, and maybe especially, when it has been forbidden. That also means anyone, which includes vulnerable groups like children and youth, can come into contact with afflicting and arousing content against their own decision: People do not share content just with friends that have the same kind of humor – they share them with friends who differ in sensitivity, sense of humor, justice, and aesthetics. Although this is true for any other form of communication, it is especially problematic with the internet which left or never had a content-environment that provided a protective framework.

5.3.2 Some Developments and Challenges in Advertising Regarding Digitalization

Many challenges can easily be transferred into the advertising area: New media and new ways to create and spread commercial messages inevitably raise new ethical questions, challenges and problems. Advertising on the internet appears to be even more ethically problematic than during the previous media changes. The net with all its possibilities, its vast coverage, the perceived closeness to other people – all these relatively new occurrences raise new kinds of problems one could not imagine when only print media, TV and radio existed.

The loss of privacy, for example, is crucial in the advertising area, too. The issue here is a relatively novel advertising method and strategy, the so called "targeting" (Bakir and Vitell 2010). The method itself is in fact not that new, it is as old as the intention to really know the audience and to adjust the content of a speech, text etc. to be able to connect with the audience or the recipients. But in times of changing media, especially with the start of "Google Analytics", a service from Google that started analyzing data traffic on webpages around 2005, the quality of targeting has changed. Now targeting, or: "Online Behavioral Advertising (OBA) is the practice of tracking Internet users' online activities to deliver ads that are more likely to be relevant to them" (Cranor et al. 2014, p. 1). Targeting in this new quality is still in its infancy. But nevertheless, any information about the online movements of internet users, the potential customers of a product, is considered to provide an indication of their interests, wishes and preferences, is therefore very valuable for advertisers and marketers. It is more than understandable that advertising companies have developed ways to get access to this data, to gain insights into their target groups with the aim to implement their advertisements more effectively in the right place, at the right time, to a more appropriate audience than ever before – at least that is their hope and plan. This kind of advertising method is ethically questionable to the extent that it, first of all, uses personal and private information, and it uses it to result in a decision the net user would not have made without these inserts. It is questionable, because this is not necessarily seen as unethical and manipulating: Some people in fact appreciate getting offers that match their actual interests. Some say that in times of an overwhelming product variety, people need some kind of presorting in order not to lose orientation. But some people could find it intrusive, because they have never been asked whether they wanted to be tracked and analyzed. Some could grasp it as a subtle and unwanted seduction.

An additional potential problem with advertising and digitalization has to do with the previously mentioned social and uncontrollable dimension of the internet, i.e. primarily advertisements' spreading and the question of who is getting in contact with them. It can be problematic, because there is almost no possible regulation of *when*, on *which* pages and especially to *whom* advertisements are shown. It means that anyone, not just targeted groups,[8] could get in contact with potentially unethically distributed commercials, anyone with a computer and an internet connection. The difficulty is that such commercials can, because of their tenuous protective framework, not only be viewed intentionally but may also be encountered involuntarily.

This uncontrollability is the main point here, one of the main reasons for the increasing importance of both the question and the answer of "who is responsible?"

5.4 The Concept of Responsibility

Before answering the question of "who is responsible?", it is necessary to take a brief look at the main aspects of the ethical concept of responsibility, that is at questions of how this concept is defined and which dimensions are related to it. The

[8] This quality of internet and interactivity stands in paradoxical contrast to the previously described enablement of advertisers to personalize advertisements, to place their ads more efficiently and fitting to the recipients – but it's not necessarily a disadvantageous paradox.

may be affected by the person's action itself and/or its consequences and side-effects. This could be the acting person herself, other (future) persons, other (future) beings, the (future) environment etc. In the discussion of these examples the focus was on vulnerable groups of persons like children, youth or living beings in general, together with the *norm of judgment* of reducing or avoiding (possible) harm and suffering – despite the fact that harm sometimes is a very subjective thing. Problematic with this norm of judgment is any kind of "sex-sells"-advertisement or commercials glorifying violence. The problem here is not just that people see those commercials; it is that these commercials have an impact, for example in consolidating and deepening oversimplified stereotypes and questionable views of the world and ethical decision making (Chatzidakis and Mitussis 2007). Those stereotypes and values could be transmitted to other persons and future generations etc.

5.4.4 Who Is Responsible?

Besides the aspects of *to whom* and *on which norm of judgment advertisements* (which is here just one case of *for what*) can be problematic, there is one last and most important aspect. It is the question of *who is responsible* for such problematic advertisements that in the end developed lives of their own, advertisements that (somehow) got into the internet and that way became available to anybody, even children or other vulnerable groups, at any time. This question seems easy to answer: It certainly is the advertising agency. But, as already mentioned, central circumstances of responsibility changed in times of digitalization and internet commercials. The question of "who is responsible" is now much more complicated to answer than it was in times of just non-digital media, and it has to do with the development of the internet as a social network, with the noted uncontrollable internet.

To begin with some general notes about "*who*" can be responsible: It refers to the question of what kind of being or entity can appropriately be responsible for its actions. Some criteria have to be met so that an individual can be held responsible for the action, its consequences and side-effects. It needs "a subject that is able to accept a task of doing something or to act and, as the case may be, to give an account on oneself"[11] (Höffe 2010, p. 37; translation by authors). Responsibility "can be attributed not only to a natural person but also to 'legal persons', thus a club, an association, even the state and likewise 'naturally' a commercial enterprise"[12] (Höffe 2010, p. 37; translation by authors). Furthermore, the subject needs to have

[11] The original reads: "[Das Sprachspiel der Verantwortung braucht] ein Subjekt, das Aufgaben zu übernehmen oder Handlungen auszuführen und gegebenenfalls Rede und Antwort zu stehen vermag."

[12] The original reads: "[In Wahrheit lässt sich aber eine Verantwortung] nicht nur natürlichen Subjekten, sondern auch 'juristischen Personen' zuschreiben, also einem Verein, einem Verband, selbst dem Staat und 'natürlich' ebenso einem Wirtschaftsunternehmen."

the ability to *act* (not just to behave). That means the subject has to have the ability to voluntarily intend what he or she is doing, and additionally, to consider every imaginable circumstances, consequences and side-effects that could follow this action. The person that can be held liable for his action must have been free in his decision and performance to do so. For explaining the concept of responsibility it is important to briefly explain what "voluntarily" means and in which circumstances this criterion is, or more importantly, is not, fulfilled. First of all, it is a matter of *freedom of action*: Nobody, no situation, no bodily condition, no social system, nothing should have forced an individual to (not) do it. Second of all, a "necessary condition for a voluntary act is *knowledge* about the exact circumstances; nescience about them, that is what we can preliminarily conclude, negates voluntariness"[13] (Ricken 2003, p. 103; translation by authors). And that, in fact, is the almost more important definition of freedom: To be able to overlook and overthink the differing (ethical) reasons for or against an action and then, with a view to these reasons, to voluntarily decide whether to do it or not.

To summarize this point: Responsibility is based – amongst other things – on knowledge about one's own actions and both their consequences and side-effects, on free will and free decision for this action. It is corresponding with actions, not with coincidences or happenstances, it is always dependent on a normative or evaluative background and standard, and finally there has to be someone or something (possibly) being affected by this action, even if it is just the acting person herself.

Only now it is possible to ask for "who" is responsible – for example for creating a questionable advertisement or/and the consequence of its viral existence. In order to reveal *who* is responsible for ethically questionable advertisements like at least two of the examples, the first step should be to detect the most relevant, initiating action and *subsequently* its consequences.

5.4.4.1 Advertising Agencies

The first view on the initiating action will rightly identify the *creation* of the commercial itself. The question now is: Who is responsible for creating advertisements which obviously will be banned from broadcasting sooner or later and which could possibly go viral and hurt other people? It is, without any doubt, the advertising agencies and their personnel themselves. First, they act by creating the advertisement voluntarily, they also know, prospectively and just as well as any other accountable person, about their duty to take responsibility for their own actions and the consequences. Second, they know about ethical standards and codices in their field of work – they know what is legal and illegal, and they know what is "bad" and "good", and what probably or certainly will get banned or the order to withdraw it by self-regulatory institutions. Third, they know very well about advertising effects

[13] The original reads: "Notwendige Bedingung für die Freiwilligkeit einer Handlung ist die Kenntnis der Einzelumstände; deren Nichtwissen, so können wir vorläufig festhalten, hebt die Freiwilligkeit auf."

and consequences – after all, this is what they are seeking. The field of advertising therefore is, not least because knowledge is power as well as money, well investigated and tracked down, so that advertisers usually, if they are "good" i.e. persuasive, obtain a great amount of knowledge about study findings on how ads work and why some persuade and others do not. Advertising practitioners know scientific findings about stimulating and arousing consumer wishes, they know about best practice and, if they are good, how to set affecting elements and what kinds of reactions they may cause, they know that showing an almost naked woman is offending for some individuals and that decapitating a cat, even if it is not real, is horrible to see for a lot of people.

And fourth, they *know* about and take advantage of the uncontrollable paths their creations could find online, they know about the importance of the internet for (almost) everyone's daily life. The movement towards a socialized digitalization, the new role of the media user opened up quite remarkable new possibilities and initiated novel forms and strategies to create advertisements and campaigns. Advertisers know they can reach almost every person at any time practically immediately, and additionally they can use more and more sophisticated technologies like targeting to place their ads more efficiently and fitting to the recipients. They realized the new and more active role of the *produser* and his or her new approach to media content – and they took advantage of our interest in expressing, profiling ourselves and connecting to each other. The former recipients and now communicators are not only invited but *asked* to share pictures, sounds, films and other audiovisual products – or advertisements[14] – and to let them go viral.

One could assume that some advertising practitioners could take advantage of the uncontrollable internet.[15] They know, that advertisements that are reputed to violate, overstep cultural values or to be otherwise ethically questionable are more interesting for the recipients, that it is more promising to create provoking commercials. Many people are fascinated by forbidden or banned content.

In fact, there seems to be a proliferation of "misleading, harmful or offensive" (ASA, n.d.a) viral commercials, mostly in the form of video clips, which the "Advertising Standards Authority" in the UK or the Deutsche Werberat in Germany would never have allowed the release of, or that were very likely to be or already banned in any other medium. It is also interesting to see that actually "banned" commercials can be found very easily on the internet, e.g. via Google-search, and they do not even disappear after many years. To get an idea of a reason for the conceivable proliferation of such provocative advertisements, one could, on the one – and more theoretical – hand, look at cultural changes in general. There is more media

[14] The webpage http://www.carbuzz.com/news/2012/6/28/The-Most-Controversial-Car-Commercials-of-All-Time-7709506/ for example says under each commercial: "Loved The Video? Share It!"; suggestions of a sharing channel are facebook or twitter.

[15] This question is aimed to be answered in the authors' research project at the University of Tübingen: "Advertising Ethics in Times of Medial Change". Part of that research cover questions like this: How are advertising practitioners dealing with the fact that their messages could reach anybody – children, youths and vulnerable groups of persons – at any time?

content than ever before and subsequently it is getting more difficult to attract the audience's attention. Additionally, the advent of highly commercialized and competitive ideals in western developed countries appears to make the "survival of the fittest" more aggressive. So, provocative advertisements could be just one sign of more aggressive and extreme environment. Without loud, maybe provocative or aggressive messages and pictures, videos, texts are unlikely to be seen and perceived. The same is also, and maybe even more true for advertising: In a more and more ..."heavily advertised market [and] breaking with traditional values may attract the attention of the target audience and build up a unique brand identity..." (Gelbrich and Roschk 2008, p. 54).

On the other – applied – hand, it seems to be a good approach and method to take a look at handbooks and compendia particularly written *by*, for example, marketing researchers or advertising practitioners *for* advertising practitioners. One could examine recommendations on how to get the attention of a potential customer, on what kind of qualities and criteria should commercials fulfil to make sure that they attract interest and attention, tips and strategies on how to create a "word-of-mouth" recommendation and how to initiate a viral marketing campaign. Findings to these areas of exploration could explain advertising agency's intention to create an obviously irritating commercial which is likely to get banned.

There are a great number of guidebooks for "viral marketing" mainly written by advertising practitioners, communications experts (one could just search for the words in a well-known e-commerce company and gets an astonishing result). There is, for example, "Viral Marketing – How to induce word-of-mouth advertising deliberately and use it lucratively"[16] by Sascha Langner in Germany (Langner 2009). He hands out advices on what leads to a successful, i.e. viral campaign and lists amongst other things "entertainment" and "new and exceptional" as criteria that contribute to an ad that could go viral. What is really interesting is that he cites quite a few commercials as examples *par excellence*. Two of them were referred to above in this paper: the ad with the decapitated cat and the other one with the monster head. As another example for a handbook – out of hundreds, as already hinted at – there is a book with the notable title *Kick Ass at Viral Marketing: How to Go Viral for Business Success* by Cyrus Kirkpatrick (2014). Here he lists "Ten Viral Dynamics", three of which are really interesting for this matter: "Challenges Social Norms", "Extremely Funny" and "Truly Controversial". The frequency of the word "extremely" (used in four of the ten "viral dynamics") or any other superlative adjective is revealing as well: It seems that only the "extreme" is interesting enough to get the attention of the recipients, and the extreme is at least not far away from stepping over the mark and being beyond the pale. So, for commercials that are supposed to go viral and be successful it seems essential to be "extremely" funny, entertaining – and last but not least challenging to social norms. This advice clearly appears to include commercials that could be too brutal, too sexist, and unethical in any way for self-regulatory institutions to release them. Such an "extreme" com-

[16]The German title reads: "Viral marketing: Wie Sie Mundpropaganda gezielt auslösen und Gewinn bringend nutzen."

mercial appears to be the best way to attract the attention of the potential customers of the advertised product – at least that is what (aspiring) advertising practitioners obviously learn from handbooks. "Significantly more than traditional advertising, viral advertising relies on provocative content to motivate unpaid peer-to-peer communication of persuasive messages from identified sponsors. While emotive content has always been the key to capturing audiences' attention in advertising, viral advertising relies on increasingly raw content for actual distribution" (Porter and Golan 2006, p. 35). This could actually explain why advertising practitioners falsely claim that their ads were banned: The forbidden and banned advertisements are usually more interesting than the usual. So, it seems that advertising practitioners are following the well-known maxim that "there is only one thing in the world worse than being talked about, and that is not being talked about" (Wilde 2005, p. 4).

Another "advantage" of the uncontrollability besides the increase of attention for apparently unethical ads could be the justification, that one can only be held liable for things that are under the respective actor's control and that one can voluntarily want (see Ricken 2003, pp. 100 f.). The uncontrollable ways of the internet are *not* under control, so an advertiser could argue that he never wanted his commercial to develop its own life. Moreover, they could advance the argument that they cannot be held liable for a commercial they have already withdrawn (if, as is mostly the case, self-regulatory institutions demanded so) but that is still in the internet. But this exact justification is, at a closer look and in ethical terms, profoundly wrong and untruthful, as the following text section will try to show.

One central step of this argument is deceiving, because there is important information about conditions when "nescience […] negates voluntariness"[17] (Ricken 2003, p. 103; translation by authors). Nescience *only then* negates voluntariness and accordingly the duty to accept responsibility for the action when the nescience *itself* is *not voluntary*. But if "nescience is a result of the [free, authors] will"[18] (Ricken 2003, p. 104; translation by authors), it does not negate voluntariness for the action. This means for an advertising practitioner, who knows that there is no possible way to withdraw a commercial that has already gotten into the internet and may even be viral, that his nescience about the online ways of his created contents is a voluntarily nescience over where to set the starting point of ethical acting and awareness. One could even assume, that they do not only *know* about the uncontrollable internet, but that use and want it, for example to get a broader reach – or to not being held responsible for anything regarding their spread commercial (Martin and Smith 2008).

So, the creators of unethical advertisements are not at all free of any charges even if they cannot know everything that could happen to their ad content. Because rather than arguing to be completely powerless against the uncontrollable internet it would be better to ask the following question: "'What *are* the causes over which we have some control and before which we do not stand entirely helpless?' These we may call the responsible causes" (Clark 1916, p. 214), as Clark states. This is a good hint at where and when, at which step of their work advertising practitioners should begin to

[17] The original reads: "Nichtwissen […] hebt Freiwilligkeit auf."

[18] The original reads: "Unwissenheit ist eine Folge des Willens."

think about their actions and resulting consequences. It is easy to see that if the starting point of *control* or *no control*, knowing and nescience was only set at that significant instant where the content already got into the internet, that point really *is* too late.

With this knowledge about the (relatively) new possibility that anyone can be reached online by any advertisement at any time, advertising practitioners in fact have to be and act more cautious and thoughtful than ever regarding what (ethical) quality and kind of advertisement they release. Hence they have to establish higher – not lower – ethical standards and principles for online advertisements because children could see these commercials, and even if these ads were banned, they could not be removed from the Internet. That is why they have to start their own ethical considerations and reflections *before* they even create the advertisement – they have to raise ethical standards on their *own initiative*. It is important that regulations and ethical guidelines are defined and settled, namely by the own branch, which seems to be the precondition to in a way "intrinsic" regulations and ethical principles. Thus, there should not (only) be a regulation from the outside but also an insight into one's own responsibility for (ethical) values and the well-being of a society.

5.4.4.2 Ethical Standards Authorities

There is another actor that can be held responsible for unethical advertisement – the already mentioned self-regulatory institutions. It is their duty to monitor the advertising area, also in the internet, and diminish ethically disturbing commercials. As a matter of fact, self-regulation institutions like the Deutsche Werberat and the ASA already acknowledged their responsibility concerning viral-going online advertisements and commercials in the year 1997. They call themselves the appropriate authority for codices and ethical standards for any kind of advertisement. They are responsible when the content of the commercial was created by the advertising practitioner himself and solely its distribution was relinquished to the consumer (Deutscher Werberat n.d.b). But for them it really is not as easy as it was to fulfil their responsibility: Most of the times they do not *know* about an advertisement until it went online or public. Furthermore it is almost impossible (or at least very complicated) for self-regulatory institutions, law, guidelines, or any codes to be able to prevent commercials like the described ones from entering the internet and going viral. This impossibility becomes apparent by the mere fact that despite given orders to withdraw a commercial, a lot of them are still online and can be viewed by anyone. Times have changed for self-regulatory institutions, and they have to develop new approaches to deal with such new kinds of problems.

5.4.4.3 Advertising Companies

Another entity could and should be held responsible: the companies that commission advertisements from advertising agencies. One could even say that they are the most important and initial actors in the advertising field. Advertising companies usually have vague ideas of how their product should be advertised and they communicate them in an open competitive bidding, leading to a pitch.[19] The companies decide which advertising agency wins this pitch; if an advertising agency does not meet the company's ideas or expectations they will not win the pitch and miss the budget volume. Advertising companies therefore have a crucial influence on how advertisements are created and distributed, for which media and communication channels they are created and so on. They can urge advertising agencies to create "unethical" commercials in order to get attention for the product. But in the end, and even though one could say advertising companies are the most important actors in the field of advertising, they are not the only reason for the creation of ethically questionable ads. To lose the pitch and the budget volume is not a good argument to obey unethical instructions. The consequences of losing a pitch or even the client will not threaten the future of the agency (see Ricken 2003, p. 106), the advertising agency could say no.

So, there are at least three actors that can be held responsible for unethical advertisements: the advertising practitioners, self-regulatory institutions or the advertising companies. But what about the distribution of those ads? Are these three actors really the only ones who can be held responsible?

5.4.4.4 Internet User – The *Produser*

There is a fourth and increasingly important group of actors which has indeed "digital responsibilities" (Ward 2014, p. 47) for the (ongoing) existence of ethically questionable advertisement: It is the group of internet users.

As previously noted in *Time* Magazine, the magazine *Advertising Age* declared "the consumers" to be the advertising agency of the year 2006 (Creamer 2014) – not without reason. They arc in a way doing the advertiser's job (Lawrence et al. 2013), or at least help them with getting their advertisement promoted. Each person is connected with every other person, they exchange not only images, music, writings and advertisements, but also opinions, values, arguments and so on. Everything can be shared in no time, and hence *produsers* play a very important part in contributing to the spreading and ongoing existence of ethically problematic content of some advertisements. Internet users are actors, they are in a way market and business participants and, as such, they have to consider and think about their responsibility for their own actions, about the responsibility towards society.

It is not only the advertising practitioner who has to take over responsibility (although they are the starting point in this regard and therefore they play an important role) – it is also the individual internet user. Although the user cannot know about *ethical codices* of the advertising agencies or the standards authorities and they legally do not even have to care about these ethical standards, it is all the more important to acknowledge: "But where the law has not spoken, every man must

[19] "Pitch" is a term of art inter alia for the advertising area. It is a competition for a new contract with a company/business between advertising agencies to represent their product.

decide" (Clark 1916, p. 223) and also raise ethical standards on their own initiative. Even if internet users can often not be held responsible legally for spreading "unethical" advertisements, they can be held responsible *ethically*. Every person has to deliberate about his or her own responsibility not to (uncritically) distribute (if it already exists) insulting, lying, misleading, fascistic and disreputable contents – due to the fact that internet content loses its protective framework and nobody, especially not children and youth, can exactly anticipate what they are about to watch. Each individual has to accept and shoulder his or her own responsibility, for the actions and their consequences – not least to protect and to sustain media freedom and freedom of expression. Because of the increased interdependency and everyone's possibility to prod*use* it is all the more true that "private individuals can act collectively where one alone is helpless and get results which would be impossible for the official machinery of government" (Clark 1916, p. 226).

5.4.5 Advertising as a Special Ethical Case

One could criticize these ethical concerns with a view to a more general or so called "macro level": The potential numbing due to aggressive video-clips just seems to fit our times and therefore it does not appear to be a specific problem of advertising. In fact, far worse videos can be seen by anyone on the internet and there are way more severe problems in the world. So, why should there be complaints about video-commercials which show, for example, a computer animated decapitation of a cat, whereas there are *real* videos of *persons* being decapitated?

There are several reasons to justify ethical concerns particularly about questionable advertising: First of all, there is no reason at all not to criticize unethical content just because there is much worse content. Secondly, "...advertising merely mirrors society as it is [...]." (Ambler 2008, p. 48), or at least that's what is expected from advertising. And it may be precisely the crux of the matter: One *expects* advertisement to be a mirror of society. Advertisements show in a sometimes extreme way what is "in" and established mainstream. If an advertisement shows brutal or sexist images, this could mean that cruelty or discrimination is already (or still) in the established mainstream of society – and this "being *in*" to act cruel or discriminatory against living beings is a problematic issue.

The third argument is that advertising is always connected with commercialization and, hence, instrumentalization. "Considering Kant's general approach, we can claim that the media's use of sexuality and violence as a marketing instrument constitutes unethical behavior. It is clear that the media institutions abuse sexuality [or violence, authors] in order to attract more viewers, that is, for only selfish" or just instrumental ends, moreover "without considering the negative consequences they cause" (Bayraktar 2013, p. 5).

This is not a complete list of arguments on why, in some cases, advertisements may appear more ethically problematic than other media content, but it might explain why advertisements are more likely to provoke ethical concerns.

5.5 Conclusion

This paper has shown that the question of "who is responsible?" is, in times of new media and digitalization, difficult to answer. And it showed the urgency of reflecting and including the new and more and more important role of every single internet user. They are not only *users* of the net, they are *produsers* of internet content, they share their opinions and values and are able to start social movements. "You" as everyone is not only the most important "TIME's person", "you" is also a very successful "Advertising agency" – "you" is a market participant with more and more power and influence. This new power of "you" does not absolve the actual advertising practitioners from their responsibility *not* to create ethically questionable advertisements. It does not absolve (self-) regulatory institutions from intervening and setting higher ethical or legal standards – this is essential to protecting vulnerable groups of persons against unwanted brutal, discriminating content and is necessary to sustain media freedom and freedom of expression. But it is also necessary for every individual to think about their own actions in the net, which includes consequences and side-effects. To end with Clark: "The scope of personal responsibility is broader than ever before, not narrower" (Clark 1916, p. 217).

References

AdvertJury. 2013, May 26. *Gibbs – SR toothpaste*. [Video file]. http://www.youtube.com/watch?v=-bULgPaQej4. Accessed 30 Nov 2015.

Ambler, Tim. 2008. Advertising. In *The international encyclopedia of communication*, ed. Wolfgang Donsbach, 43–49. Malden [et al.]: Blackwell.

Anderson, Craig A., Akiko Shibuya, Nobuko Ihori, Edward L. Swing, Brad J. Bushman, Akira Sakamoto, Hannah R. Rothstein, and Muniba Saleem. 2010. Violent video game effects on aggression, empathy, and prosocial behavior in eastern and western countries: A meta-analytic review. *Psychological Bulletin* 126(2): 151–173.

ASA. Advertising Standards Authority. n.d.-a. *About regulation*. https://www.asa.org.uk/About-ASA/About-regulation.aspx. Accessed 30 Nov 2015.

———. n.d.-b. *Sanctions*. https://www.asa.org.uk/Industry-advertisers/Sanctions.aspx. Accessed 30 Nov 2015.

———. n.d.-c. *Online sanctions*. https://www.asa.org.uk/Industry-advertisers/Sanctions/Online.aspx. Accessed 30 Nov 2015.

Bakir, Aysen, and Scott J. Vitell. 2010. The ethics of food advertising targeted toward children: Parental viewpoint. *Journal of Business Ethics* 91(2): 299–311.

Bayertz, Kurt. 1995. Eine kurze Geschichte der Herkunft der Verantwortung. In *Verantwortung: Prinzip oder Problem*, ed. Kurt Bayertz, 3–71. Darmstadt: Wissenschaftliche Buchgesellschaft.

Bayraktar, Ahmet. 2013. Marketing the media with sexuality and violence: Is it ethical? *Journal of Academic & Business Ethics* 7(1): 1–10.

Becker, Alexander, Christian Mehr, Heino Heinrich Nau, Gerson Reuter, and Dagmar Stegmüller. 2003. *Gene, Meme und Gehirne: Geist und Gesellschaft als Natur; eine Debatte*. Frankfurt am Main: Suhrkamp.

Bruns, Axel. 2008. *Blogs, wikipedia, second life, and beyond: From production to produsage*. New York [et al.]: Lang.

Chatzidakis, Andreas, and Darryn Mitussis. 2007. Computer ethics and consumer ethics: The impact of the internet on consumers' ethical decision-making process. *Journal of Consumer Behaviour* 6(5): 305–320.

Clark, John M. 1916. The changing basis of economic responsibility. *Journal of Political Economy* 24(3): 209–229.

Conger, Sue, Joanne H. Pratt, and Karen D. Loch. 2013. Personal information privacy and emerging technologies. *Information Systems Journal* 23(5): 401–417.

Cranor, Lorrie Faith, Hoke Candice, Leon Pedro Giovanni, and Alyssa Au. 2014. *Are they worth reading? An in-depth analysis of online advertising companies' privacy policies*. Research Conference on Communication, Information and Internet Policy (TPRC 2014), Arlington, VA, USA.

Creamer, Matthew. 2014. Ad age agency of the year: The consumer. *Advertising Age*. http://adage.com/article/news/ad-age-agency-year-consumer/114132/. Accessed 30 Nov 2015.

Deutscher Werberat. n.d.-a. *Öffentliche Rügen*. http://www.werberat.de/ruegen. Accessed 30 Nov 2015.

———. n.d.-b. *Deutscher Werberat und Online-Werbung*, link to "*Verlautbarung*". http://www.werberat.de/deutscher-werberat-und-online-werbung. Accessed 30 Nov 2015.

Drumwright, Minette E., and Patrick E. Murphy. 2009. The current state of advertising ethics: Industry and academic perspectives. *Journal of Advertising* 38(1): 83–108.

Funk, Jeanne B., Heidi Bechtoldt Baldacci, Tracie Pasold, and Jennifer Baumgardner. 2004. Violence exposure in real life, video games, television, movies, and the internet: Is there desensitization? *Journal of Adolescence* 27(1): 23–39.

Gelbrich, Katja, and Holger Roschk. 2008. Advertising, cross-cultural. In *The international encyclopedia of communication*, ed. Wolfgang Donsbach, 50–56. Malden: Blackwell.

Grossman, Lev. 2006. *You – Yes, You – Are TIME's person of the year*. http://content.time.com/time/magazine/article/0,9171,1570810,00.html. Accessed 30 Nov 2015.

Höffe, Otfried. 2010. Soziale Verantwortung von Unternehmen: Rechtsphilosophische Überlegungen. In *Corporate Social Responsibility in der Wirtschaftskrise: Reichweiten in der Wirtschaftskrise*, ed. Michael S. Aßländer and Albert Löhr, 35–48. München: Rainer Hampp.

Jenkins, Henry, Sam Ford, and Joshua Green. 2013. *Spreadable media: Creating value and meaning in a networked culture*, Postmillennial pop. New York: New York University Press.

Jocson, Josiah. 2014, July 21. *K fee commercial #1*. [Video file]. http://www.youtube.com/watch?v=aNBGfzoacw4. Accessed 30 Nov 2015.

Kant, Immanuel. 2005 [1797]. Die Metaphysik der Sitten. In *Immanuel Kant, Werke in sechs Bänden*, ed. Wilhelm Weischedel, Vol. Vol. 4. Darmstadt: Wissenschaftliche Buchgesellschaft.

Kirkpatrick, Cyrus. 2014. *Kick ass at viral marketing: How to go viral for business success*. Media Enterprises L.L.C.

Krahé, Barbara, Möller Ingrid, L. Rowell Huesmann, Lucyna Kirwil, Juliane Felber, and Anja Berger. 2011. Desensitization to media violence: Links with habitual media violence exposure, aggressive cognitions, and aggressive behavior. *Journal of Personality and Social Psychology* 100(4): 630–646.

Langner, Sascha. 2009. *Viral marketing: Wie Sie Mundpropaganda gezielt auslösen und Gewinn bringend nutzen*. Wiesbaden: Springer.

Lawrence, Benjamin, Susan Fournier, and Frederic F. Brunel. 2013. When companies don't make the ad: A multimethod inquiry into the differential effectiveness of consumer-generated advertising. *Journal of Advertising* 42(4): 292–307.

Martin, Kelly D., and N. Craig Smith. 2008. Commercializing social interaction: The ethics of stealth marketing. *Journal of Public Policy & Marketing* 27(1): 45–56.

McFall, Liz. 2008. Advertising, history of. In *The international encyclopedia of communication*, ed. Wolfgang Donsbach, 91–97. Malden et al.: Blackwell.

Meme. n.d. In *Oxford dictionaries*. http://www.oxforddictionaries.com/definition/english/meme. Accessed 30 Nov 2015.

Morewedge, Carey K., Young Eun Huh, and Joachim Vosgerau. 2010. Thought for food: Imagined consumption reduces actual consumption. *Science* 330(6010): 1530–1533.
Mullin, Charles R., and Daniel G. Linz. 1995. Desensitization and resensitization to violence against women: Effects of exposure to sexually violent films on judgments of domestic violence victims. *Journal of Personality and Social Psychology* 69: 449–459.
Porter, Lance, and Guy J. Golan. 2006. From subservient chickens to brawny men: A comparison of viral advertising to television advertising. *Journal of Interactive Advertising* 6(2): 30–38.
Rankin, Catharine H., et al. 2009. Habituation revisited: An updated and revised description of the behavioral characteristics of habituation. *Neurobiology of Learning and Memory* 92(2): 135–138.
Richards, Jef I. 2008. Advertising ethics. In *The international encyclopedia of communication*, ed. Wolfgang Donsbach, 77–82. Malden [et al.]: Blackwell.
Ricken, Friedo. 2003. Der Begriff der moralischen Handlung. In *Allgemeine Ethik. Grundkurs Philosophie. Bd. 4*, ed. Friedo Ricken, 91–117. Stuttgart: W. Kohlhammer.
Sagar, Amin. 2014, December 2. *Sportka cat commercial funny videos, funny video clips, funny movies, viral videos flv.* [Video file]. http://www.youtube.com/watch?v=2t70nC1IgWE. Accessed 30 Nov 2015.
Schudson, Michael. 2013. *Advertising, the uneasy persuasion: Its dubious impact on American society*. London: Routledge.
Smith, N. Craig, Patrick E. Murphy, Alina Reibetanz, and Markus Scholz. 2015. Marketingethik – Ein Überblick. In *Corporate social responsibility*, ed. Andreas Schneider and René Schmidpeter, 721–734. Berlin/Heidelberg: Springer.
Stapf, Ingrid. 2010. Tod und Sterben. In *Handbuch Medienethik*, ed. Christian Schicha and Carsten Brosda, 391–405. Wiesbaden: VS Verlag für Sozialwissenschaften.
Strenziok, Maren, Frank Krueger, Gopikrishna Deshpande, Rhoshel K. Lenroot, Elke van der Meer, and Jordan Grafman. 2010. Fronto-parietal regulation of media violence exposure in adolescents: A multi-method study. *Social Cognitive & Affective Neuroscience* 6(5): 537–547.
TheBdscraps. 2012, March 3. *Bulova: World's first television advertisement.* [Video File]. http://www.youtube.com/watch?v=8JenAyMmZ68. Accessed 30 Nov 2015.
Toffler, Alvin. 1980. *The third wave*. London [et al.]: Collins.
TomTomOfficial. 2014, July 22. *Alexandria Morgan runs strapless.* [Video file]. http://www.youtube.com/watch?v=Ur0qPdMhrag. Accessed 30 Nov 2015.
Turkle, Sherry. 2011. *Alone together: Why we expect more from technology and less from each other*. New York: Basic Books.
van Eimeren, Birgit, and Beate Frees. 2013. Rasanter Anstieg des Internetkonsums – Onliner fast drei Stunden täglich im Netz. *Media Perspektiven* 7(8): 358–372.
Ward, Stephen J.A. 2014. Radical media ethics. *Nordicom Review* 35(Special Issue): 45–52.
Wilde, Oscar. 2005. *The picture of Dorian Gray (1890)* (The complete works of Oscar Wilde. The Picture of Dorian Gray. The 1890 and 1891 Texts) vol. 3, 1–165.
Wimmer, Rainer. 2011. Verantwortung. In *Neues Handbuch philosophischer Grundbegriffe*, ed. Petra Kolmer, Armin Wildfeuer, and Hermann Krings, 2309–2320. Freiburg/Breisgau/ München: Alber.

Chapter 6
The Position of Female Homeworkers in a Global Supply Chain: How Do Capitalist Labor Market Practices Interplay with Gender Ideologies?

Farah Naz

Abstract With the expansion of global capitalism since the later part of the twentieth century, homeworking has become an integral component of the global production organization. Although it was expected that homeworking would decline with the industrialization, the situation is, in fact, exactly opposite to what was expected. The involvement of homeworkers is on the rise in global supply chains and the employment of workers under poor working conditions is driving down the labor conditions. These new production arrangements have fueled the debate about the working conditions and associated responsibilities in global supply chains on a much broader scale. This paper aims at contributing to these discussions by focusing on female homeworkers in a garment supply chain of Pakistan. A qualitative study was designed to explore the intricacies of female home-based work in global supply chains and to develop theoretical insights relevant to the institution of homeworking. This study shows that women's involvement in homework within the private sphere of the household is shaped by the interplay of gender ideologies and capitalist labor market practices, spreading responsibilities in the case of homeworkers. Therefore, existing notions of economic responsibility in laissez-faire economics are not adequate to deal with the issues of homeworking in global supply chains.

6.1 Introduction

Despite the fact that the garment sector contributes significantly to the employment and economic growth of the developing world, it is often criticized for ethically questionable labor practices (Soundararajan and Brown 2016). Over the last two decades, the garment industry has also become the focus of a great deal of attention in debates on globalization and labor, due to women's increased involvement in

F. Naz (✉)
Alpen-Adria University Klagenfurt, Klagenfurt, Austria
e-mail: fanaz@edu.aau.at

M. Haase (ed.), *Economic Responsibility*, Ethical Economy 53,
DOI 10.1007/978-3-319-52099-5_6

classified GCC chains into two types: buyer-driven and producer-driven commodity chains. Producer-driven chains are mainly governed by the large transnational companies (TNC) and have centralized governance structures, whereas buyer-driven chains are controlled by retailers, brand name merchandisers and trading companies. The garment industry is a buyer-driven system of governance. There is intense competition among the producers that drives down prices in the international market, because sourcing companies are in a position to switch factories or countries in order to benefit from a small price reduction (Oxfam 2004). Brand name companies and retailers further protect their profit by demanding high quality and low-priced products from the supplier at short notice. Six to eight fashion seasons in the year have become the norm in the Western market, which has built up time pressure on the producers. This pressure ultimately translates into pressure on the work force in the form of unpaid overtime and sub-contracting and outsourcing. A large number of the female homeworkers are deeply integrated into the closely-knit local/global supply chains. Although there is not much data available about home-based workers due to their invisibility, it is estimated that approximately 80% of all home-based workers are women located at the lowest nodes of commodity chains (Mehrotra and Biggeri 2007; ILO 2011; Chen 2014).

6.2.3 Home-Based Work: Concepts and Interpretations

Home-based work includes all kinds of remunerative work carried out inside the home. There are two prevalent, but contrasting images about working from home. The traditional perception about working from home is more pessimistic and evokes the image of low-paid and low-skilled manual work performed in unsafe surroundings, often involving the labor of children and unpaid family helpers, whereas the optimistic image is of highly paid and skilled professionals, technicians, and managers conducting business operations from their homes. In reality, home-based work is more heterogeneous in nature and it ranges from labor-intensive semi-skilled work to high-tech capital and information-intensive professional work with considerable diversity in the terms and conditions of work experienced by different groups of home-based workers. Homeworkers are a sub-category of the home-based workers, who work from the home for factories, mostly on piece rate. Largely, they are involved in industrial out-work.

The International Labor Organization (ILO) adopted a Homework Convention in 1996 (No. 177), which uses the term "homeworker" for a person who carries out work for remuneration in the premises of his/her own choice, other than the workplace of the employer, resulting in a product or service as specified by the employer, irrespective of who provides the equipment, materials, or inputs used. The ILO convention on homework requires that ratifying states ensure the equality of treatment between employees and homeworkers in their national policies. Homeworkers constitute a particularly vulnerable category of workers due to inadequate legal protection, isolation and weak bargaining position (ILO 2014).

There are two major strands of debate around the issues of women's labor force participation in the new production model. One group is optimistic about the transformative potential of female labor force participation (Chhachhi 2006; Kabeer 2004). It is claimed that current changes in the world system have extended the opportunities for women workers, previously excluded due to their limited human capital and their cultural constraints. Homeworking, along with self-employment, part-time work and temporary contracts in sub-contracted production chains are seen as a boon for the women, since they have to continue with their care work in spite of their wage labor. Homeworking is thus viewed as having some advantages for mothers with young children to care for. Meanwhile, opponents take it as another form of female exploitation through biased labor market practices that naturalize women's role as caregivers and constrain women's opportunity structure in the labor market and society. The integration of the household into capitalist labor processes has tended to reinforce patriarchal relations and sharpen the gender inequalities (Elson 1995; Pearson 1998).

6.2.4 Women's Empowerment and Agency: Contested Terrain

There is an ongoing debate in feminist and development literature about the implications of women's paid work within the domestic sphere of the household from the perspective of their empowerment and agency. Empowerment can be defined as the capacity of the individual or groups to make choices and transform these choices into desirable forms of action. It is evident from the existing studies that the individual capacity to make choices does not automatically lead to women's empowerment, for the reason that a choice can only be made in the first place, if a person has agency and appropriate opportunities exist for making choices and getting at least some of the desired results (Alsop et al. 2006). Agency is the ability of an individual to envision and make choices. Many factors constrain the individual ability to make choices, because individual choices and actions are embedded within a framework of a given society (Haase et al. 2016). Therefore, individual agency may be hindered by the cultural context and everyday realities of a person's life.

Social institutions that are a reflection of shared ideologies also play a very important role in shaping women's perceptions about their abilities. These ideologies are so deep-rooted that the women themselves cannot fully perceive the disempowering impact of these gendered ideologies (framework of ideas). Women themselves see their dis-empowerment as befitting morally virtuous and socially appropriate behavior. In many patriarchal societies, women accept the right of men to engage in domestic violence as 'Doxa', which is seen as a natural and common phenomenon (Kabeer 1999). Therefore, normative structures of society play an important role in determining and shaping individual choices. In many cases, patriarchal norms are so deeply embedded that women are not always aware that their habitual choices undermine their own position with regard to their own agency, their rights in the broadest sense. They may fail to appreciate that their 'desirable' behavior is not natural, but rather tends to be socially constructed (Alsop et al. 2006).

6.2.5 Conceptualizing Economic Responsibility

There is a tradition to reflect on the idea of responsibilities of business. In this section, the intellectual underpinnings of various dimensions of the concept of responsibility are explored, which are relevant for the ascription of economic responsibility in the case of poor working conditions of female homeworkers in the global supply chains.

There are two dominant paradigms[2] in history that define the relationship between business and morality of larger society, namely; the theory of moral unity and the amoral theory of business (Shepard et al. 1995). The theory of moral unity in pre-industrial *Gemeinschaft* societies rests on the assumption that only one set of moral standards exists within a society and economic entities are not considered as "ethical sanctuaries" (ibid, p. 580). The underlying assumption is that social relations and economic activities are socially embedded and governed by the same set of rules, value and norms. In contrast, modern societies are characterized by high levels of social differentiation (Weber 1968; Habermas 1981) as compared to pre-industrial societies and shift from *Gemeinschaft* (pre-industrial) to *Gesellschaft* (industrial) societies, marked by individualism, social fragmentation, weak family ties, and competition. There is also a shift from integrated social institutions to a high level of functional differentiation. Therefore, in capitalist societies, institutions designed for carrying instrumental goals are governed according to the tenets of rationality. From the perspective of neo-liberal economic theory market participants are viewed as rational actors whose only desire is to maximize their utility, and economic responsibility is not beyond what is defined in the laws. According to this perspective business relationships are not immoral however, they are not subject to the same moral constraints and practices covering other areas of social relationships (Shepard et al. 1995).

Consequently, in the long-standing tradition of the liberal market economy, responsibilities of commercial agents are narrowly defined and restricted only to negative duties. The core assumption in orthodox economic theory termed as Euclidean economics (Clark 1921; 132 ff.) is that business is a special domain within society with its distinct morality that derives its efficiency from the self-interest of mutually benefiting commercial agents. The market is portrayed as a neutral force linked to economic individualism and personal preferences (Stehr et al. 2006). The neo liberal economic theory paradigm has limited space for particularism, sentiment, and morality, except for the minimum morality that is defined by law. However, contemporary debates on the moral responsibilities of businesses

[2] "Paradigm" means the shared cultural understandings that define (1) the place of social institutions in society and (2) the relationship between social institutions and individuals (Shepard et al. 1995, p. 579).

that operate internationally have begun to challenge this established principle and intuitions that the morality of commercial life ought to be a minimum morality (see also Hsieh 2013), and moral reasoning is gaining ground to explain market behavior (Dubbink and Van Liedekerke 2014). Clark argued that private enterprises cannot be governed solely by private interest.

> We are coming to see that our everyday business dealings have more far-reaching effects than we have ever realized, and that the system of free contract is by itself quite inadequate to bring home the responsibility for these effects. We have begun to realize the many inappropriable values that are created and the many unpaid damages that are inflicted in the course of business exchanges (Clark 1916, p. 217 f.).

The application of the restrictive economic responsibility model in traditional business economics has striking implications for global society. It leaves the most pressing problems in the domain of supererogatory action[3] and reduces them to issues of mere philanthropy and charity (Clark 1916). Therefore, a more adequate concept of responsibility is required for the collective age to solve multidimensional large-scale problems (Wettstein 2012). The normative vacuum created by the dilution of the *homo-economicus* model needs to be filled by altered or new norms and ideas. However, transition from one to another mode of thought is fraught with challenges and contradictions. The debate over the appropriate duties of commercial agents has been articulated, particularly in discussions on international business, to demonstrate that the morality of commercial life cannot exclude all positive duties. However, within existing literature, there is a divide on the issue of grounding positive duties either as inescapable moral duties ensuing from the liberal tradition (Young 2010; Hsieh 2013; Dubbink and Van Liedekerke 2014), or to conceptualize positive duties as an alternative vision of responsibility termed economics *of responsibility* (Clark 1916), in which business recognizes its responsibility for the public interest (Scherer et al. 2006; Scherer and Palazzo 2007, 2011).

6.2.6 *Macro Context of the Case: Mapping the Supply Chain*

The knitwear industry is an almost totally export-oriented industry in Pakistan. It is a highly profitable industry, earning valued foreign exchange. During the last few years, the segment of knitwear has shown a substantial rise in exports. Export of knitwear increased from $464 million in 1992–1993 to $1.842 billion in 2013–2014 (Sajjad 2014). There is fierce competition among the manufacturers, both at the global and national level. This situation is further exacerbated by drastic changes in the trade rules after the expiry of the ATC Agreement on Textiles and Clothing

[3] Supererogation is the technical term and a theoretical construct for the class of actions that go "beyond the call of duty." Roughly speaking, supererogatory acts are morally good though not (strictly) required. Although common discourse in most cultures allows for such acts and often attaches special value to them, ethical theories have only rarely discussed this category of actions directly and systematically(Heyd 2007).

(ATC) at the end of 2004. The knitwear industry in Pakistan has come under great stress since the phase-out of the quota. It has been severely affected by the low-priced and high-quality goods from China, India, Bangladesh, and Cambodia. Knitwear was one of the most flourishing sub-sectors of the garment industry in Pakistan, but 77 exporting units have already closed since the expiry of the quota system. Of the closed knitwear units, 31 units were based in Lahore. Irfan Textile Limited (ITL) was established in 1990 and is now a leading knitwear exporter in Pakistan. It has set up three modern production units for knitwear in Lahore. ITL was the largest quota holder in Pakistan in category 338 (cotton knit shirts) of men's knit to the USA, enjoying comfortably high margins during the quota regime. However, after the quota expiry it came under strain and now faces fierce competition in the global market. Export margins on the products in general have decreased in a highly competitive global market without the guarantee of a secured quota.

Figure 6.1 is intended to facilitate an understanding of the complex nature of the garment production process that has widened the scope and responsibility of different (socially and geographically situated) actors in the wake of economic restructuring. There are six main tiers of this production chain. A small number of retailers and brand names govern the chain. They are located in the advanced countries and have greater access to and control over the Western consumer market. They have their own buying houses and they also control research and management, whereas production is carried out in the middle part of the chain. ITL, which carries out the

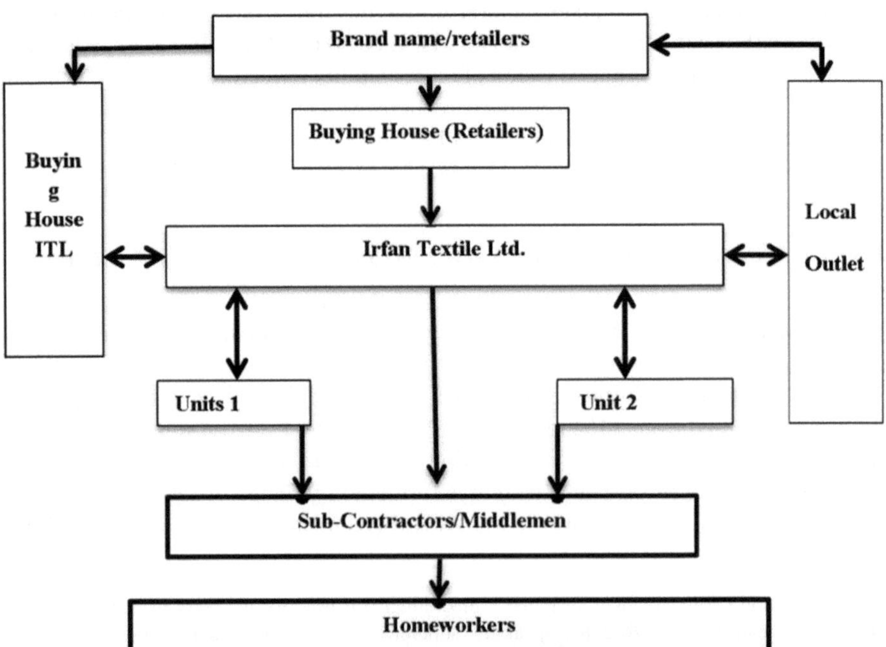

Fig. 6.1 The supply chain of Irfan Textile (Pvt) Ltd. (Source: Author)

assembly line manufacturing, is located in the middle of the chain. ITL was used as an entry point in this research to locate the homeworkers and analyze their working conditions in complex and multi-layered subcontracting garment supply chains of Pakistan. ITL also has its own buying house in New York and receives most of its contracts (approximately 70%) through this buying house, which gives ITL some control in this supply chain. Irfan Textile also produces for the Famous Brand, who is the retailer for Hang Ten (USA), Jockey International (USA), Slazenger (UK), and Dunlop (UK) in Pakistan. They have acquired the licenses to design, manufacture and distribute the clothing in Pakistan for the above-mentioned brands.

A large part of what follows remains focused on the empirical case of the garment industry of Pakistan. As such, it draws on the theoretical framework outlined in the paper to analyze the situation of female homeworkers in a garment supply chain of Pakistan. Empirical material is used as an example to illustrate the existence of broader patterns as well as structural and actor-oriented aspects of homework. Structural aspects include the type of work, working conditions and associated responsibilities, whereas actor-oriented aspects are mainly concerned with the meaning of homework for homeworkers themselves.

6.3 Research Methodology

A qualitative study[4] was designed to explore the intricacies of female home-based work in global garment supply chains and to gain insights relevant to the institution of homeworking. Case study[5] is a research method to explore and understand complex issues and is widely used for the holistic and in-depth investigation of the phenomenon (Eisenhardt 1980; Eisenhardt and Graebner 2007). Case study also helps to emphasize the rich, real-world context of the phenomena. In this research, a case study of a garment-producing firm facilitated a deep-level exploration of the structure of the garment industry and helped to elaborate important insights about homework. The purpose of this case study was to provide a rich description of the situation of homeworkers within the supply chain in order to further develop and focus insightful research questions, which have been developed mainly on the basis of theory. In this case, the justification of the research strategy rests on the importance of investigating homeworking within the context of a supply chain to gain a more holistic understanding of the phenomenon.

[4] Two important paradigms mostly followed in qualitative research are positivist and interpretive (for more discussion see Lincoln and Guba 1985). This research followed the interpretive paradigm and the ontology that is based on the assumption that reality is constructed and can be multiple. Whereas the epistemological stance of the study is that inquiry is inductive and value driven and hence generalization is not possible.

[5] According to Yin (1981, p. 23) the case study research method is "an empirical inquiry that investigates a contemporary phenomenon within its real-life context; when the boundaries between phenomenon and context are not clearly evident; and in which multiple sources of evidence are used."

This case study enabled the researcher to provide valuable insights into the working conditions, nature of work, production relations, and empowering potential of homework in the garment supply chains of Pakistan and to identify key issues with policy implications for governance and the improvement of homework. While locating the role of female home-based workers in the global supply chains, including their invisibility and marginalization with regard to work and labor rights, the paper uses in-depth interviews and non-participant observation as tools for data collection and analyzes their perceptions and their access to labor rights in particular. This case study was conducted at three levels of analysis. Interviews were conducted at the level of the firm, at the level of the sub-contractor and at the level of the homeworkers. The research sample was drawn from a population through snowball sampling. In order to locate the homeworkers and obtain first-hand information about the working situation of homeworkers, ITL, was used as an entry point in this research. Lahore was selected as the main area for study for the reason that it is one of the largest garment-producing cities of Pakistan. This became an important starting point that helped the author to trace homeworkers in the supply chain and to establish independent contact with them. Once the initial contact had been established, it became easier to trace other homeworkers through neighbors or residents in the same locality. The author's position as a middle class Punjabi[6] woman from Pakistan helped her to contact female homeworkers, who represent an otherwise hard-to-reach population.

In order to overcome data challenges, systematically collected data were mainly organized around theoretical framework and the research question being asked. Interviews were conducted in person at homeworkers' homes and careful consideration was given to the framing of questions to avoid bias. Interviews were recorded on a digital recorder and the duration of interviews ranged from 35 to 60 min. Interview data were transcribed and themes were identified for analysis. In order to cope with the challenges of biases, varied informants were selected to obtain diverse data. The sample was comprised of twenty homeworkers, one subcontractor, and two management staff.

6.4 Empirical Evidence

The rapid growth of the garment export industry in Lahore, Pakistan during the past few decades has opened some new windows on income-earning opportunities for poor women in Lahore and its surrounding villages, where agriculture is no longer able to provide the livelihood for the entire village population. Increased trends of outsourcing through sub-contracting processes in the garment industry have helped women with limited or no marketable skills to earn cash income to supplement their family needs within the private sphere of the home (Chen et al. 1999). However, the conditions under which they are incorporated in the wage labor process are a matter

[6] An ethnic group of Indo-Aryan peoples, originating from the Punjab region, found in Pakistan and northern India.

of great concern from the perspective of human rights, and labor rights in particular. The following section deals with the major themes that emerge from the analysis of empirical data.

6.4.1 Structural Relations and Conditions of Work in the Garment Supply Chain

Production costs in Pakistan are comparatively high for various reasons, such as high labor cost, higher utility costs, and higher financial costs as compared with India, China, and Bangladesh. Therefore, despite having enough orders, manufacturers are having a difficult time meeting the demands at a cost that is feasible for them due to the high unit cost of production. Tight delivery schedules are also reported as a problem for the manufacturer. They usually have no more than 90 days from the day of the order to the delivery of the products. There is also fluctuation in the orders (informal interview with a manager of the garment production unit of ITL). Therefore, the firm has to use different organizational strategies to become more competitive and flexible by transferring the pressure to the bottom of the chain. The following excerpt from an interview shows that in order to be competitive the firm uses multiple managerial strategies. Sub-contracting is one of the most common strategies adopted by the manufacturers to remain competitive in the market.

> Outsourcing is widely practiced by the garment manufacturers in Pakistan. We do not indulge in these practices. We own three units with large manufacturing capacity, therefore we do not need to outsource our work. However, in peak seasons we may bring women into the plant for work. These women also bring their young daughters with them to help them in their work. We do not employ women without checking their valid ID cards. These women are paid on a piece rate basis. We ensure that they can earn on average 5000 PKR (44.1 Euro) per month; that is our minimum wage level (Interview with male Garment Production Manager ITL).

It was found that ITL engages in both horizontal as well as vertical sub-contracting practices. In horizontal sub-contracting, work is sub-contracted by ITL to two other sibling factories in the same city. Dying and fabric painting is mostly sub-contracted to other small units. In the case of large orders and short delivery periods, the company adopts two main strategies of sub-contracting. One of the strategies adopted by the management is to hire a temporary workforce for a short period or to engage workers in overtime. Hiring of workers for a short period is an innovative type of sub-contracting, widely practiced in new production models, in which workers are brought inside the plant to complete the task during a short period. These temporary workers do not have any formal job contracts or other labor right entitlements. During the fieldwork, it was revealed in an informal interview with the manager of a garment production unit that these temporary workers, mostly women, are paid on the basis of piece rate. The company does not feel that it has obligations towards these workers. They do not even maintain records concerning these workers, their hours or production levels and pay.

Although it was denied by the manager, field research revealed that outsourcing is another strategy adopted by the management to reduce the cost and time of production (Mudambi and Venzin 2010). ITL also hires temporary piece rate workers through subcontractors. Three permanent female supervisors who work in the quality control section also serve as sub-contractors for ITL. According to the information generated during the fieldwork, the two main types of task that were mostly outsourced by ITL were hand embroidery and fabric painting. Work is sub-contracted through different agents. The company does not have any direct contact with the homeworkers. In cases of outsourcing, work is sub-contracted through intermediaries. These intermediaries have the formal contract with the firms on some basic terms and conditions. The terms and conditions are fixed regarding the time and the quality of the work. Sub-contractors mostly work for many firms at a time. They receive the orders directly from the factories and maintain their own network of homeworkers. There is intense competition among the sub-contractors and they are highly reluctant to disclose information about their workers. These sub-contractors enter into the category of self-employed entrepreneurs. They do not have a steady flow of orders. No firm is bound to give them the contract. Sub-contractors work under great pressure. They have to provide good quality work within a limited span of time; otherwise they are in fear of losing their customers.

Sub-contractors have a dependency relationship with the exporting firms. They do not have any control over the process of production, but they keep a check on the quality of the sub-contracted work. Sub-contractors have limited bargaining power and have to accept low rates for their orders. Mapping of this supply chain helped in the analysis of the relative position of various actors within the chain. One of the major problems reported by the female sub-contractor interviewed during the field survey was the delaying tactics used by the factories in making payments. The location of workers in different tiers of the chain determines their position and bargaining power in the hierarchy of the relationships. As shown in Fig. 6.1, international retailers and brand names are at the top end. As the drivers of this supply chain they extract maximum profit without sharing the risk involved in production and market fluctuations. Female homeworkers, who add high value to the products, are located at the lowest end of the supply chain. It is clear from the mapping of the garment supply chain that various actors in the supply chain are linked to each other in a system of structural and institutional relations (Young 2010).

It has been established from individual responses of female homeworkers that the earnings of one member was not sufficient to meet the family's basic subsistence needs. Apart from economic insecurity, many sources of social insecurity, including poor housing conditions, limited access to health care, the high burden of health care expenditure, and the low age of entry into home-based work, are also explored. It is revealed from the information generated through in-depth interviews with homeworkers that most of them belong to the lowest economic strata of Pakistani society. The majority of female homeworkers live in tiny one- or two-room houses, where living conditions are over-crowded, and where there is almost nothing in terms of amenities or facilities nearby. Poor hygiene and ventilation are problems for all the homeworkers and their families. With three earning members per family,

Table 6.1 Socio-demographic data of respondents

Age	**10–18 years**	**06**
	19 and above	14
Marital status	Married	14
	Un married	04
	Other	02
Education	Literate	05
	Illiterate	15
Family members	Up to 5	03
	More than 5	17
Training	Yes	01
	No	19
Contribution to family budget	Minimum	1500 KR. (approx. 13.3 Euros)
	Maximum	7000 PKR. (approx. 62 Euros)
Reported breadwinner	Male	16
	Female	04
Reasons to take homework	Poverty	16
	Choice	04

Source: Field notes

the labor of young children is involved as well as that of women and men (Mehrotra and Biggeri 2010). A family size above five persons (see Table 6.1), which applies to the majority of respondents is large in relation to the size of the accommodation, which must also serve as a workspace for the women homeworkers.

Homeworkers, who were interviewed during the field research, reported very low rates of payment. Rates vary according to the type of work. In the case of hand embroidery, for one "Booti" (single small pattern of embroidery), they usually receive two PKR. It takes approximately one hour to complete one pattern. This means that if they work for eight hours per day they can earn 16 PKR. per day and 480 PKR. (approximately 5 Euros) per month, which is not sufficient to take care of the entire family's needs. However, some of them are able to earn more, e.g. one of the interviewees reported that she had received some training in machine embroidery and is able to earn approximately 7000 PKR. per month through homework (approximately 53 Euros). In principle, it is assumed that homeworkers have more opportunities to organize their work independently, but their decisions have repercussions for their income and livelihood security (Baylina and Schier 2002). Therefore, for many homeworkers, this flexibility of homework amounts to self-exploitation involving long hours of work without rest or leisure time in order to secure their livelihood and save their future opportunities for cash income. Unpaid family help is also desired in case of intensive work schedule and demands for delivery of products.

In line with the existing research findings (Mehrotra and Biggeri 2010), this research also reveals that children are withdrawn from schools to share the economic burden of their families and avoid schooling costs. Young boys are withdrawn from the schools to work as casual laborers or as unpaid family helpers with their fathers. Girls and boys are withdrawn from schools due to poverty-related reasons and girls are expected to share the housework from an early age. Girls as young as six or seven shoulder the domestic responsibilities of their mothers, and also contribute to homeworking with their mothers. This reflects the urgency of having more earning hands to meet the basic subsistence needs of the family. Homeworkers are producing for international brands, but their contributions are neither recognized in official economic discourse nor at the household level. Findings of the study support the notion that the scope of the actors is often global in scale and everyone stands in relation to mutual obligations in the garment supply chains. Grounding responsibility on the basis of neoliberal norms of the egoistic homo economicus, it is hard to reconcile a transnational system of interdependence and dense economic interaction. In modern production organizations, responsibility is grounded in the objective systemic institutional relations in which we dwell together with distant others (Young 2008).

6.4.2 Ideological Construction of Homework: Gender at Work

In the social context of Pakistan, industrial homework that is carried out by homeworkers in the ITL supply chain within the private sphere of the household is constructed as a feminine activity, and does not undermine the ideological expectation of the "male bread winner" role. This feminization of industrial work contributes towards its marginalization in production relations (Mehrotra and Biggeri 2002). Female homeworkers are denied the recognition as a worker. They carry the double burden without any recognition and improvement in their life situation. Thus, in line with the existing literature on the empowering potential of home-based work, this study also add evidence to the view that homework is least likely to bring any significant change in power relations, both within the household and in the broader social milieu without some positive support (Mehrotra and Biggeri 2010).

Homework carried out within the private sphere of the household is completely blended with the other household chores. Interview data reflect that despite the fact that women are spending on average seven and a half hours per day on their productive work, it fails to bring them the recognition as a worker. In line with the findings of existing research (Prugal 1996; Burchielli and Delaney 2008; Chen 2014), information generated through in-depth interviews also confirms that women do not share a common position in the hierarchy of production relations; some workers get more work than others. Homeworkers are not a homogeneous group. Boundaries are very fluid and constantly shifting at the bottom end of the garment supply chain. The majority of female homeworkers interviewed during fieldwork reported having no formal skills or training. They utilize the traditional skills and crafts of stitching and hand embroidery that they had learned as a part of their gender role socialization in order to raise additional resources for the family. Most of the women are engaged in embroidery and stitching, which is considered a natural talent or skill for women, learned informally during their childhood as part of their future gender role socialization. Women cannot receive formal training due to the absence of supporting mechanisms and facilities where they reside. Poor infrastructure of roads, difficulties of accessibility and the high cost of transport are major constraints reported by the interviewees.

The naturalization of women's skills as part of gender role training devalues these skills rather than relegating to their work the status of valuable professional activity. Such perceptions about women's traditional skills also influence the opinion about their homework as a secondary activity by the families and by the workers themselves. Gender ideologies are so deeply embedded in society that although women are contributing to the family budget, their participation in paid work fails to bring any substantial change to the existing gendered division of labor in the household. For female homeworkers, their work is an extension of their unpaid household work and their assumed role as caregivers with responsibility for the family's welfare. They devise their own strategies to maintain the balance between their paid and un-paid care work. It is of great concern that production by the homeworkers mainly involves the un-paid labor of other female family members, mostly elder daughters, thus undermining the potential of these young girls through serious capability deprivations (Mehrotra and Biggeri 2010).

> I have been working for the last twenty years. I got one year of training in embroidery and started working for different agents. I am able to earn approximately six to seven thousand. I give my entire income to my husband because he is the head of the family and he can manage it in a better way. I prefer not to go out for work because I can earn in the house and manage the house as well. I have made my house much better through my income than what it used to be (Salma).

The only positive change that is reflected from the interviewees' responses is that it helps them to earn some money for their families, giving them a sense of pride and self-worth. They gain the confidence that they can work to bring their families out of economic stress. However, in this process, they are carrying an unequal burden of work. Although they are aware of the exploitation by the intermediaries, they are not in a position to search for better options under the prevailing strong patriarchal norms and existing opportunity structure of the society. Despite producing for international brand names and the global market, the social construction of homework diminishes homework's ability to fix responsibility or frame and claim their rights. Institutional rules in Pakistani society also lead to the ideological and social construction of female homework within the household as a secondary activity. Such a normative construction of female homework is so deeply embedded in society that homeworkers are unable to identify themselves as workers. A majority of respondents reported their status to be nonworking housewives, despite the fact that they have been engaged in homework for several years.

> My eyesight is adversely affected due to long hours of work over the previous few years. I was operated on last year and have to wear eyeglasses during work. Whom should I hold responsible for my miseries and plights? I am not a regular employee, as I do not get work regularly and I work for many agents. Why should the agent provide for my health expenditure? (Bushra)

Evidence from existing research (Baylina and Schier 2002; Kabeer et al. 2013) also suggests that female home-based workers, being located at the invisible margins of informal economies, are unable to transcend their structurally disadvantaged position within the economy and household, except for some hidden subversion. It was evident from the testimonies of homeworkers as well as a female subcontractor interviewed during the field research that rather than openly challenging the dominant patriarchal ideologies of Pakistan, they are trying to create a safe space for themselves through strict adherence to cultural practices such as veiling in public spaces in order to gain access to income earning opportunities (Haleema, female sub-contractor).

6.5 Discussion

This research began with the assumption that women's involvement in wage labor through industrial homework must have helped them to come out of the strong patriarchal controls that largely characterize Pakistani society. However, this optimism could not persist after exploring the living realities of the female homeworkers in the garment supply chains of Pakistan, which are extremely difficult in terms of living conditions, illness and insecurity of livelihood. In Pakistan, women's seclusion still stands for family propriety, in spite of dramatic economic changes in social structures, women's seclusion continues to symbolize hegemonic masculine identities. Women are therefore not encouraged to work in the public sphere, except in segregated occupations. For the middle and lower middle classes, women working in the public sphere in male dominant occupations are stigmatized. Women are encouraged to work inside the house, where their paid work is effectively disguised as an extension of the housework and is either not paid at all, or devalued in the private sphere of the household, to avoid undermining the ideological expectation of the 'male provider' role being able to sustain the family. Thus, homeworkers' choices are largely shaped or constrained by gender roles, relations within the families and by regional contexts (Baylina and Schier 2002). In rural areas where job opportunities are limited, homeworking within the informal sector is a socially acceptable form of productive activity for women. The broader social context thus gains relevance in the interpretation of the persistence of homework.

The homeworkers' situation is further worsened by the lack of supportive mechanisms for homeworkers in Pakistan. The social construction of homework as a devalued and secondary economic activity also constrains female homeworkers from claiming their labor rights. Homework is construed as secondary in official and cultural discourses and homeworkers are denied recognition as a worker, which is a clear violation of article 3 and article 38 of the constitution of Pakistan, that is, of the constitutional right to work and non-discrimination in the labor market, granted to all citizens regardless of their sex. Thus, the state is also an important factor in gendering the labor market and maintaining the ideological boundaries of the public-private divide through the official definition of workers. The veiling of female homework within the private sphere of households, which makes women homeworkers invisible in economic and political discourses, has serious implications for their labor rights entitlements and their other human rights.

Use of space for production purposes, within the private sphere of the household, embodies the possibility of exploitation. Homework performed within the private sphere of the household does not help women to acquire any kind of professional status. However, it may provide room for economic gains by giving them the opportunity to earn some income for their own and their family's needs. Despite the precariousness (Kallberg 2011; Burchielli et al. 2014a, b) of the work, the need for cash income is the major motivating factor that keeps the homeworkers working. Although the need for income might vary among female homeworkers, nevertheless, the majority of them are working for their personal and their family's survival. There are some other common denominators related to motivation, which may include factors such as the possibility of combining different tasks, or few job opportunities.

Homework provides an opportunity to turn the home into a site of economic activity, which may also provide an opportunity for women to sidestep personal, social and structural constraints that hinder their access to the labor market or prevent them from earning income or realizing their professional career. Despite the existing constraints, working at home is reported to have some positive outcomes as well, especially for single mothers or mothers with small children. Again, this is a reflection of prevailing traditional gender roles like the *mother mythos* that glorify the role of the mother as caretaker of the children (also documented in Haase et al. 2016). For women who assume reproductive work responsibilities due to their gender roles, other forms of work are difficult to engage in. Women indicated during their interviews that homeworking is important for them and something that is 'normal' in their life plans. Efforts for grounding responsibility in relation to poor working conditions of homeworkers reveal that the structure of the global apparel industry diffuses responsibility for poor working conditions, especially in the case of homeworkers (Young 2006). As shown in Fig. 6.1, at the top of the global garment industries are the brand names or retailers who are rarely the producers or owners of the factories where most of their garments are manufactured. These contractually distinct entities are responsible for bringing the manufactured clothes to the stores from which people buy them. However, firms located at the highest nodes of the garment supply chains have no legal responsibility for the policies and operations of the firms with whom they enter into sub-contracting relations. In the global garment industry, each link in the chain works under conditions of fierce competition. They are under heavy pressure from the firms higher up the chain to produce low-cost and high-quality garments under time pressure in a highly competitive environment (interview with manager).

Another important aspect of the garment industry that makes it difficult to ascribe responsibility is the blurred boundaries of employment relations. Some homeworkers revealed that they also serve as sub-contractors for the main sub-contractor, although they do not have any link with the manufacturer or buyers at the upper echelons of the chain (Chen 2014). Each layer of sub-contracting between the producer and buyer adds to the cost of the item. Homeworkers who make garments are at the bottom of the chain. Their wages are much lower than the retail price of an

6.6 Conclusion and Recommendations

It is evident from the case study of the ITL supply chain that female homeworkers contribute to the global capitalist system of production, but are invisible not only to labor market regulators, but even to themselves, in the sense that they do not identify themselves as workers (Burchielli et al. 2008). Their newly gained opportunities to earn cash income provide them with limited means to challenge the existing patriarchal values and norms of the society. One of the reasons for this dependency could be that, despite considerable effort and time spent by the women on homework, income earned through their wages is not sufficient to meet the entire needs of the family. Their work is also unstable and there is no assurance about the continuity of this work. Although their income is crucial for the survival of their families, they have a weak position in production relations. Their paid work does not bring desirable recognition for their contributions. Assigning responsibility for the plight of these workers is a daunting task in a complex and multilayered system of production. Women's involvement in homework within the private sphere of the household has diffused responsibilities in the case of homeworkers. Assigning responsibility on the basis of the existing notion of economic responsibility as it is conceived in laissez-faire economics is not adequate to deal with the issues of homeworking in global supply chains. Clark (1916, p. 213) traced the line of responsibility when he argued that the results of business action (e.g. adverse labor conditions of female homeworkers in this case) are "things over which someone can exercise control and that means they are things for which someone is responsible." The findings of this research clearly indicate that the scope of responsibility of business has to be broadened from the limited goal of profit maximization to broader goals, where various actors have opportunities to gain and claim legitimacy and business also recognizes and accepts its responsibility towards its societal goals (Clark 1916).

There are three recommendations that arise from this research, as follows:

- Organizing female homeworkers: In order to increase the income level and bargaining power of homeworkers it is important that homeworkers are organized for collective action. Organization in the form of unions or cooperatives is not only important for the economic gains, but also provides opportunities for political participation as an actor in production organization.
- Provision of training facilities: Training facilities and certification of skills will help female homeworkers to gain recognition of their work as a valuable professional activity in the labor market.
- The need for effective state legislation and enforcement mechanisms: This is needed to increase the visibility of homeworkers and will require changes both in the legal and the broader institutional environment. For example, registration of homeworkers is one possible way to increase their visibility.

References

Alsop, Ruth, Mette F. Bertelsen, and Jeremy Holland. 2006. *Empowerment in practice: From analysis to implementation*. Washington, DC: The World Bank.
Baylina, Mireia, and Michaela Schier. 2002. Homework in Germany and Spain: Industrial restructuring and the meaning of homework for women. *GeoJournal* 56(4): 295–304.
Burchielli, Rosaria, Donna M. Buttigieg, and Annie Delaney. 2008. Organizing homeworkers: The use of mapping as an organizing tool. *Work, Employment and Society* 22(1): 167–180.
Burchielli, Rosaria, Annie Delaney, and Kylie Coventry. 2014a. Campaign strategies to develop regulatory mechanisms: Protecting Australian garment homeworkers. *Journal of Industrial Relations* 56(1): 81–102.
Burchielli, Rosaria, Annie Delaney, and Nora Goren. 2014b. Garment homework in Argentina: drawing together the threads of informal and precarious work. *The Economic and Labour Relations Review* 25(1): 63–80.
Burchielli, Rosaria, Annie Delaney, and Tim Connor. 2015. Positioning women homeworkers in a global footwear production network: How can homeworkers improve agency, influence and claim rights? *Journal of Industrial Relations* 57(4): 641–659.
Burchielli, R., D. Buttigieg, and A. Delaney. 2008. Organizing homeworkers: The use of mapping as an organizing tool. *Work, Employment & Society* 22 (1): 167–180. doi:10.1177/0950017007087422.
Burchielli, R., A. Delaney, and K. Coventry. 2013. Campaign strategies to develop regulatory mechanisms: Protecting Australian garment homeworkers. *Journal of Industrial Relations* 56 (1): 81–102. doi:10.1177/0022185613498662.
Chen, Martha. 2014. *Informal economy monitoring study sector report: Home-based workers*. http://wiego.org/sites/wiego.org/files/publications/files/IEMS-Home-Based-Workers-Full--Report.pdf. Accessed 22 Feb 2015.
Chen, Martha, Jennefer Sebstad, and Lesley O' Connell. 1999. Counting the invisible workforce: The case of homebased workers. *World Development* 27(3): 603–610.
Chhachhi, Amrita. 2006. Eroding citizenship: Gender, labour and liberalization in India. In *Engendering human security: Feminist perspectives*, ed. Thang D. Truong, Saskia Wieringa, and Amrita Chhachhi, 234–276. London: Zed Press.
Clark, John M. 1916. The changing basis of economic responsibility. *Journal of Political Economy* 24(3): 209–229.
———. 1921. Soundings in non-euclidean economics. *American Economic Review* 11(1): 132–143.
Dubbink, Wim, and Luc Van Liedekerke. 2014. Grounding positive duties in commercial life. *Journal of Business Ethics* 120(4): 527–539.
Eisenhardt, Kathleen M. 1980. Building theories from case study research. *The Academy of Management Review* 14(4): 532–550.
Eisenhardt, Kathleen M., and Melissa E. Graebner. 2007. Building theories from cases: Opportunities and challenges. *Academy of Management Journal* 50(1): 25–32.
Elson, Diane. 1995. *Male bias in development process*. Manchester/New York: Manchester University Press.
Eshleman, Andrew. 2009. *Moral responsibility*. http://plato.stanford.edu/entries/moral-responsibility/. Accessed 25 June 2014.
Freeman, Dena. 2004. Homeworkers in global supply chains. *Greener Management International* 43: 107–118.
Gereffi, Garry. 1994. The organization of buyer-driven global commodity chains: How U.S retailers shape overseas production networks. In *Commodity chains and global capitalism*, ed. Gary Gereffi and Miguel Korzeniewicz, 95–122. London: Greenwood Publishing.
Gereffi, Garry, Miguel Korzeniewicz, and Roberto Patricio. 1994. Introduction: Global commodity chains. In *Commodity chains and global capitalism*, ed. Gary Gereffi and Miguel Korzeniewicz, 1–14. London: Greenwood Publishing.

Haase, Michaela, Ingrid Becker, Alexander Nill, Clifford J. Shultz, and James W. Gentry. 2016. Male breadwinner ideology and the inclination to establish market relationships: model development using data from Germany and a mixed-methods research strategy. *Journal of Macromarketing* 36(2): 149–167.

Habermas, Jürgen. 1981. *The theory of communicative action life world and system*. Cambridge, MA: Polity Press.

Hartman, Edwin M. 2000. Socratic ethics and the challenge of globalization. *Business Ethics Quarterly* 10(1): 211–220.

Heyd, David. 2007. Supererogation. In *The Stanford encyclopedia of philosophy*, ed. Edward N. Zalta. http://plato.stanford.edu/entries/supererogation. Accessed 25 May 2015.

Hsieh, Nien-he. 2013. Multinational enterprises and incomplete institutions: The demandingness of minimum moral standards. In *Business ethics*, ed. Michael Boylan, 409–422. Hoboken: Wiley.

Hurley, Jennifer, and Doug Miller. 2005. The changing face of the global garment industry. In *Threads of labour: Garment industry supply chains from the worker's perspective*, ed. Angela Hale and Jane Wills, 16–39. Oxford: Blackwell Publishers.

International Labour Organization. 2011. *Searching the invisibles: A study of home based workers in Pakistan*. http://www.ilo.org/wcmsp5/groups/public/@asia/@ro-bangkok/@ilo-islamabad/documents/publication/wcmson. Accessed 2 Dec 2013.

———. 2014. *Labour practices in footwear, textile, and clothing industries*. Paper for discussion at the Global Dialogue Forum. http://www.ilo.org/sector/Resources/publications/WCMS_300463/lang--en/index.htm. Accessed 20 June 2014.

Kabeer, Naila. 1999. Resource, agency, achievements: Reflection on measurements of women's empowerment. *Development and Change* 30(3): 435–464.

———. 2004. Globalization, labor standards, and women's rights: Dilemmas of collective (in) action in an interdependent world. *Feminist Economics* 10(1): 3–35.

Kabeer, Naila, Karisty Milward, and Ratna Sudarshan. 2013. Organising women workers in the informal economy. *Gender and Development* 21(2): 249–263.

Kalleberg, Arne L. 2011. *Good jobs, bad jobs. The rise of polarised and precarious employment systems in the United States 1970s to 2000s*. New York: Russell Sage Foundation.

Lincoln, Y.S., & Guba, E.G.(1985). Naturalistic inquiry. *Beverly Hills*, CA: Sage.

Lund-Thomsen, Peter, and Khalid Nadvi. 2010. Clusters, chains and compliance: Corporate social responsibility and governance in football manufacturing in South Asia. *Journal of Business Ethics* 93(2): 201–222.

Mehrotra, Santosh, and Mario Biggeri. 2002. *Social protection in the informal economy: Home based women workers and outsourced manufacturing in Asia*. UNICEF Innocenti Working paper no. 97. http://www.unicef-irc.org/publications/pdf/iwp97.pdf. Accessed 25 June 2014.

———. 2007. *Asian informal workers: Global risk, local protection*. New York: Routledge.

———. 2010. Children in home worker households in Pakistan and Indonesia. International *Journal of Manpower* 31(2): 208–231.

Mudambi, Ram, and Markus Venzin. 2010. The strategic nexus of offshoring and outsourcing decisions. *Journal of Management Studies* 47(8):1510–1533.

OXFAM. 2004.*Trading away our rights: Women working in supply chains*. http://www.oxfam.org/sites/www.oxfam.org/files/rights.pdf. Accessed 8 June 2014.

Pearson, Ruth. 1998. Nimble fingers revisited: Reflections on women and third world industrialization in the late twentieth century. In *Feminist visions of development: Gender analysis and policy*, ed. Cecile Jackson and Ruth Pearson, 171–188. London: Routledge.

Porter, Michael E., and Mark R. Kramer. 2006. Strategy and society: The link between competitive advantage and corporate social responsibility. *Harvard Business Review* 84(12): 78–92.

Prugl, Lisa. 1996. Home-based producers in development discourses. In *Homeworkers in global perspective: Invisible no more*, ed. Eileen Boris and Lisa Prugl, 39–60. New York/London: Routledge.

Sajjad, Zahid. 2014. *Country report Pakistan* (H-14). http://itg.net.pk/Download/Country%20Report%20Textile%20&%20Clothing.pdf. Accessed 10 June 2014.
Sayer, Andrew. 2006. Approaching moral economy. In *The moralization of the markets*, ed. Nico Stehr, Christoph Henning, and Bernd Weiler, 77–97. New Brunswick: Transaction Publishers.
Scheffler, Samuel. 2001. *Boundaries and allegiances: Problems of justice and responsibility in liberal thought*. Oxford/New York: Oxford University Press.
Scherer, Andreas G., and Guido Palazzo. 2007. Toward a political conception of corporate responsibility: Business and society seen from a Habermasian perspective. *Academy of Management Review* 32(4): 1096–1120.
———. 2011. The new political role of business in a globalized world: A review of a new perspective on CSR and its implications for the firm, governance and democracy. *Journal of Management Studies* 48(4): 899–931.
Scherer, Andreas G., Guido Palazzo, and Dorothée Baumann-Pauly. 2006. Global rules and private actors: Toward a new role of the transnational corporation in global governance. *Business Ethics Quarterly* 16(4): 505–532.
Schrank, Andrew. 2004. Ready to wear development? Foreign investment, technology transfer and learning by watching in the apparel trade. *Social Forces* 83(1): 123 156.
Shepard, Jon M., James C. Wimbush, and Carroll U. Stephens. 1995. The place of ethics in business: Shifting paradigms? *Business Ethics Quarterly* 5(3): 577–601.
Singh, Ajit, and Ann Zammit. 2004. Labour standards and the "race to the bottom": Rethinking globalization and workers' rights from developmental and solidaristic perspectives. *Oxford Review of Economic Policy* 20(1): 85–104.
Soundararajan, Vivek, and Jill A. Brown. 2016. Voluntary governance mechanisms in global supply chains: Beyond CSR to a stakeholder utility perspective. *Journal of Business Ethics* 134(1): 83–102.
Stehr, Nico, Christoph Henning, and Bernd Weiler. 2006. Introduction. In *The moralization of the markets*, ed. Nico Stehr, Christoph Henning, and Bernd Weiler, 1–28. New Brunswick: Transaction Publishers.
Weber, Max. 1968. In *Economy and society: An outline of interpretative sociology*, ed. Guenther Roth and Claus Wittich. Berkeley/Los Angeles/London: University of California Press.
Wettstein, Florian. 2012. Corporate responsibility in the collective age: Toward a conception of collaborative responsibility. *Business and Society Review* 117(2): 155–184.
Wilson, Tamar D. 2003. Forms of male domination and female subordination: Homeworkers versus Maquiladora workers in Mexico. *Review of Radical Political Economics* 35(1): 56–72.
Yin, Robert K. 1981. The case study crisis: Some answers. *Administrative Science Quarterly* 26(1): 58–65.
Young, Iris M. 2004. Responsibility and global labor justice. *The Journal of Political Philosophy* 12(4): 365–388.
———. 2006. Responsibility and global justice: A social connection model. *Social Philosophy and Policy* 23(1): 102–130.
———. 2008. Responsibility and global justice: A social connection model. In *Handbook of research on global corporate citizenship*, ed. Andreas G. Scherer and Guido Palazzo, 137–165. Cheltenham: Edward Elgar Publishing Limited.
———. 2010. *Responsibility for justice*. Oxford/New York: Oxford University Press.

Part III
Consequences: Economic Models and Economic Responsibility

Chapter 7
On the Responsibility for Economic Models and Their Use

Klaus Kornwachs

> *And laying responsibility on the environment cannot take it off the shoulders of persons so long as the environment of each of us consists chiefly of the rest of us* (Clark 1916, p. 217).

Abstract J. M. Clark's paper from 1916 about responsibility gives reason to focus on responsibility related to modelling and models in economics. First, the concept of responsibility is discussed with respect to its components, developed by discourses about responsibility in studies concerning the ethics of responsibility in technology. This enables the application of this concept of responsibility in economic ethics. Modeling in economics is analyzed from the perspective of technology studies and the philosophy of science. This allows posing questions of responsibility in a slightly modified way, since model building in the social and the natural sciences are different, even if both types of models are depicted mathematically. Models in the social sciences depict rules rather than "laws" in the strict sense. Therefore, the use of models and the communication thereof should respect these limitations. Responsibility is important for model builders as well as for those who apply models and interpret their outcomes. Thus, responsibility for the economic outcome of an economic action, if seen from the perspective of an individual, is different from the responsibility for the economy, i.e. being responsible for all our actions and decisions, effects and side effects for all people involved. The latter includes the responsibility of economic scholars for their models and for the use thereof.

K. Kornwachs (✉)
University of Ulm, Humboldt-Center of Humanities, Ulm, Germany

Office for Culture and Technology, Argenbühl, Germany
e-mail: klaus.kornwachs@uni-ulm.de; klaus@kornwachs.de

M. Haase (ed.), *Economic Responsibility*, Ethical Economy 53,
DOI 10.1007/978-3-319-52099-5_7

7.1 Introduction – Clark's Fascinating Foresight

John Maurice Clark (1884–1963) was a very influential economic thinker who inherited his talent of economic thinking from his father John Bates Clark (1847–1938). The latter was a representative of the so-called neoclassic economists whereas his son became an institutional economist, known as a leading member of a countermovement against the contemporary neoclassicism with its focus on marginal utility (Nutzinger 2009, p. 470). J. M. Clark's work respecting economic multipliers, the dynamics of the market economy and the theory of the acceleration principle founded his fame (Clark 1917), despite his refuse to join the trend that had become popular after WW I, i.e. to mathematize economics. He might be seen as a forerunner of today's conviction that the formalization of economic insights might be very elegant, and it might be a necessary precondition for making quantitative forecasts, but the power to make good explanations and forecasts is limited by an incomplete knowledge of boundary conditions[1] and by a categorically questionable application of the models[2] as well. In any event, J. M. Clark called for a translation of mathematically formulated models and model results into the ordinary, everyday language (Pribram 1992, p. 1076 and Clark 1947).

It might be astonishing that many bibliographies of his work do not even mention his paper "Changing Basis of Economic Responsibility" (Clark 1916), written in a time when a first change of paradigm took place in theorizing about the nature of the processes in economy. It was the transition from Ricardo's theory of values, and from the doctrine of "laissez faire", corresponding to the simplified Darwinian sayings of the "survival of the fittest", towards a more dynamic conception, in which the developments of technology, society and institutions play an important role (Pribram 1992, p. 773 ff.). Ricardo's assumption about rational behavior was not compatible with the rise of American Pragmatism, put forward by Charles Sanders Peirce, William James, and John Dewey. According to them, instincts, habits, thinking in terms of functionalism,[3] and direct experience began to play a pivotal role. Moreover, the avoidance of speculative theories about the intrinsic nature of man, or about the true nature of economic processes became important. Institutional aspects were increasingly understood as significant: Thinkers started to perceive institutions as a kind of collective acting in order to control and steer individual decision making and behavior (Pribram 1992, p. 670). All these movements may have led J. M. Clark to re-think economic responsibility in his 1916 paper.

Nevertheless, Clark described the change that happened in his time and, which had impressed him so much, in a way, which today reminds us of the very modern problem of responsibility diffusion in a complex interconnected and globalized

[1] To solve the equations of a mathematical model explicitly, it is necessary to make realistic assumptions about the boundary conditions, i.e. the initial values of the independent variables at time $t = 0$ and further constraints like upper or lower bounds of variables. Very often, the boundary conditions are not sufficiently empirically known, or there is no realistic assumption feasible at all.

[2] Discrete events cannot be modeled by continuous variables and vice versa. Moreover, it seems to be categorically wrong, to model institutional facts like physical, i.e. natural systems.

[3] Functional approaches hold only interest in how to do things effectively with respect to a given goal and refrain from theoretical groundings as, for example, in rational theories.

world. Beside the problem of how to legitimate interventions of the state or the government, Clark observed that the idea of personal responsibility (e.g. a person is blamed for an accident) had been shifted to social responsibility – characterized by the "compulsory compensation which blames nobody" or the distribution of responsibility between the state and the industrial system, respectively (Clark 1916, p. 211). In his eyes, a vague concept of systemic determinism started to replace the concept of free will. The determining factors are considered more and more as significant and responsible causes for joblessness, incapacity, bankruptcy, etc. Thus, Clark thought his contemporaries saw unemployment as a disease of the economic system, and – as a consequence – unemployed people and criminals as victims of the social order.

Although Clark (1916) did not himself define the term "responsibility", he made a clear distinction between responsibility and causation: An event can only be a matter of responsibility, if someone who has had control over a relevant situation has caused the event within this situational framework or arrangement. Clark wanted to maintain this control as long as possible: It is necessary that "we do not stand entirely helpless" (Clark 1916, p. 214). Clark referred to two essential elements of the classic responsibility concept: According to the classical model of responsibility, to be responsible for something presupposes having brought it about with intent, and to be subject of punishment or reward for this by somebody (Bayertz 1995). However, the new problem he was facing is the fact that the environment[4] was now considered as a cause of many obstacles and catastrophes, with respect to both individual and societal prospects. This environment also includes unexpected and remote causes, closely interconnected with the nearer causes (Clark 1916, p. 212). His view is indicative of a conscious perception of the intensified global and interconnected interactions within a complex world economic system.

The example with sunspots discussed by Clark in a somewhat ironic manner represents a very modern point of view: An economic system may be so weak and unstable, that some damages like a change of weather due to sunspots will harm its functionality. Beside the fact that Clark could not yet know about the vulnerability of our worldwide communication systems with respect to electromagnetic storms, sunspots may serve as a paradigm for external and uncontrollable disturbances of a system. Are the sunspots responsible for an economic breakdown? The answer is no, since in this case responsibility rests with the people who had missed making the economic system stable against such possible disturbances.

> In a system of private production with enormous use of capital, involving the staking of industrial fortunes on a distant future, any irregularity is intensified in some quarters (Clark 1916, p. 214).

Today, we know empirical and theoretical systems of that kind, on the one hand from the experiences of the Global Financial Crisis, and on the other hand from modern modelling using nonlinear equations and chaotic dynamics.[5] As it is gener-

[4] Not yet to understand as an ecological term, but as the surrounding living conditions with respect to social, financial, private and economic issues.

[5] Cf. Lorenz (1993). For more recent developments in the application of physical models using thermodynamics, see for instance Richmond et al. (2013); for more advanced models in "Econophysics", see Slanina (2014).

ally known, the mathematical description of such models shows an extreme sensitivity against a slightest change of relevant boundary conditions.

When dealing with models, we always have to ask whether the "real economy" does really behave as the model suggests. If we have good reasons to assume, that the dynamics we can observe has been modeled adequately, we could ask, according to Clark: who may be responsible for the inadequate and chaotic behavior of such a part of reality? Is it the human being, who is in charge of fixing the boundary conditions and controlling the process, i.e. the manager? From this type of processes, we know that we cannot control it completely since the preparation of the control parameter and initial conditions can never be done adequately by human action, not even when it can be enhanced by technology. Thus, we rather assume a responsibility for those people who have designed, installed or supported, or even failed to prevent such a sensitive economic system that is not controllable. In terms of the ethics of responsibility, we can move from the classical concept of responsibility that implies controllability and imputation, to an altered concept, discussed by Bayertz (1995) as well. Due to the increasing division of labor, the responsibility for an action or its consequences is reduced to the responsibility to fulfill a task within a large mechanism, but without robust routines (Bayertz 1995, pp. 34 f.).

Any understanding of systems, may they be of a technical or economic nature requires a model or at least a kind of preliminary or pre-theory. Models, theories, explanations, methodological rules how to develop a model, or standards in science, are the work of man. Moreover, the analysis of the economy has to deal with institutional facts, not with natural or brute facts. The difference is obvious: The law-like statement: "All bodies do fall equally fast", or: "I cannot remove more coins than there are within my purse", describes a natural fact, which cannot be altered by man's will. The statement: "My overdraft is actually 3000€" describes an institutional fact. It is possible – in principle – that negotiations can change the upper limit by a contract with the finance institute. Institutional facts can also be observed and they are constitutive for models in economics, but they can be changed by human actions, and they can be removed and re-installed by consensus.[6] Thus, we are not responsible for physical reality *sensu* brute facts, tentatively described by Newton and other scholars, but for the existence and the shape of institutional facts. Economic patterns observed by economists or statisticians are not natural or brute facts, but institutional patterns. The term "we" includes – generally speaking – the model builders and model appliers as well as those, who are shaping technologies, and design economic processes and institutions with the help of man-made models.

Having started with Clark's remarks, the article intends to focus on the responsibility related to modelling and models in economics. First, the concept of responsibility is discussed with respect to its elements, developed by the discourses about responsibility in studies about the ethics of responsibility in technology. This allows

[6]The difference between institutional and natural (brute) facts has been widely discussed by Popper (1947, Vol I., Chap. 5, pp. 49 ff.) and used by Searle (1969, Chap. 2.7, pp. 50 ff.), who showed that the success of speech acts like to promise something to somebody requires some minimal institutional facts.

us to perceive responsibility in the light of widely discussed approaches to economic ethics. As a first result, the idea is rejected that economics is a value-neutral science and its models are free from moral considerations. After that, in line with Clark's paper, the question is raised, whether the economic crises may have changed the basis of economic responsibility. This article looks on the building and application of models in economics from the perspective of technology studies and philosophy of science. This allows posing the question of responsibility in a slightly modified light. Thus, from a point of view in philosophy of science, model building in the social and the natural sciences are different, even if both types of models are expressed mathematically. Models in social studies express rather rules than "laws". Therefore, the use of models and the communications thereof should respect their always given limitations. A responsibility is seen for model builders as well as for model appliers. Thus, the responsibility for the economic consequences of an economic action, if seen from the perspective of an individual, is different from the responsibility for the economy, i.e. being responsible for all our actions and decisions, effects and side effects for all people involved. The latter includes the responsibility of economic scholars for their models and for the use thereof.

7.2 Responsibilities Revisited

The concept of responsibility has regained attention in Europe and particularly in Germany with the work of Hans Jonas (1984) "Imperative of Responsibility". Nevertheless, the book was more or less a settlement with "Prinzip Hoffnung" of Ernst Bloch[7]; moreover, it did not provide a systematic conceptualization of responsibility. In his book, Hans Jonas focused on technology as the object of responsibility, and he pointed out that the problem of collective ethics could break new ground. However, he did not cover the economy as an object of responsibility, beside a critique of Marx's ideas of utopia as the future of man and the emergence of the classless society.

7.2.1 Dimensions of Responsibility

Conducting a more systematic analysis, Hans Lenk and others like Günter Ropohl (Lenk 1991 and Ropohl 1996, pp. 74 ff.) have introduced manifold dimensions of the concept of responsibility. According to their view, the question: "*Who is responsible for what?*" must be answered by specifying the following dimensions:

(a) The object (for what),
(b) the subject (who – this may be a person, a group or an institution),

[7] This is one of the reasons for the fulminate success of the book and its frequent citation by conservative circles. The book is an outright rejection of any utopia.

(c) the instance (to whom),
(d) the time dimension (how long the subject is seen as responsible),
(e) the possible sanctions (repair, compensation, reward and punishment), together with the question of liability, and
(f) the time horizon (i. e. the timely duration of effects and impacts of human actions).

Ropohl has shown that one can find many types of responsibility, if one combines the dimensions mentioned above, that is, not all dimensions have to be considered in all types of responsibility.[8] Later, Armin Grunwald has introduced two further dimensions:

(g) Responsibility with respect to the general rules accepted by a community,
(h) Responsibility relatively to the actual state of knowledge (Grunwald 2010).

All these dimensions have been applied within a broad discussion about the responsibility of engineers for the effects and side effects of technology development and use (Hubig 2003, pp. 31–49 and pp.105–130; VDI 1991, 2000, 2002).

When coupling the concept of responsibility including the dimensions (a–f) with three idealized and simplified types of ethics (Kutschera 1982) – ethics of duty (1), teleological ethics (2), and intentional ethics (3), there are *prima facie* three partially exclusive possibilities to specify the object of responsibility:

1. An individual is responsible for the action he is performing or has performed. If one has to judge criminal acts, or if an individual has violated his duties or rules of conduct, this view is preferred. This view is also important for the design of regulations concerning punishment and reward.
2. An individual is responsible for the effects and possible side effects of his actions. There is a certain distinction between the circumstances as to whether side effects were predictable or not.
3. An individual is responsible for the intentions, motivations, purposes, and interests he has or he pursues when performing an act.

The contemporary ethics discussion has ceased to draw on this classification since, firstly, neither scholars nor everyday discussion uses a pure type of such ethics and, secondly, none of the three simple versions mentioned above can avoid massive fallacies in morally judging concrete cases (Kutschera 1982, Kornwachs 2000). Thus, an approach to responsibility ethics is preferred in which not only the result of an action counts, but also the judgment is important whether there has taken place a violation of certain values[9] due to the action itself. In all communities,

[8] Indeed, Ropohl (1994) spoke about a "combinatorial explosion", and therefore it is reasonable to restrict one on concrete types. Within this paper, we specify these restrictions as follows: the subject of responsibility is a person or a definable group of persons. The instance is a person or a material institution with acting persons within it, where the object of responsibility is an act or the effects of an act (even if not predictable), where the time horizon is pragmatically limited and the possibility of liability should exist.

[9] The meaning of the term "value" within the context of ethics is given by examples like health, life, welfare, freedom, equality, safety, stability, harmony, etc. and characterizes given or intended

there are certain values considered as inviolable under any circumstances.[10] Therefore, the doctrine according to which "*the end may justify the means*", indicating a crude teleological ethics (type 2), can be avoided. Thus, responsibility ethics includes an ethics of duty to a certain extent, i.e. they imply the duty to avoid the violation of sacrosanct values. We are responsible to fulfill our duties, as long as these duties do not violate established values and rights of oneself and of others. It is clear that in this field dilemmatic conflicts are unavoidable. If one accepts the ethical conviction, that the conscience should be respected and that nobody should be coerced to act against his conscience, this type of ethics (type 3) can be included within the responsible ethics, since the conscience become an instance of responsibility (dimension c). Here we emphasize the respect for the question of conscience (germ. Gewissensentscheidung) as a higher leveled value. Of course, the definition of such inviolable values, and the definition which priority relation may be acceptable in case of conflicts between values is quite different in various cultures, classes, groups of interests and so on. Thus, there is a well-known discussion whether they may be inviolable values at all (Joas 1997).

Another approach, related to the first possibility above, is the distinction between first order and second order responsibility. The first kind is related to the responsibility for actions and individual tasks, the second requires taking responsibility generally to evils and states, which should be eliminated or whose occurrence should be avoided, even if the individual is not at all involved in their existence or occurrence (Gosepath 2006, p. 393). According to this distinction between primary and secondary responsibility, one can argue that economic model builders are responsible for the quality of their model – the intended outcome of their activities. One could also argue that they have to take care that their models are used within the limits of their validity and that avoidable "operating errors" can be prevented. On the other hand, the actors and designers of economic processes are responsible for the use of models, with which they design and rule this processes, and how they do it.

Here the question of the subject of responsibility arises: Who is responsible for the quality and possible performative effects of models? Is it a group of scholars as a collective entity? Are the individual developers of the model responsible, or is it the institution in which the model builders perform their work? We will come back to this problem of collective responsibility in Sect. 7.7.

---

states of institutional, i.e. man made facts, whether they fulfill a good for man (*bonum physicum*). Sometimes there is a close relation between values and virtues like justice or truth, which relates more to a judgment about human behavior (*bonum morale*). Conceptions of values have different sources: religious convictions, considerations in natural law, culturally fixed patterns, and results of ethical reflections in philosophy and anthropology. Originally, the term "value" denoted a measure of an economic good. Philosophy has adopted them in the nineteenth century. The author is convinced that ought not to be reducible to utilities, preferences, or advantages. Nevertheless, there exist relations of priorities between values.

[10] Such inviolable values can be presented in a hierarchical way according to Human Rights, see Kornwachs (2000, pp. 91 f.), Nida-Rümelin (1996).

7.2.2 The Possible Diffusion of Responsibility

When accepting approach (2) above to an ethics of responsibility, a severe problem emerges with the responsibility for unforeseeable side effects. In technology and in engineering ethics this problem is not yet solved.[11] The question is whether one can "moralize probability", since we are used to express the degree of uncertainty of our knowledge about possible failures or the impropriety of a decision (i.e. concepts like risk, reliability etc.) in terms of probability (Grunwald 2010, 2011; Bechmann 1993). The well-known problem of decision making under uncertainty has a close relation to this.[12]

J. M. Clark perceived a second severe problem – the above mentioned diffusion of responsibility. The responsibility relation turns to be quite fuzzy, as soon as one begins to shift the subject of responsibility from an individual to a group, or to a collective, e.g. to a board of trustees, or even – as a vague and abstract way of speaking in some discussions – to society. According to the "Polluter Pays Principle", the person causing the damage is responsible for these consequences, and the sanction is at least the obligation to compensate the damage up to a maximally possible degree. The instance of this responsibility, i.e. the person or institution this responsibility is owed to, can be the person or the organization, which is the owner of the damaged issues (which can be immaterial, too). In case of a violation of law, the person who has caused the damage is responsible to a court. Or, if accepted, the person might be responsible to an arbitration commission. Roman law and its concept of responsibility has focused on individuals and on the possibility to individual sanction, i.e. to punish persons, not firms or other organizations.[13] However, we face today that the subject of responsibility can be a collective or an institution like a firm or an authority. The same holds for the dimension of instance (cp. 2.1), since the instance cannot be only an individual, but also a group or organization. There are very often statements like: "*we feel responsible to our clients*", or "*politicians are responsible to the parliament*" etc.

There have been attempts to solve the problem of collective ethics. One position is to apply the responsibility concepts only to individuals.[14] Beside fines, further

[11] Nevertheless, the National German Academy of Science and Engineering (acatech) stated, referring to the Ethical Guidelines of the German Association of Engineers (VDI 2002): "As far as their responsibility for technology is concerned, engineers must ensure the quality, reliability and safety of their technological products. They are also considered to be jointly responsible for ensuring that people are properly informed about how to use technological products, so that they are used correctly and avoidable operating errors are prevented. The guidelines place particular emphasis on engineers' strategic responsibility for taking account of undesirable developments and the potential for deliberate misuse, and recommend that they ensure the conditions for responsible behavior when designing a piece of technology, i.e. that they enable the user to operate the technology in a responsible manner." Cf. Kornwachs et al. (2013), p. 38.

[12] Supposed that there is a measure for incompleteness of information like Fuzzy measures, the problem can be treated in formal models. Cf. e.g. Fodor et al. (2000).

[13] Nevertheless, practically the Romans punished the whole family of a wrongdoer.

[14] Only individuals are able to control their actions according to rules, commandments and prohibitions (cf. Zimmerli and Aßländer 1996, p. 305).

legal sanctions like punishment are not applied in Western legal systems. The other position is supported by the idea of Patricia Werhane (2007), i.e. to conceptualize enterprises as secondary moral actors. Nevertheless, there must be some relation between individual responsibility and corporate responsibility (Heidbrink 2012, p. 15). These relations have been discussed in different approaches,[15] which attempt to conceptualize organizations based on the study of corporate decision processes, as subjects of responsibility. Most of the concepts envision a one-side relation: The action in question (the object of responsibility) – a cooperative decision process – is influenced by the actions of the organizational members, but they cannot be explained in or reduced to terms of individual action. Thus, collective actors bear responsibility for their actions, but this responsibility is very difficult if not impossible to be reduced to individual responsibilities.

As a rule, the diffusion of responsibility starts where one is unwilling or unable to specify clearly the dimensions of the concept of responsibility mentioned above. If the instances of responsibility are named very cloudy as society, history, or even God, one may perhaps suspect that this is an attempt to veil responsibility relations. Hence, in a case of concrete damage, this instance cannot execute sanctions or claim a liability.

Against the backdrop of Clark (1916), it could be expected that the concept of responsibility plays an important role in economic ethics. Actually, this type of discussion, long before the discussion about responsibility in technology studies,[16] has reached economic ethics and business ethics in the first half of the last century (Abend 2013). Since the second half the discussion faces the rise of the importance of the shareholder value idea, ecological problems, growing joblessness, and the globally widening gap between the rich and the poor.[17]

Meanwhile the Global Financial Crisis and the breakdown of the validity of many economic models based more or less on the paradigm of mathematically classical state-space approach and its deterministic dynamics,[18] has led to a new discussion about ethics in economy and in economics as well.[19]

[15] See a list of such approaches in Maring (2001), pp. 264 ff. The discussion about this topic is still controversy; Jonas (1979) calls it a new territory of ethics. Responsibility of institutions is discussed very early in Hubig (1982). See also Ropohl (1987, 1994, 1996). There is an ongoing debate about this problem; cf. Zimmerli (1991). My own position has been developed in Kornwachs (2000), pp. 46 ff.

[16] Cf. Lenk (1987). See also further contributions in Lenk and Ropohl (1987).

[17] For the history of economic ethic, see Noll (2010), particularly for the development in the 2nd half of the twentieth century Caspari et al. (2009). Concurrently one can observe the debate about the so-called Corporate Social Responsibility (CSR). Nevertheless, this debate did not cover the concept of responsibility from an ethical viewpoint; it is suspected that an important motivation to practice CSR is to satisfy stakeholders. Cf. Branco and Rodrigues (2007).

[18] Cf. regular textbooks in economics. It remains questionable until today whether utility can be measured directly, and whether this can be subject of calculus. This has been criticized already by Mayer (1932), pp. 147–239; cited according to Pribram (1992), pp. 775f.

[19] Cf. Kirchgässner (2009) Emunds (2014). Münch (2015) has shown, that the Global Finance Crisis can be characterized by dilemmatic structures which have produced many factors of the crisis, e.g. lack of personal liability, real estate bubble, low interest rates and complex finance products, and moreover detachment of the investors from the original credit risks. The actions of the proponents involved in such

The discussion started anew with more phenomenological[20] questions, based upon the obvious. Many questions were posed in economic scholarship, such as: Who is responsible for the Global Financial Crisis; is there a group of unscrupulous managers and bankers at work; is there any parliament responsible for laws and weak regulations not reaching far enough; have economic models proved to be wrong? Looking on all the breakdowns of so many private households, the question concerning the causes arises: The people involved in the financial system – to whom are they possibly responsible? Who are the winners and the losers? Who will punish whom, who can compensate, what about justice and fairness? There are more questions than answers and the public discussion started to speak about the crisis of economic science, apparently unable to predict the disaster and to propose measures against it.[21]

We should also take into account that any attribution of responsibility (i.e. to specify the dimensions (a–h)) is not a fact, but an act, done by individuals, groups, and/or institutions. In a society, characterized by division of labor, this attribution of responsibility is managed according to rules, which themselves require a justification (Grunwald 1999). This responsibility is always embedded within a social context with attributions, obligations, and expectations (Grunwald 2014).

To this point, we have more or less discussed the responsibility concept, originating from the ethic of responsibility and further developed by the discourse about technology assessment, engineering responsibility, and the problem of far reaching effects of decisions in technology studies. Today, there seems to be a very complicated relation between several groups representing the economy, for example, industry associations and scholars, studying ethics in the economy, for example business and economic ethicists. On the other hand, there are tensions between business and economic ethicists and economists.[22] We are interested in these conflicts, as far as they are related to the use of economic models. Since models in economics are increasingly used not only to make predictions,[23] but to shape and to control large scale economic processes, it may be reasonable to take a look at concepts of ethics applied in technology studies. There is a certain analogy: The engineers have the same problem: They invent, shape and control large scale processes in technology with considerable impacts for the life of all. All these impacts are difficult, if not impossible, to predict.

dilemmatic structures have been judged morally negative, i.e. as irrational, egoistic, and greedy. It is nearby impossible to act in a responsible way in a dilemmatic situation, see Sect. 7.7.2.

[20] Such phenomenological questions do not yet aim at achieving evidence based answers. They have given rise to merely a collection of seemingly obvious observations, facts and data without drawing on hypotheses or models.

[21] Very early, cf. Bell and Kristol (1984). Even in textbooks this discussion can be found, cf. Engelkamp (2013), Vorwort zur 5. Auflage, p. VI. As a rule, critiques have been coined along the obvious crisis, not along an immanent scientific dialogue. Cf. e.g. Ronge (2015).

[22] Cf. the Memorandum for a Renewed Economy (Thielemann et al. 2012).

[23] Cf. very early Smolinski (1968), obviously overestimating the possibilities of prediction, further Weber (1996), Hanke and Wichern (2009). Today, the claim is more modest towards pattern recognition and prediction according to Hayek (1967), who was influenced by Karl Popper; cf. Hayes (2009).

7.3 On the Relationship of Economic Actions and Morally Judgeable Actions

In order to situate some basic lines in economic ethics, we use here a formal framework for the generation of concrete systems of normative statements, i.e. particular and different morals. This framework has been developed for the solution of ethical issues in technology studies, but it seems to be broad enough to be used, tentatively, also in business and economic ethics (Kornwachs 2000, 2004a, b).

7.3.1 *A Theoretical Framework for Ethics: Principles and Values*

The definition of a concrete ethics as a basic reference for the study of morals in societies is given by a set of more or less accepted principles[24] and a set of moral values (like life, safety, health, common and individual welfare, quality of life, sustainability, and possibly others).[25] There are only a few fundamental principles that have been offered in the history of ethics, like the Golden Rule, the Categorical Imperative, or the principles established by reflections of natural rights. The values are interrelated by priority relations, since nearly all values are in conflict with each other. Hence, we are not living in a perfect world and thus we have to face ambiguous situations on a regular basis in which we are forced to make a decision. It is possible that an individual or an institution changes this priority relation with time. Moreover in different cultures we can find different priority relations, but a considerable intersection between the meanings of the values.[26]

Both, the ethical principle(s) and the set of chosen values, are more or less independent. A moral is a set of normative statements, which can be founded on or even derived from prioritized values and the principle(s). Virtues such as justice, fairness, charity etc. are only patterns of value-oriented actions; they should not be confused with values.

So-called normative statements (they contain terms such as "is forbidden", or "is allowed", "is morally good or bad") express norms. For example, life may be a primordial value and the Golden Rule has to be applied. If we do not want to be treated with the result to lose our live, we should not act by threatening other men's life. The normative statement: "Thou shalt not kill", expressing the protection of

---

[24] The foundation problem of principles like the Golden Rule or Kant's Categorical Imperative will not be discussed here; cf. Kornwachs (2000). Ethical principles recommend an assessment procedure, addressing whether the own behavior is adaptable for a generalization. Whether the result of this assessment procedure is desired or not, can be judged by applying the values. For this, each value has to be transformed into criteria, which must be met.

[25] Values like freedom or equality are dispositive values – they can only be defined as presuppositions for other values.

[26] See the references to the project of World Ethos, e.g. Küng (1991), Küng et al. (2012).

This theory assumes that the contemporary way to act in economic processes has been developed in interaction with the formation of institutions providing the constraints for individual action. This way to act can be expressed in the form of rules. According to these rules, a correspondent way to act can be observed empirically in economical processes. Thus, Karl Homann, a proponent of this way of thinking, argues that it is not only or not primarily the task of economic ethics to delineate how an individual should act under given conditions. Here the teaching of suitable virtues may be sufficient. In his view, the task lies in finding an answer to the question of how morals and norms can be enforced within the economy as well as within society (Homann 2009, pp. 328 ff.). Incentives play an important role, and the design of adequate institutions is a necessary, but no sufficient condition for morally acceptable behavior in economy and society. Additionally, the moral commitments of individuals have to be taken into account (see Homann 2009, p. 331).

Nevertheless one could argue that strong monism (d) may pave the way for an "economization" of our thinking, because all "advantages", even those not able to be quantifiable like health, a long life, a good life *sensu* Aristotle, dignity, freedom, trust, feelings of happiness, peace and so on, are counted as abstract economic issues (Homann 2009, p. 334). This kind of ethics in terms of economics *sensu* Homann is convinced that the actors obey moral norms, derivable from values that are not primordial economic ones, only if it is – generally speaking – not detrimental for them (Homann 2009, p. 336). Thus, the assignment of responsibility becomes dependent upon the respective conditions: Morally very well appreciated or not acceptable circumstances cannot be attributed to the actions or intentions of the actors, but to the boundary conditions due to existing institutions, which may force the actions of individuals systematically into a certain direction (Homann 2009, pp. 328 f.). This does not exclude the possibility of individual responsibility, but it becomes embedded into a kind of collective responsibility for the design of adequate institutions. Thus, the individual responsibility for actions is shifted into a responsibility for the conditions of actions. Here we may suspect again a certain diffusion of responsibility, remarked by J. M. Clark, as mentioned above. To sum up Homann's understanding of economic ethics,

> Economic Ethics (in German 'Wirtschaftsethik', author) can be understood as an *ethics with an economic method*, or, this may be equivalent, as an *economic theory of moral. …* it has both meanings: Ethics for economy (genitivus objectives), and ethics due to economic calculus (genitivus subiectivus).[29]

This double meaning can only be understood if one accepts that the values primordially valued by economic actors (not by the economic ethician) are economic ones and that the individuals choose on the basis of their preferences. Notice that values are not identical to preferences[30]; only the choice of the priority relation between values can be interpreted as a preference. It may be the case, that different individuals have different priority relations between their values, even against the background of the

[29] Cf. Homann (2009), p. 335; transl. by the author, emphasis by Homann.

[30] This is a long-standing debate; it may be sufficient to refer to the position of Zimmerli and Aßländer (1996), who interpret values as preferences; against this equation, see Hansson (2004), Chap. 2.

same ethical principle. Thus, a lot of people may agree with the categorical imperative of Kant, but some may prefer life and health as the most important values, whereas the other may favor national honor or values with reference to religious beliefs like grace. In position (d), there are no criteria to legitimize for such a choice beside the priority of the economical values. Often, this is an advantage to society as well – if individuals choose to trade with each other instead of fighting religious conflicts. Choice according to (d) is due to the individual objectives to optimize one's own advantage. Many people may accept this, comparing it with their own interests and feelings. Nevertheless, acceptance is not yet sufficient for legitimation (Thielemann 1998, p. 15).

This approach has been criticized as an attempt to avoid morality, i.e., moral convictions and moral feelings in economic ethics (Pies and Meyer zu Schwabedissen 2005). In an economic world ruled by competition and established economic ideologies, the implementation of ideas like solidarity between all men or ecological ideas like sustainability and livable future should be done in accordance with criteria that are "compatible with incentives" (Homann 1996, p. 182).

The above mentioned approach of integrative monism (position (c)) requires the development of an extra economic ethic with new and general principles, since the complexity of economic processes, particularly the problem of controllability, needs new insights into decisions under uncertainty (for examples, Gilboa and Schmeißer 2009; Kochenderfer 2015). Approach (c) assumes that a new integrative business ethics is required for the study of these problems (Ulrich 1992, 2008; Koslowski 1991). Peter Ulrich, the main proponent of this approach, observes a drift between a functional logic of economy, in accordance with present mainstream economics, and the responsibility for the impacts of economic action.[31]

Here the priority relations between values are altered and other values, not reducible to benefits or advantages of individuals, only begin to play a role.[32] Approach (c) includes views from philosophical anthropology, because Ulrich sees economics and the shape of the economy as dependent on the respective conception of man. It is possible to distinguish approaches of this type according to the answers to the question, whether the human being is only a rational decider or more, and if so, whether it is possible that rational decisions can lead to immoral actions and undesired effects in the economy (Zimmerli and Aßländer 1996, p. 296).

7.3.3 Homo Economicus as a Moral and Rational Subject?

The famous concept of homo economicus has been criticized very often and very early – it is easy to show that many of our everyday economic decisions are not compatible with the narrow economic approach to rationality (Wellas 2012). The

[31] Cf. Ulrich (2008), p. 13, cited from Gerlach (2009), p. 864.

[32] If values and their connections to some anthropological issues like conjectures about the nature of man can be established with recourse to good reasons, this type of ethics belongs still to the cognitive types of ethics. Cf. Kutschera (1982).

backdoor for the homo economicus is not only the fact, that subconscious wishes and desires, unveiled by psychology, are counted as rational factors when weighing the pros and the cons for a individual decision. It is rather the assumption that a human being should be nothing but a rational decider, if the subject is interacting with other subjects. Proponents of this hidden or inner rationality claim to explain apparently irrational decisions in the light of long-term rationality, and they are arguing with the above mentioned psychological factors in terms of utility or advantages (Weißenberger and Hirsch 2013, with relation to Krishnan et al. 2005). Nevertheless, the exploration of individual decisions has brought new insights, and Reinhard Selten started with experimental Game Theory and found other types of behavior like altruism (Selten 1971 pars pro toto).

If one defines the concept of advantage as a difference of utilities which some individuals may have in the same situation, or the difference between utilities of different options, then the utilities themselves can only be estimated (at least in a comparative measure) within the realm of a concrete situation and a theoretical conception thereof, i.e. by a model. Here we have to distinguish between decisions of an individual person and interdependent decisions of many actors. For instance, Game Theory delivers such models for the estimation of payoff functions in market models. In Game Theory, it is supposed that each of the players tries to minimize the maximal loss and to maximize the minimal profit. This Minimax-Theorem is a conjecture about the decision rule a rational player would obey. It facilitates model building and makes calculations possible. This is an approximation and its plausibility is grounded only in mathematical reasons, not in Psychology or in any measurement of utility. Nevertheless, Game Theory is a good tool to model such situations with different options, and even John Rawls (1999) has required that social equality and economic fairness should be arranged according to this principle as a rational guide. Today, Game Theory has been further developed by experiments as well as by theoretical research (Camerer 2003).

Economics investigates processes with interdependent decisions made by many actors; therefore, it seems to be a good modelling strategy to assume economic rationality for all individuals involved. As long as it is conceded that this approach makes it easier to develop mathematical descriptions, this could be accepted as a first step in a research strategy to find overall characteristics of such processes. Nevertheless, it cannot be expected that such a strategy applies in all times and circumstances, if the basic assumption has nothing to do with social reality on the individual level. It must be admitted that the problem of how to come from individual behavior to the formation of institutions and the structures within the society is not yet solved.

An uncountable number of books about business ethics have been written, and firms, companies, scientific and expert societies have published rules of conducts, guidelines, and standards for their respective areas and disciplines.[33] Nevertheless,

[33] A review is given by Zimmerli and Aßländer (1996) and Korff et al. (2009). For codices within the realm of technology see VDI (1991, 2000, 2002), EFCA (2011), FEANI (2006) etc. An overlook about estimated 400 guidelines gives Maring (2001). For approaches to economic development, see e.g. IEDC (2008), but the book of Starr (2011) has started a rather late onset debate,

business ethics and economic ethics have been developed *before* the Global Financial Crisis, and *before* the most recent crisis of economic sciences started. However, all these initiatives and reflections could not prevent the crisis.

Today, we seem to be faced with an overall global dynamics of economies, which can be described as "irrational" because we do not understand it. Thus, an explanation of such dynamics is desired; and it remains questionable whether overall narrow rationality assumption has a satisfying description to offer.

Thus it is hardly surprising that the question is discussed controversially whether the two dominant conceptions of rationality within economics really cover all aspects of psychological and social realities. Amartya Sen criticized the rationality assumption as internal consistency of choice as well as the rationality as maximization of self-interest or personal welfare.[34] According to Ulrich's approach of a discourse ethics, a possible way to find an extended rationality including these factors could be to enable participation, i.e. to listen to the voices of those affected more than before (Ulrich 1993, p. 294).

We plea for the view that economic actions as well as economic action conditions can be the subject of moral judgments. Moreover, economics as a science and as a social practice is the subject of moral judgments with respect to its impacts, too.

Consequently, one cannot consider economics as a neutral science, making only descriptive models free from moral concerns.

7.4 Has the Economic Crisis Changed the Basis of Economic Responsibility?

Today, we find ourselves in a situation comparable to when John Maurice Clark wrote his article. It is remarkable how up-to-date his arguments sound, for example, with respect to the role of the state: How far a government or even a state can take responsibility for a breakdown of an entire economic sector (Clark 1916, p. 227), an argument nowadays significant with regard to the bailout of "banks too big to fail". He proposed the implementation of institutions, designed by the enterprises themselves, which express the responsibility of their creators. Actors should develop rules according to which each enterprise has to act in a responsible way instead of supporting the

---

whether economists should have a Code of Ethics. The AEA (American Economic Association) has released Extensions *to Principles for Author Disclosure of Conflict of Interest*; cf. AEA (2012). In Germany there are rules for good scientific practices for university teachers (VHB, Verband der Hochschullehrer für Betriebswirtschaft), in: http://vhbonline.org/en/ethics as well as a Code of Ethics, put forward by Verein für Socialpolitik, an association of more than 4000 economists, in: https://www.socialpolitik.de/docs/Code_of_Ethics.pdf. Nevertheless, to my knowledge, there is no general Code of Ethics for stakeholders in economy, i.e. people charged with far reaching decisions on national or international level.

[34] Sen (2002) relates on the so called "traditional revealed preference theory" (TRPT), by Samuelson (1938) and others, and its modern version: contemporary revealed preference theory (CRPT), put forward by Ross (2014). For an evaluation of this debate, cf. Hédoin (2015).

prevention of fair competition (c ibid.). More recently, this issue has been revisited in terms of institution-building and the self-commitments of enterprises (Pies et al. 2009).

Clark believed that legislation could not develop laws governing everything. For him, the question of responsibility was related to the legitimacy of implementing rules. Thus, it is necessary to formulate reasonable constraints under which a great degree of freedom remains possible. Therefore, it is necessary for the legislator to know what is happening in the economy in general and in businesses in particular. Otherwise, legal regulations could produce obstacles for a successful and fair economy. As a future ideal, Clark (1916, p. 227) hoped:

> Perhaps in some future century we may even venture to ask business men's advice on proposed laws for the prevention for unfair competition without the uneasy feeling that their purpose in giving of their wisdom is to make the laws ineffective and keep things as they are.

Today we know that without the expertise of professional consulting and law firms, some special bills for regulating the economy cannot be developed. The knowledge of experts in ministries, authorities, and parliaments is too limited with respect to the complex finance sector. Nevertheless the apprehension of Clark that egoism and self-interest may rule, the advice given in such cases is not too far-fetched. Clark (1916, p. 210) criticized his time: "We have inherited an economics of irresponsibility" and his statement intended to counter-argue this attitude. We could vary this statement today into "We have inherited also an economy of irresponsibility".

Subsequently, we identify three issues that are usually connected with the last economic crisis. Those issues should not be confused with the economical causes of the crises; to discuss these causes should remain reserved at this point to the economy itself.

7.4.1 Double Standards of Moral

The growing commodification of nearly all issues in daily life, in politics, in art, in education, in science and so on, has been surely supported by the transformation of some socialist regimes into other political and economic orders after the fall of the Berlin Wall in 1989 and by the globalization. Nevertheless, this happened in Western World long before this date. As a theoretical mirroring of these processes, Nobel prizewinner Gary Becker (1976) has put forward the identification of economic thinking with rational behavior by reducing social, psychological, institutional, and individual values to utilities and preferences.[35]

There is no reason to blame only the already well-known stakeholders and agents like managers, politicians, producers, marketing people, merchants, dealers, shareholders, owners as such and their servants as causes of economic dysfunctions. There are rather many additional players like users of services offered (customers,

[35] Becker (1993) contains early contributions translated into German.

consumers, or clients); moreover, we have to take into account scientists, publishers and the media.

Discussions about responsibility during the Global Financial Crisis were actually misleading and characterized by double standards of moral. Many organized protests against the closure of plants and industrial sites, aimed by the shareholders to outsource the production into cheaper countries. Nevertheless, most consumers are looking for a bargain with the cheapest clothing and do not worry about where our trousers have been stitched. We are protest voters and "Schnäppchenjäger"[36] at the same time. We are against the displacement of production capacities into foreign countries, but we prefer to spend our holidays abroad. Within the national debate, we are fighting for jobs, but we appreciate growth and innovation, and we accept without moral outrage the Western competitiveness as a preservation of the wealth gradient between the North and the South. We exercise solidarity with remote living conditions, but we are quite tough managers of our own living. As citizens, we are acting like socialists, and as customers, we behave like the rational optimizer of our own advantage. Here we can find exactly the divided morality described in the previous subsection in terms of position (a).

This quasi-schizophrenic behavior can be considered as similar to what John Cassidy (2009) has named "rational irrationality". It describes a perfectly reasonable behavior on the individual level, but it becomes disastrous when "aggregated in the market place". He compared this behavior with the old game of Music Chair[37] and the situation modelled by the well-known Prisoners Dilemma: subsequent reactions to what others are doing in the same situation produce a dangerous feedback. Each attempt to improve the own situation makes the general situation worse. Nuclear warfare has a comparable inner structure with its logic of deterrence and mutual assured destruction. Under attack, it is reasonable to strike back, but the consequences would be catastrophic for the whole world.

7.4.2 Globalization

The recent state of globalization is not fate – it is work of man, and a consequence of a development long ago. Colonization was one of the triggers for the development of international markets. The decision to remove the brakes, to enable a free flow of people, capital, goods, information, labor, and ownership accelerated the process of the world economy after the abandonment of the Bretton-Woods system of fixed exchange rates in the first half of the 1970s. The globalization process has not been caused, but it has been supported and accelerated by the converging development of information- and communication technologies in the 1980s and 1990s. They facilitated the

[36] This is a typical German expression for somebody, who is on the hunt for a bargain.

[37] In Germany it is known as "Journey to Jerusalem": "When the music stops, in terms of liquidity, things will be complicated ... but as long as the music is playing, you've got to get up and dance" (Cassidy 2009, p. 32). Cassidy is a former Wall Street CEO from City Group.

7.5 Models and Model Building

Any making of economic models starts with a – perhaps implicitly made – decision in philosophical anthropology: What is man? What is his role in society? In what processes does he play a role? In which system he is considered an element? What an individual is used to do under "normal" or constrained conditions? Is it striving for happiness and good feelings, or for some advantages, driven by economic rationality? Answers to these questions determine the formal definitions used in model building, and how the objectives of the parties or players in an economic process can be formalized, since such presuppositions influences the estimation of the payoff functions.

All these decisions are influenced by culture, by socio-economic issues, by everyday experiences, and by currently dominant doctrines, of course. The selection of data as relevant presuppositions of model-building is another option that is influenced by explicit and implicit assumptions about the "nature" of man as an active member of an economic system and about the "nature" of economic processes. The technology of Big Data allows finding quickly unknown correlations in data sets, collected for many other purposes.

7.5.1 The Impact of Ideas from Philosophy and Metaphysics on Model Building

Philosophy and metaphysics influence model building. It can be shown that American Pragmatism, denying all metaphysical entities, is incompatible e.g. with Ricardo's assumption, according to which the labor and all the efforts, applied when forming or producing an object, induces an inner value as an ontological property of this object, regardless of any later (trans)actions and uses. For a pragmatist, there is no such thing as a value directly introduced into an object due to labor. This metaphysical assumption reflects the conviction that an effort, made to produce a product against recalcitrant nature and with suffering and sweat, cannot be lost – it must be conserved within the product that becomes more precious than the former and unprocessed piece of material. Karl Marx has adopted this view and extended it with Ricardo's concept of added value (German: *Mehrwert*). This allowed Marx to moralize the famous difference between exchange value (*Tauschwert*) and value given by socially necessary abstract labor-time (*Arbeitswert*). This simple example shows how metaphysical concepts give rise to certain conceptualizations as a very starting point when forming models.

Another example may show this effect in a similar way: If one discusses different views in ethics when comparing family-owned Small and Medium Enterprises (SMEs) of China and Germany (Buder 2014), one can also find different basic philosophical and religious concepts. Business ethics according to the Protestant ethic, described by Max Weber (2002) on the German side, and the sayings of Confucius with his concept of universal harmony and the rule of family on the other side, are the main determining factors to conceptualize work and economy. Both "ideologies" have different consequences: The Confucian predominance of family, self-cultivation, harmony, and piety, i.e. "to cultivate yourself, to harmonize the family, to rearrange the state and to bring peace to the world"[45] leads to a certain ethos – i.e. to increase wealth and happiness in the interest of the own family. As a contrast, the Calvinist ethos regards the duty to fulfill all tasks of the profession, because economic success is an indicator of one's own salvation and God's merciful choice (Weber 2002). Both concepts lead to different economic behavior and to different models as a means to justify the different types of economic performance.

It is essential to know which concept of man is explicitly or implicitly applied when starting to conceptualize economic processes. What kind of entities a theory should contain (transactions, goods, services)? What kinds of activities – transactions like exchanging goods, or paying debts, or borrowing an object; or offering a share – should be judged from a moral point of view? Is it sufficient to analyze processes in terms of utility? Is a transaction only a flow of material with certain intrinsic properties, or is this merely a communication act, including promises, trust, and certain types of social behavior? This very much depends on the theoretical concepts chosen to describe the research subject.

In Philosophy of Science, and additionally in Cybernetics, in General Systems Theory, and in Computer Science, particularly in Software Engineering, the model building process has been investigated very extensively. From a formal point of view, there are several common steps, when building a model.

7.5.2 The Model-Building Process and Model Functions

One starts with a selection of an area, a part of social reality, and creates a "Universe of Discourse". For us, it contains phenomena, observations of single events, and repeated processes. If we already have some sort of a pre-theory allowing us to formulate conditions for what we can observe, then we can define the type of variables (nominal, ordinal scales etc.), and these types also define the type of measurement. The measurement of the variables, called observables, delivers the values. If the values can be ordered according to time or other parameters, then we can call them data. At this point, we already consider a colloquial description of properties, events, or processes from this chosen area to be a model. Such a simple non-formal description uses concepts, which bring together observed things with imaginable things and vice versa. Such a description in everyday language may be very simple, but it is a model, which can be formalized gradually. The model building process is regarded as a transformation from a very simple model to a more sophisticated,

[45] Confucius (1992): Liji and Daxue (Book of Rites, The Great Analect), Chap. 2. See also Gu (1999), p. 35.

formalized, potentially mathematical model which is applicable for a series of so-called model functions (Stachowiak 1973; Zeigler 1978; Kornwachs 1985).

One can use a model to describe structure and behavior of the observable area, to make forecasts about the dynamics of observables or for explanation, i.e. to look for the causes of certain structures or behaviors one assumes to be present in the original.[46] For all these functions of models, the selection of the relevant observables and variables may be different and the mathematical type of the formal model may be different, too.[47] There is an interaction between the model functions and the selection process of variables: What may belong or not to the chosen selection of the observable area? Therefore models have different structures, as they are used as means of calculation with different purposes such as simulation, making forecasts and simulations (i.e. producing new data), or controlling technical or economic systems, to derive further hypotheses which could be tested, to test data sets for inconsistencies and to give ideas for further experimental and theoretical research.[48] It may be that explanation and forecast will lose their importance in the age of Big Data, since here the software selects the essential variables by the mean of only formal criteria.[49]

It should be taken into account that models are frequently used in clusters of slightly modified or alternative models. Moreover, in most cases in social studies we cannot figure out cause-effect relations, but only some observable mechanisms or regularities, which we must investigate further (Ylikoski and Aydinonat 2014).

Many models are highly formalized, since the model builders tend to use mathematics and numerical methods and are strongly supported by computers – firstly to perform the calculation itself and secondly to an increasing extent to transform simple, natural language based models into mathematical models. I.e. the computer supports the model building process by means of a meta-model.[50]

Although models seem to be useful descriptions of processes and things with a certain power in forecasting and explanation, the use of models is not limited to this descriptive function. If one uses a simulation model in order to get better knowledge

---

[46] We exclude here form models as toys or in CAD and 3-D printing.

[47] Thus, there is a difference between a model for used to make an explanation and one to make a prediction. Not every explanation model is able to make a forecasts (like the models, based on evolution theory in Biochemistry – they can only explain the history of evolution). Some models for prognosis (e.g. models which use least-square-fits, Kalmann filtering or exponential smoothing etc.) are not able to deliver explanations of the observed processes in terms of cause and effect relation.

[48] We subsume here decision models as a subset of models for control purposes, since each control process includes decisions, and each decision is a part of a control process.

[49] A first attempt to do that can be found in the method of Reconstructability Analysis; cf. Klir (1976). A formal criteria to make a selection, i.e. to define a so-called mask which selects the variables is for instance to vary the mask according to the minimal entropy principle.

[50] This "Computer Aided Modelling" (cf. very early Zeigler 1978) uses well-developed tools with very comfortable user surfaces. Nevertheless, it is not farfetched, that the computer-aided formulation of a model becomes more and more dependent upon the available tools. For special applications in economics, see, e.g., Schwaninger and Mandl (2012) and other contributions to EUROCAST Conferences (Springer Lecture Notes in Computer Science 1989–2015).

about the dynamics in an electric network (like stability, overload etc.), the simulation results can be used immediately to calculate what actions could be taken to control such a net and to keep it stable. In this case it is obvious that a model is used in a control modus – it tells us, what we ought do, if we accept the model. The critique of the World Model of the Club of Rome mainly aimed to the immediate consequences to take early actions against the threatening collapse (Meadows and Meadows et al. 1972). As will be shown later, this normative modus is predominant and the most frequent way of use of economic models. Thus, description is no neutral model function, but also usable as a means to change the described observable area, i.e. as an instrument with the purpose to interact with it. Mostly, the creator (an individual as well as a research team) of the description has an objective, what he wants to do with the model. To shape and control processes is a predominant objective when model building in technology, and in applied sciences. Due to different self-understandings in economics, which reach from theoretical or "pure" science up to an applied or even action science (German: "Handlungswissenschaft"), the mentioned objectives are different.

Building models has many presuppositions, shared by various disciplines. This holds for natural sciences (with the predominant model functions of forecast and explanation), for social studies as well as for economics (where reliable predictions are very often impossible due to the complexity of the observable area), as well as for techno-sciences, where the question of the quality of a model is closely connected with the reliability of the technical function.

There is a stock of methods, procedures, and descriptive tools, with which models can be developed, unfolded, and designed. Beside the colloquial language approach as an embryonic state of model,[51] there are many concepts, which are independent of the subject area. Thus, cybernetics as applied control theory has brought nearly in all fields of science a mathematization of the described processes with the help of state space approach. This approach is well known in the natural sciences, in technology, and even in economics. This approach considers all taken n variables as essential, and forms an n-dimensional space. A point in this space is the state of the system at one moment, showing which values all the variables have in this very moment. A dynamics can be described by a trajectory, i.e. a successive series of points ordered according to time. In order to calculate the future development of the system, one needs the timely solution of the system equation (as the kernel of the model). With the help of defined boundary conditions, it is possible to make forecasts about the future dynamics of the model. If one has only a recursive formula instead of an analytical solution, one can calculate the future dynamics gradually from an initial point. The mathematics for this approach is well known since the canonical formulation of classical Newtonian Mechanics by Hamilton and others. This approach is very suggestive, but it can only be applied successfully when the relevant variables are expressed as continuous and unlimited entities. In cases when the state space or the partial spaces of the independent or dependent variables are limited (e.g. restricted control spaces), one runs into difficulty to find

[51] Nevertheless, a language to do this is not yet a model of the described selected realm of reality.

exact numerical solutions. Moreover, the kernel equation or recursive formula can be nonlinear and may show extreme sensitivity with respect to the initial conditions. In all of these cases, one is forced to make use of approximations or to simplify the model. This is done by neglecting variables, which are considered as not essential characteristics or by applying statistical methods, in order to enable the calculations and to keep them simple.[52] This simplification always runs the risk of cutting off "essential" properties of the model.

Of course, there are other tools offered in the stock of methods. Discrete functions enable us to design models with discrete variables at certain points in time in order to simulate path-dependent events or point processes.[53] This is done very successfully, when dealing with control problems in production processes in which continuous, i.e. flowing and discontinuous impact processes must be coupled.[54] In this case, the model is applied to control a process directly.

7.5.3 Models and Systems

In the previous examples, the model depicts a system. Not every formal system is a model of something (e.g. logic systems like predicate calculus or the system of chord transpositions in music), but models can be developed with the help of systems theory.

Since the system concept is used in very different meanings in the literature and in various disciplines, it should be clarified here what kind of definition is preferred by the author of this paper: A system is a formal description of a section of perceivable or imagined reality or of abstract entities. To say "something is a system" means, it can be described in terms of system description language. The formal description is oriented to mathematical tools. Elements of a system are subsystems, which are not subject of further analysis and description. They are taken as last and least units. They can be described as small black boxes with a definite input-output relation, i.e. its elementary behavior. The relations between the elements and between the subsystems define the structure of a system. This may be done on different hierarchical levels. The elementary behavior is expressed by the timely change of the quantitative values of variables of the elements and can be described either by tables, mathematical functions, or equations. The overall behavior can be

[52] The same holds for the methods of System Dynamics. They are difference- no differential equations as results of modelling causal relations as feedback-slopes. It is possible to calculate with hybrid, i.e. continuous and discrete time variables in time discrete steps. The problem of this modelling method is its sensibility for the choice of initial conditions. The models of the Club of Rome (Meadows et al. 1972), have been revised gradually; a review see Bardi (2011, p. 3): "The warnings that we received in 1972 … are becoming increasingly more worrisome as reality seems to be following closely the curves that the … scenario had generated". Cited acc. to http://en.wikipedia.org/wiki/The_Limits_to_Growth#cite_ref-27.

[53] Like discrete event-oriented simulation; cf. Zeigler et al. (2000).

[54] Like assembly line (continuous) production and batch production.

calculated with the knowledge of the elementary behavior of all elements or subsystems and of the structure, if a separation between independent and dependent variables is possible and a satisfying approximation to linearity is possible.[55] Such system description can help to build up a model of a selected realm of an observable area (things, processes) or of a fictional reality. A system description is a model if it can be used to fulfill the model functions: explanation, simulation, and forecasting. A system description which is only describing and which does not fulfill any of the mentioned model functions is not yet a model.

The description of a selected realm of an observable area in order to make a model of it, can be regarded as a system if it fulfills some formal conditions: Variables, subsystems, elements and structure must be defined. The calculation of the overall behavior in order to make predictions or simulations depends on the knowledge of the behavior of the elements and the structure. This can lead to unsolvable equations. It is due to the decision of the author of this kind of description, which elements and relations are belonging to the system and which do not. The description of such a section of reality in terms of system theory is shortly called a "system". It can be used as a model with all common model functions. Thus, a system is not an ontological entity within the reality, but a description of some section of reality, made by an author, who is – as a modelling individual – interested to use this description for his purposes.

When we talk about the "System of Finance", we mean the description of a section of the financial world, modeled with help of system-theoretical terms. These are Black Box, behavior, structure, element, function, hierarchy, stability, state space, dynamics, subsystems, independent and dependent variables etc.[56] Thus, systems theory is a tool for description. A system itself is only a description, not an entity in terms of classical ontology within the selected realm of reality.[57] Therefore, each system, i.e. each description has an author. This will be relevant when we discuss the responsibility for models. This implies trivially the social construction of each model to a certain extent.

---

[55] For formal definitions, see Mesarovic (1972); or Klir (1969), Zeigler (1978), Zeigler et al. (2000).

[56] All these terms have an exact meaning due to definition, mostly home in mathematics and engineering. Cf. paradigmatically Klir (1969) or Padulo and Arbib (1974). It is not very helpful to use these concepts in sociology without respecting its original meaning. This has led to confusions and to enormous waste of time due to trials to redefine them in discussions. Thus a definition like that from Anthony Giddens (1976): "To examine the structuration of a social system is to examine the modes whereby that system, through the application of generative rules and resources is produced and reproduced in social interaction" is not very helpful. It reminds to similar vague definitions of system concept e.g. in Luhmann (1985) and Giddens (1979), which conceptualize systems as ontological, existing entities. See controversial critiques, e.g. Obermeier (1988) or Ropohl (2009). Of course, other methods like Game Theory, Linguistics, Stochastic, and Logic are offered to be applied in model building, too.

[57] Cf. Kornwachs (2004a, b). This position avoids ontological commitments about systems.

Not every model need be a formalized or must be a mathematical one. If one refrains from explicit forecasting of time dynamics of processes,[58] other concepts allow an explanation of or an understanding of a process, resulting in dynamical and structural changes. Besides mathematical modelling, we use metaphors and analogies from one field of knowledge or disciplines to compare and explain phenomena in terms of other fields of knowledge and disciplines. Thus, the formalized, mathematical description of a model does not tell us more than we have already applied to build it up. Nevertheless, the calculation, as a production process of formal consequences of this knowledge, can provide new insights (simulation, visualization, forecasts etc.).

7.5.4 The Social Construction of Reality

When we start with model building, we use images, patterns of experience, and as Steffen Groß proposed, symbolic forms, introduced and explained by Ernst Cassirer.[59] These forms cannot be formalized and they cannot be reduced to cause-effect-patterns as law-like expressions, and they are not only reports about isolated processes or human acts. They are something in between – they are observable patterns in culture and society, which we produce when we act in social and economic life. The other way around, these structures influence the way we behave, think, and act. Even in one and the same disciplines, different forms may occur. Thus the reported switch from the ideas of free will to:

> determinism, [from] individualism to public control, [from] personal responsibility to social responsibility (Clark 1916, p. 210)

may serve as an example for the change of the preference of forms. These forms are different in different fields, they are specific for them, and they can serve as an orientation in cultural studies as well as in economics (Groß 1999). Thus, the idea of an ideal, undisturbed market can be used to form a simply structured model, but the model tells us only the numerical consequences of this idea. It does not tell us whether the simplified idea is adequate, it tells us only, when comparing field data and simu-

[58] What can always be done to a certain extent using Least Square fit methods or Exponential Smoothing or Monte Carlo Methods, presupposed the process can be modelled according to the same variable type.

[59] Cf. Groß (2011), p. 419, with relation to Cassirer (2004), p. 187. Forms are defined as cultural patterns, with which interpretations of science, culture and society are made. The cultural patterns are different due to socializations within a society; e.g. thinking only mechanically or in holistic or ecologic terms. Thus, the way to think or to speak in social subsystems like engineering, economics, politics, or in religion are quite different. Cassirer call this "the expressive function (Ausdrucksfunktion) of thought, which is concerned with the experience of events in the world around us as charged with affective and emotional significance, as desirable or hateful, comforting or threatening". Cited according to Stanford Encyclopedia of Philosophy, in: http://plato.stanford.edu/entries/cassirer/#4.

lated data, to which extend they may fit together. The interpretation of the accordance is again strongly dependent upon the goals we want to pursue with the model.

Due to formalization, frequently the equations are too complex, not solvable, with too many variables etc. One can go back iteratively, repeating the steps mentioned above. It is difficult to simplify the original model while preserving the essentials. This step is performed very often with respect to a better, i.e. a faster and prone calculation. The approximations are justified by the expectation that only small changes in the result of simulation runs may occur.

Formalization includes the procedure of symbolization, i.e. the substitution of everyday verbal expression by a sign, representing a category of the selected formal language. This is an essential vertex of the modelling process. Symbolization happens quite late within the steps of modelling and is a presupposition of formalizing. This can be demonstrated in two examples, in Logic as well as in economic modelling. If one tries to formalize a statement, e.g. "all swans are white", one has to firstly select the categories in which one will use the signs in a potential formula. If one selects the linguistic categories of verb and noun phrases, adjectives and auxiliary verbs, we get a formal phrase grammar of this statement. Using logic categories like quantifiers, we get a logical expression. In both cases, we have a different kind of formalization, hence we have symbolized with different categories. In each case, this is a result of an interpretation: It depends upon our decision, with which category we want to formalize and this has to do with the purpose of the model. Potentially, in linguistic categories the expression is formalized in order to win a translation into another language with another vocabulary and another grammatical structure. In the case of logical categories, one uses this kind of expression to make conclusions and to test the truth condition of the consequences.

Beside these very simple examples, one can state that each equation we can find in theories, which fulfill a modelling task, is the result of such formalization procedures (including some formal transformations). This procedure always includes acts of selection and interpretation.

We can use a model, if it is expressed in a suitable form, to produce consequence statements. This can be generated by logical conclusions or transformations of grammatical structures in the case of our examples above. In the case of equations (algebraic or as differential equations), one can use the solutions (exact or approximate ones) and calculate them concretely with the help of boundary conditions and initial values. For this, the calculus of logic, or syntax, or algebra is used as formal machinery. In principle, mathematics is ruling this machinery. Results, produced by this machinery, are formal expressions, which can be de-formalized, i.e. reinterpreted in terms of the "real-world meaning", i.e. with the concepts used to observe the observable area. Such formal, reinterpreted statements have a "real-world meaning" inasmuch as they relate to experiences, which can be translated into everyday language and communicated.[60] Any solution of the prize equations

---

[60] We cannot circumvent or exceed the level of description. Therefore, theoretical derived statements about existence of something are rather a *façon de parler*, but no statement about the world. They formulate merely hypotheses that are preconditions to the possibility of descriptions. To

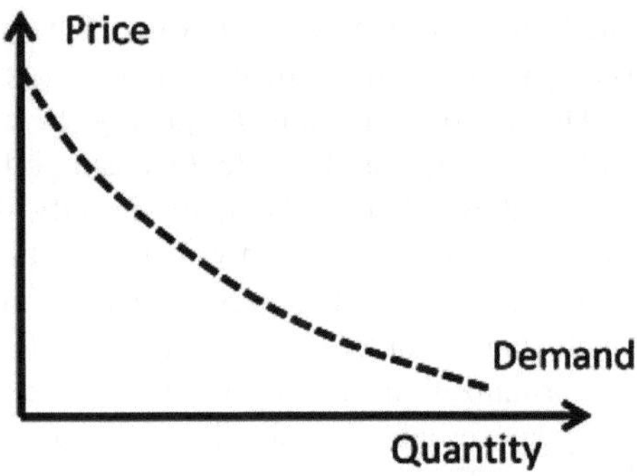

Fig. 7.1 "Law of demand" model

(according to Fig. 7.1) has to be interpreted as a set of consequences of the presuppositions we have put into the model. If the statements about the assumptions we have made (like an undisturbed idealized market for only one good without any other interactions) are assumed as statements about the model world, then it is not yet clarified, why we are allowed to interpret the deduced statements also as statements about the real world. This is not even clarified yet in physics![61] First, we are dealing only with formal statements as formal consequences of other, presupposed formal statements.

There are many necessary presuppositions for the substantiation of the conjecture that a formally correct statement, deduced from an algorithm or a calculus, represents an empirically true statement about the real world, i.e. to "conclude"

avoid misunderstanding, we exclude here for social sciences Hempel's paradigm (Hempel 1965, 1969, 1973) about the simple reducibility of theoretical terms to empirical terms and vice versa.

[61] The solutions of Maxwell's Equations about electrodynamic waves are symmetric in time. But only solution propagation in the time direction from par to future can be observed. Such the extension of the set of possible derivable statements is often greater than the set of statements, which can be interpreted in accordance to experience. The other way around, sometimes two different mathematical descriptions of the same area can be equivalent. Thus, it took a certain time, until in Quantum Mechanics the Heisenberg model (using matrix calculation) and the Schrödinger approach (using differential equation) were proven as equivalent. Both methods were very successful with respect to the assessment of the relation between theory and evidence. Cf. Simony (1995), pp. 439–450; see also Werner Heisenberg's discussion with Ernst Schrödinger and Niels Bohr in Heisenberg (1969), pp. 101–115. While the overwhelming success in forecasting natural processes as well as the internal (mathematical) unity of the mentioned models justified their use, but the choice of the categories (basic terms like matrices or differentials) to formalize the model was not yet justified only by the success. Even the conclusions from formal truth of a calculated result to its empirical truth presuppose many preconditions, which are not self-evident. If one believes that the book of nature is written in terms of mathematics, certain justifications of these conclusions may be given. Nevertheless, such a belief is a metaphysical commitment, concerning the status of mathematics, according to a saying of Galilee in Saggiatore (1623), Chap. 6. The question is still in discussion: Is mathematics telling us something about the physical or societal world? Is it an invention of man, or is it a necessary precondition for the possibility to make meaningful propositions about nature? Anyway, if we draw such conclusions, nothing is said about the nature of the nature. All this holds not only for brute, i.e. natural facts, but also and *a fortiori* for institutional facts. Therefore, a model in economics does not tell us something about the "nature" of the economic world.

from formal truth to empirical truth, as is done in the Natural Sciences[62] and sometimes in economics.[63]

1. The statement, representing the premises, formalized correctly[64] according to the chosen categories, must be empirically "truth definite", i.e. it is possible to consider it as empirically true or not, depending upon given data or experiences. When considered as empirically true, and when correctly formalized, it is considered also to be formally true. This step has no other justification than its practical utility.
2. The algorithm, i.e. the rule-based proceeding of the formula's manipulation must be truth preserving, i.e. the result must be formally true within the context of the algorithm or the calculus.[65]
3. The reinterpretation of the deduced formal expression (e.g. as a solution of an equation) must be performed with the same categories used by the forgoing formalization.
4. The categories must be chosen in such a way that the value of what is called a variable (or entity) can be observed in a real-world situation, e.g. as institutional or brute fact. The algorithm, i.e. the procedure, with which the deduction has been made, must preserve the categories. Thus, the variables and their respective values must be definable in the same realm, when observed and when calculated.[66]
5. The re-interpretation of the formal expression into a proposition about the world, observable with help of the given variables of the model, presupposes the same context, and the same knowledge of formalization and re-interpretation. Even this step has no justification besides its practicability.

The requirements 1–5 are necessary conditions and more or less formal ones. They do not require some relations between ontological issues and formal structures, but they are conditions for the possibility to make testable statements. Moreover, they avoid ontological commitments.

Formalizing and modelling of processes in nature and economy are themselves social processes. This is not done without objectives and purposes, and these

[62] In natural sciences like physics, the formal truth of a statement can only be judged within the realm of a theory. The theory is expressed in mathematical terms. If the theory is considered empirically valid within the accepted range of measurement errors, i.e. without any successful attempts to falsify it, the formal truth is a presupposition for the hypothetical empirical truth of the statement. Otherwise, it cannot be used for calculation. Cf. Poser (2001), Chap. V, pp. 104 ff.

[63] Cf. as an early example Porstmann (1986), pp. 95 ff. The discussion is closely connected with the problem of naturalism in economics. If a formally correct theory is accepted to describe economic reality to a certain extent, the derivable statements should also describe parts of economical realty. A critical review is given by Jackson (1995).

[64] The term "correctly" means here that the statement is expressed as well formed formula.

[65] In formal logics, this property of rules is called *salva veritate*. This is the well-known requirement for computability at all.

[66] If a model has been built, in which the counting of goods can have no negative values by definition, a calculated negative result cannot be interpreted anymore within the realm of the model.

objectives and purposes find their way into the choice of categories, they influence the selectivity, and due to this, the inner structure of the model.

7.5.5 *Model Interpretation: An Example from Economic Textbooks*

The well-known price-demand model from microeconomic textbooks is often read as a law-like relation – with some statistical variations – between the change in the supplied or demanded quantity of a homogeneous good and the price for this good in a market (Fig. 7.1). If one tries to formalize this allegedly statistically proven market dynamics, then the assumption of linearity in the model is very seductive, also with respect to didactic use.

It is easy to "read" the model behind Fig. 7.1 in different directions[67]: This depends on which variables are conceptualized as independent variables and as dependent ones. Prices and quantities are expressed as continuous, positive, and definite variables. In a simplified version, the relations between the variables are written as linear mathematical functions.

Taking the classical linear form of the so-called inverse demand function approximately as (*): $Q(P) = a - b \cdot P$ with P as price for a good, and "a" embodies the effect of all factors other than price that affect demand, i.e. if the curve intercepts the price axis for $Q = 0$. "b" is the slope of the curve as plotted in Fig. 7.1. Here the variable P="price" is taken as independent (horizontal interpretation). A statement like: *If ceteris paribus the price of a good increases, the demand will fall* is a consequence of equation (*).Thus it is easy to calculate the revenue function, the marginal revenue, the profit function and the marginal profit, if the price-demand function P(Q) and the cost function for production are given.

If one solves equation (*) to the (**): $P(Q) = 1/b \cdot (a - Q)$, the demand becomes the independent variable. It is possible to make statements like: With a given demand, the prize the consumer is ready to pay for it can be estimated by equation (**) (vertical interpretation).

Consider a statement such as "The market rules the states of the system according to supply and demand": If ceteris paribus the demand of a good increases, the price will go up; and when ceteris paribus the supply increases, the price will go down.

Nevertheless, in this very simple model, the chosen categories may be subject to some objections.

The values for prices P and quantities Q can be observed quantitatively over time and the curves may be interpreted as a linear or polynomial fit of the point clouds representing observed prices and demands. Thus it is possible to calibrate the

---

[67] Normally, the x-axis represents the independent variable. Nevertheless, this is a convention. It not used in cases, when business bar charts are used for independent nominal variables (nominal variables or structure variables; e.g. countries). Here the y-axis is recommended. Cf. International Business Communication Standards (www.ibcs-a.org).

parameters "a" and "b". Statistical analysis can reveal correlations: These are only observed correlations with possibly considerable statistical fluctuations: The curve in Fig. 7.1 can be seen as a least square fit of a cloud of observed points in the P–Q plane for the same object. Everybody knows: to conclude from a correlation to a causal relation without knowing the generating process within a realm of a good theory is a fallacy.[68] Beside, a market with only one good is not observable in reality. We have it to do with an idealized model, but with some explanatory power.

The demand curve is viewed from top left to bottom right. This negative slope is "explained" using the two laws of Hermann H. Gossen (1810–1858). His first law is the law of diminishing marginal utility and is also labeled as saturation law. The second law of Gossen is the law of compensation benefits and is also called marginal utility balancing rule (Gossen 1927). In his interpretation, Blaug (1980, p. 163) writes:

> Thus, the early pioneers of demand theory really had only two choices: to follow Augustin Cournot and Gustav Cassel in asserting downward-sloping demand curves as crude empirical generalization, or to deduce the law of demand from a set of primitive assumptions about economic behavior.

In order to characterize the model, the question is whether the plot in Fig. 7.1 with respect to the equations (*) or (**) is really "justified" within the realm of statistics by observations, and whether it can be interpreted as a law-like statement.

The statements, which are derived from this model, cannot be observed in all cases in the real world, i.e. in concrete economic processes. The "law" has empirical exceptions. If a baker has some buns left at the end of the day, he will sell them not according to the number resting in the cradle as required by the model. Sometimes, after a certain time, when he decides to make a clearance sale he will lower the prices, sometimes not. In other cases, one can observe that the price of a product is constant despite increasing demands – people are waiting patiently to purchase the product, even if it is not available – see Apple's iPhone. Sometimes, agents of supply and of demand even act contradictory to the model: In the very beginning when the market is opening, goods are offered at a discount in order to provoke demand, even if the availability of goods is still low. Moreover, the so-called Snob-effect can be observed: Here increasing prices will produce an increasing demand. This may be the case when dealing goods, whose brands are status symbols with high prestige for the consumers. These goods are also called Veblen goods.[69] There are also known other exceptions, e.g. the so-called Giffen-effect with inferior goods, i.e. the consumers buy more as the price rises.[70]

The market model represented by Fig. 7.1 assumes ideal conditions: homogeneous goods, no individual preferences or interactions between customers, no time delays and complete information about all relevant market data for all participants, etc. All models are more or less idealized representations. The question concerning the law-likeness is defined in natural science as follows: A law-like statement speci-

[68] This is the well-known induction problem, discussed already by D. Hume (1748).

[69] They are named after Veblen (1899), who described drastically the conspicuous consumption as a status symbol of the leisure class.

[70] Inferior goods are more in demand at lower income, firstly reported by Marshall (1895), p. 208. Cf. also Blaug (1980), p. 163.

fies a universal regularity, which holds independent from place and historical time for a certain realm, i.e. within certain limits of validity. "A true law-like statement is called a natural law" (Mehlberg 1980, p. 3). A fact-like statement, represents, if empirically true, local conditions and circumstances, i.e. facts (ibid.). These facts can be decisive as boundary or initial conditions within a model.

Using this distinction *mutatis mutandis* for the textbook model above, the equations (*) or (**) are simplified expressions of statistically collected observations, i.e. condensed fact-like statements. Law-like statements should be derivable from a theory and calibrated with experience and empirical observation. The step to go further in sociological studies is to find statistically better correlations with improved correlation coefficient r^2. Applying a regression analysis, resulting in equation (*) or (**) already presupposes that a causal hypothesis can be formulated. This causal hypothesis is taken from the two "laws" of Gossen, whereas these "laws" are again condensed observations of human behavior. They cannot be taken as a theory.

According to Blaug (1980, pp. 159 ff.), one could characterize the "law of demand" not as a causal or deterministic law, but as statistical "law" or better regularity, which can be used to build more complex market models. Simplified models should not be rejected from the beginning due to their simplicity, but it should be kept in mind which epistemological character they may have. Unfortunately it is very seductive, to present in textbooks statistical laws or fact-like regularities as causal or deterministic laws. This is also misleading for economic decisions when based upon the application of such fact-like regularities.

7.6 On the Interpretation and Use of Models

7.6.1 Three Ways to Deal with Models

In the social sciences, there are options to interpret such an abstract, highly idealized model. We consider three of them

1. The equations are used to build a model for the explanation of observed data. If the data are used, to calibrate the parameters like "a" and "b" in equation (*) or (**), it is possible to compare the structure of the "theoretical" curve with the observational data. If the parameters "a" and "b" can be estimated elsewhere, the model can be used to make prediction within the realm of statistical uncertainty. Very often, this uncertainty makes it practically impossible to make any predictions.
2. The model delivers a hypothesis about the self-understanding of the individual market players. The expectations and convictions of the players explain the characteristics of the curves.
3. The model, based on the equations above, is a hypothesis about the interaction between market participants. Therefore, it rather recommends us what we could do, when we are suppliers and producers and what we have to accept, when we

are consumers, if we accept a particular economic goal, i.e. to act like the homo economicus. This normative approach to the understanding of models informs us how we should behave, if we want to make a profit as a seller or to avoid a disadvantage as a consumer. This educative function of the model abandons the original context of a merely explaining or forecasting model during the re-interpretation of the formal curve in Fig. 7.1.[71]

Thus, we are not only dealing with a fact-like regularity like a curve or table like in case (1) and (2), but also with an implicit rule to act in case (3).

7.6.2 Laws, Regularities and Rules

Natural laws and law-like statements may be judged according to their formal and empirical truth, ie, whether rules are effective or not. Moreover, rules have another logical form.[72] Whereas a law is more or less an implication (if A is given, B will be always the case), a rule rather says "If B is wanted as a goal, you *must* apply A." It is a very general ends-means-relation. A rule is not true or false, but effective or not.

This can also be applied to statistical laws and fact-like regularities. The corresponding rules for a statistical law are: If A is given, B will be the case with probability p. The corresponding rule to act is: If B is wanted as a goal, it is recommended to apply A and the result can be expected with the probability p. For a fact-like regularity like: If A is given, the table, curve, equation etc. shows that B and vice versa, the correspondent rule to act is: If B is a goal, look for the correspondent A in table, curve or equation or vice versa.

This is a very important difference between rules and law-like statements, and the philosophy of technology and engineering has explored these structures in more detail. Here a technological theory is understood not as a set of consistent natural laws, but as a set of coherent and effective rules about how to act technologically. The foundation of the rules by natural laws is given only implicitly and tentatively: If we know the natural law, that A will generate B under certain circumstances, and if we want to have B, it is a reasonable rule, to try A in order to get B with respect

[71] Even Hermann H. Gossen (1927, p. V, Preface) stated: "Und wie die Entdeckungen jenes Mannes [Kopernikus] es möglich machten, die Bahnen der Weltkörper auf unbeschränkte Zeit zu bestimmen, so glaube ich mich durch meine Entdeckungen in den Stand gesetzt, dem Menschen in untrüglicher Sicherheit die Bahn zu zeichnen, die er zu wandeln hat, um seinen Lebenszweck in vollkommeneren Weise zu erreichen".

[72] A rule: "If B is wanted, try A" or shortly "B per A" contains not only a statement, describing a state B as a conditional obligation, but also a statement, describing an action A, which must be put into practice. This form is logically and semantically different from the form "if A then B", in which a causal law and statistical or observed regularities can be expressed "B per A" contains variables for actions, and modalities of obligation. The table of effectivity is not coextensive with the truth table of an implication. For details see Bunge (1967), Chap. 11, p. 121 ff., Kornwachs (2012), Chap. B1.4-B1.5, pp. 212–224.

to the circumstances.[73] Despite of this close relation, this foundation (the so-called pragmatic syllogism) is not a logical but a pragmatic relation.[74] In other words, physics does not found technology, but it makes the effectiveness of technological rules more plausible. Thus, it is possible to act successfully in technology according to a technical rule without knowing the founding natural law behind it. Nevertheless, a successful application of a rule does not ground the empirical truth of a corresponding natural law and vice versa (Kornwachs 2012, Kornwachs et al. 2013).

Exactly this seems to be the fallacy in the understanding of many models in economics: The successful application of rules, derived from fact-like regularities, as contained in Fig. 7.1, cannot found a theoretical relation between the variables as shown. This is given by the assumptions from which the model is derived. In any case, it is not justified to speak about "market laws" in terms of brute or natural facts, which we could not escape. The exceptions described above have shown very early in the history of this model, that we cannot speak about a law. Nevertheless, many models in economics are not only used in a descriptive, but also in a prescriptive way as rules which correspond to the fact-like regularities.[75]

7.6.3 The Performative Character of "Laws" in Economics

Considering what we have discussed in the last section, a model is not only a (mathematical) description, suitable for explanation, prediction or simulation. Even verbal or qualitative descriptions, which aim to explain economic processes in terms of cause and effect of entities, the dynamic of which can be observed with appropriate means, are already models as well. Pure descriptions, only reporting about observations, refrain from causal explanation. Nevertheless, with the means of Big Data, it may be possible to find hitherto unknown correlations which may be candidates for putting forward statistical or even causal hypotheses and which can be empirically tested afterwards.

One can distinguish between empirical variables like rates of demands, stocks, quantities of goods, production quotas etc., and theoretical variables like utility or

[73] In natural sciences, the circumstances should obey the requirement of ceteris paribus. This requirement is hardly to fulfill in real-world economic processes. In natural sciences, the problem is known as the stable preparation of the boundary conditions within an experiment. Since one has to do with brute facts, it is easier to specify the requirements of ceteris paribus and to prepare them to a certain extent.

[74] Cf. Kornwachs (2012), Chap. B. in English in Kornwachs (1998).

[75] As an example for the hope of many scholars in economics concerning laws of economics: "Saying that there are laws of economics does not imply that we will ever be able to make perfect predictions about the economy, but it does imply that we might someday have a far deeper understanding of economic phenomena than we do today. It also means that economics in the future may be able to make prescriptive recommendations about business and public policy with a level of scientific authority that it has not had before" (Beinhocker 2007, p. 13). It could be regarded as a research program to investigate more complicated models with respect to the arguments above. As a treasure for the study models, see e.g. Mäki (2002) and Morgan and Knuuttila (2012).

diverse indicators like capital commitment or Net Operating Profit after Taxes.[76] Theoretical variables are mostly calculated on the basis empirical entities, but they are not observables. Thus, the concept of utility for instance is a theoretical term. It has been argued very early, that this concept could not be observed directly and that it may not be applied as a continuous variable in infinitesimal calculus without fallacies.[77] As we have seen in the discussion about Fig. 7.1, the observation of some behavior in real economy, modeled as fact-like regularities, gives occasion to interpret them as a set of rules regarding how to behave economically (case 3). In this case, we could speak about a rule-model, based on fact-like regularities. A rule-model cannot make predictions about the dynamic of a process like a law-based model, solving equations with respect to boundary conditions and assumed causal processes. Nevertheless, rule-models are not only descriptive, saying that the observance of such and such rules can be observed in economical processes, but they have a performative potential. They contain a conditional call to action. Thus, there are some temptations to make prescriptions with these models about what should be done, if certain results are expected. The rule-model can only be related to fact-like regularities, i.e. at least to observations. These do not yet found a corresponding model based on law-like statements

A brief remark should be made about the role of Game Theory. This is a mathematical frame to calculate the payoffs of the own action possibilities depending upon the possibilities of the other player(s).[78] If one decides to maximize the own payoff and to minimize the options of the counterpart, Game Theory allows to calculate the best strategy. Thus, Game Theory does not tell us, how people behave in real processes, but it shows the consequences for the calculations of the payoffs, if one selects certain rules, consisting of ends-means relations. In other words, the use of Game Theory presupposes already the knowledge or assumption about the rules. These rules can be provided by rule-models.

Additionally, it is possible to use Game Theory in experimental economics. The behavior patterns figured out by experiments can be used to find more realistic hypotheses about rules (Davis and Holt 1993, Berninghaus et al. 2010). Optimal strategies may have been calculated and elaborated by analysis of possible strategies, depending upon the rule-models, and calculated with the help of Game Theory. But – how runs the story, if people do not behave according to proposed optimal strategies, and if they act in an altruistic way for instance, as done in the experiments by Reinhard Selten (1971) and others? In such cases the rules must be changed; obviously, we have "another game". Thus, the rules, according to which the game is played, are not laws. The existence of rules and the fact that they are obeyed or not, are institutional facts, expressing interests and compromises, goals, wishes and ideas about optimal behavior in thinkable situations. Therefore, it is reasonable to

[76] Moreover, these indicators are defined in a different way according to different microeconomic schools, and they are used in different ways for different purposes; see textbooks in Business Administration.

[77] Cf. Mayer (1932), according to Pribram (1992), pp. 775 f.

[78] Founded 1944 by Oskar Morgenstern and John von Neumann (1953).

use Game Theory for experimental research. Another task is to refine Game Theory as a mathematical tool for modelling.

7.6.4 *Objective Based Uses of Models and Their Limits*

Objectives can influence the interpretation and use of model as well. First, objectives in using a model determine directly, which of the variables of the model should be taken as dependent (caused or output) variables and which as independent (causing or input) variables. Second, the elaborated rules can be obeyed or not. As experience shows, some people did act against the rules, as the Global Financial Crisis has proven. A mere rule-model cannot predict whether the rules will be obeyed or not. It expresses regularities, elaborated by some observations and conjectures about capital or interest rate markets with a lot of idealized presupposition about the probable motivation of players, acting at a financial market. The consequences of the fact, that rules are either obeyed or not, would even be hard to predict, if any.

Thus, there are no right models or wrong models; what we can do is only to improve them. To do this, we can try to reduce the number of exceptions for which the model is seen as not (yet) valid. A weaker model has more exceptions than a stronger one. Judging models can only be done in comparative terms.

In an article discussing the Hicks-model of a market with three goods,[79] Paul Krugman (2000) wrote:

> In the long run, what this says is that we haven't really got the right models. The small models haven't gotten any better over the past couples of decades; what has happened is that the bigger, more micro-founded models have not lived up to their promise. The core of my argument isn't that simple models are good; it's that complicated models aren't all they were supposed to be. But pending the arrival, someday, of models that really do perform much better than anything we now have, the point is that the small, ad-hoc models are still useful.

This reminds philosophers of the "morale par provision", exercised in Descartes thinking about ethics.[80] Before we can build a huge church like a cathedral, we must first build some builders' huts and some shacks where we can live for the time while the building is under construction. The same holds with ethics: before we can for-

[79] Cf. Hicks (1937); later the so called IS-LM model (**I**nvestment-**S**aving/**L**iquidity preference-**M**oney supply) based on the simple model of a market with three goods X, Y and Z, Z serves also as numéraire, presented in Krugman (2000), p. 35, Fig. 1. The model assumed that bonds and money could be treated equally to goods. The IS-LM model has been criticized, because the interest rates are "made" by Central Banks according to some political rules; cf. Romer (2002).

[80] Cf. Descartes (1997), p. 37. English: "And finally, as it is not enough, before commencing to rebuild the house in which we live, that it be pulled down, and materials and builders provided, or that we engage in the work ourselves, according to a plan which we have beforehand carefully drawn out, but as it is likewise necessary that we be furnished with some other house in which we may live commodiously during the operations, … I formed a provisory code of morals …" In: http://www.gutenberg.org/files/59/59-h/59-h.htm#part3.

mulate a complete ethics as a comprehensive theory of morality (i.e. the cathedral), we must apply some rules of thumbs – the huts – of a provisional morality.

Analogously, the small ad hoc models in economics do not claim to explain everything like a theory, because they are too small for that. Thus, scholars should perhaps be more modest when proclaiming a theory for the purpose of recommendations, policy advice or consultancy.

Models are used according to their functions as mentioned in the foregoing Section. However, any model can be used for purposes outside the intentions of the model builders. Economic models do not only serve for as a forecast or explanation tool, but are used in policy and law making, too. Moreover, they serve as recommendations to implement structures according to their findings. This is what Steffen Groß (2014a) has mentioned as the performativity of economics.

Economists act as scholars when developing and publishing models. Above all, they influence the economic processes by proclaiming fact-like statements in economics like law-like, i.e. natural laws.[81] Thus, a wrong trust is induced, a trust for allegedly science-based forecasts of dynamics, whereas such statements are only expressing rules and some consequences of the assumption that these rules may be obeyed by the players.

Therefore, we must not only take the model as a means, but must also consider the proclamation thereof and the communication about it. Despite of all that, it is not meaningful to restrict the developments of models, but we should take care with what claims a model is communicated to industry, politics, and the public, since it is easier to publish the strength and rigor success of a model than to talk about its limits. The latter is a duty in serious academic work. Sometimes, this seems to be forgotten when the medial communication allows only for short time conditions. Thus, it is not only necessary to put emphasis on the responsibility for the quality of models, but also to the responsibility for the way how they are communicated and used. Even at the very moment when a model and its results like forecasts or explanations etc. are handed over to the acting deciders in politics, management, and beyond, the realm (i.e. object) of responsibility of economists as scientists is extended to an economic responsibility.

Thus, we have to look for which types of ethics of responsibility could be well suited to the problem of normativity and performativity of economic models.

---

[81] As Hans-Werner Sinn stated: "Seit es unser Fach gibt, steht es im Konflikt zwischen dem sogenannten Primat der Politik und den Gesetzen der Ökonomie. Nicht nur der Fall des Eisernen Vorhangs hat mich davon überzeugt, dass die Gesetze der Ökonomie sich letztlich durchsetzen werden. Mittel- bis langfristig ist keine Wirtschaftspolitik erfolgreich, die diesen Gesetzen widerspricht." In: http://www.boerse-online.de/nachrichten/aktien/ifo-Praesident-Hans-Werner-Sinn. "Since its existence, [economics] is in conflict with the so-called primacy of politics and the laws of economics. It is not only the fall of the Iron Curtain that has convinced me that the laws of economics will prevail ultimately. Medium to long run, no economic policy is successful which contradicts to these laws" (transl. by the author). This is in contrast to a more modest attitude: "(F)ew modern economists would claim that economics has so far produced more than one or two laws" (Blaug 1980, p. 161).

7.7 Responsibility for the Development and Use of Models

In this section, we ask how the analytical concept of responsibility, unfolded in Sect. 7.2, can be applied to the act of model building, of communicating models, and economic decision-making in the case of public policy.

To do this, we must consider the performative character of models in economics, i.e. that the knowledge expressed by a model, published and discussed in economics as well as in public policy and in the economy, has a certain controlling effect and impact upon the actions and decisions of people believing in it (Groß 2014b). Since there are no clear criteria in economic sciences of how to develop better models than the former ones and with which arguments they possibly may be supported or rejected, the responsibility for making models in this field becomes highly delicate.[82]

7.7.1 The Different Realms of Responsibility

We discuss comprehensibly the responsibility for building models, for the communication thereof and for decisions made by economic, political and other actors based on these models using some of the dimensions of responsibility (a–h) and the simplified types of ethics (possibilities 1–3) in Sect. 7.2.1.

When talking about a framework for ethics, normative statements express norms, and they can be justified and derived by principles (or imperatives) and values (cf. Sect. 7.3.1). Within this realm, the judgment of actions and decisions is oriented towards normative statements. Here, to build models in economics *and* to communicate them in politics and the economy is an economic action with intentions, effects and impacts. To build a model in academic world is not yet an economic action, unless it is done as a paid job. An economic action is an action with the help of and/or within economic structures with economic intentions and/or economic impacts and effects.

[82] In many critiques it is suggested that one can find always a set of data set which "verifies" a model to a certain extent, since the constraints are not or cannot be kept stable (Brodbeck 1998). Moreover, the validation of a model, comparing simulated data with collected field data, can be done with respect to different objectives: Validation with respect to function: How the model reacts for extreme values and how is the basic structure of the "curves"? Validation with respect to theory: Do the generated data fulfill the expectations about the model theoretically? Here we do not need necessarily data from the field. Validation with respect to the result: Which deviations between field data and simulated data are still acceptable? This can be answered e.g. by methods of intervals of coincidence. Nevertheless, in all this methods it remains a question of consensual acceptance.

7.7.1.1 The Realm of Model Building

The subject of responsibility (dimension b) is the individual researcher or scholar in economics. The instance may be the scientific community as well as the customers in contract research. The object of responsibility (dimension a) could be the intention or motivation (see type three in Sect. 7.2.1), the duty to strive for a better quality of the model than for foregoing one to his best knowledge. The best known sanction is the loss of reputation. The question remains, whether the chosen categories and concepts are really adequate for the modelling purpose.

The unpredictable effects of decisions in a global and interconnected economy do not allow simple rules of the game like the model of markets tending to equilibrium. This model has its roots in mechanical thinking with the belief that things can be controlled through adjusting a few parameters. As it is known (Sen 1999), the behavior of the participants in the "market" is very often not rational; we have irrationalism, fear, altruisms, ideologies, greed, and other reasons to act. As Steffen Groß (2011) has shown, one of the shortcomings of economics using exclusively this concept of behavior is that it does not distinguish clearly enough between behavior and action. A behavior can be modeled as a certain dynamic in a state-space approach, and it requires some invariant properties; e.g. that one can move patterns along the timeline. Acts are individual events in time, space and social contexts and personal situations, and therefore in history. Single acts are hardly predictable.

Can we really suspect that some economics models are made with obviously weak presuppositions, with unclear basic concepts, and non-transferable types of theories, designed by irresponsible scholars or research projects detached from economic experience? The answer is no, of course. Nevertheless, many of the models are inspired by mechanics, using mathematical analogies. There is no doubt that we need models to cope with the complexity of our economic world, and that it is a predominant task of economics as a social science, to find better models and theories. Today it is highly questionable whether social processes can be conceptualized with the concepts of classical physics at all.[83] Thus, rule-based models seem to be more helpful.

The preconditions for such kind of models fail. The models used are applying the concept of state, i.e. to a certain point in time we have a defined set of values of all relevant variables. The belief is that each state is determined by the forgoing state and this give rise to formulate a dynamic of states in terms of an equation. This

[83] Brodbeck (1998), Chap. 2, has shown and criticized the mechanical roots of model thinking in neoclassic economics. Classical physics means here: (D) Deterministic types of system description, i.e. each state in the state-space is defined by a unique function of forgoing states; (L) Locality, i.e. in each time point there is only one state existing in state-space; (P) Predictability, i.e. the future states are predictable if the dynamic equation and the forgoing states are known completely. This holds also for relativistic physics and statistical system descriptions like in thermodynamic. It can be shown that Quantum mechanics violates – according to different interpretations – all these conditions; chaotic systems fulfill (D) and (L), but violate (P). Cf. Kornwachs (2008). Nevertheless, social processes has been tried to be modelled by physicists within the context of synergetics and sociodynamics. Cf. Weidlich (2002).

concept of distinction allows forecasting the next state and it suggests some quasi-objectivity. This alleged quasi-objectivity is dangerous, because it hides the fact-like character of this model. We have it t do with institutional facts. It is not a description of reality, but a rule-model how to act economically. We have the effect that the economic reality "resembles" the model (Blinder 2000). Therefore, the model itself is regarded as an orientation for behavior and this can be object of a moral judgment. In other words, one is responsible for the effects of rules when writing models as rules for economic systems. Economics is not a linear causal system, which can be controlled by models with an explanatory force and by preparing boundary conditions, but economics is as well as economy an area with intentions, purposes, goals, actions, and interactions – indeed a complex adaptive and self-referential system. For all these phenomena, we still have weak models, i.e. with many exceptions. It is a matter of responsibility to concede this fact openly, too.

7.7.1.2 The Realm of Communicating Models

For many economists, the communication of the models discussed is an academic duty. Due to its performative character, communicating a model in economics is already an economic act. The author is convinced that each action in economy should also be the subject of ethical and moral judgments.

The object of responsibility is the act to communicate a model not only in scientific community but towards possible users of the results, i.e. explanation, forecast, simulation, rules etc. Such an act is performed within a certain specified context, on which the effects will depend. It makes a difference whether a model is communicated in mass media or in an academic journal. The subject is not quite clear – it can be an individual as well as an institution (research institute, university etc.). Thus, to communicate a rule-based model, and to proclaim it as an economic "law", should be considered as not very responsible, because it could support a misleading use of models. It is a duty to communicate the limits of the model, too. As an instance we could see the community of the potential users of the model and its results.

7.7.1.3 The Realm of Model-Based Decisions

Models are used to initiate, trigger and support decision-making in politics, the economy, and beyond. Decisions have impacts – these can be distinguished in direct and side-effects, in effects foreseeable and not, and in desirable effects and undesirable ones.

It seems to be obvious that the idea of personal responsibility for all economically inadequate decisions, based on communicated models, cannot be maintained in general, as Clark (1916, p. 210) has pointed out. Nevertheless, we have to avoid diffusion of responsibility, which can be observed very clearly, when its instance starts to become fuzzy. Whereas the instance of responsibility of a board of a company is quite clear, even to be responsible to the assembly of the shareholders, the question cannot be answered easily, to whom a designer of an economic model or the writer of a program for electronic stock trading may be responsible.

A possible and careful extension of the realm of responsibility should be taken into account. Such an approach would require that companies do not only bear a responsibility with respect to shaping the framework of rules, but also have a system responsibility with respect to maintaining the functional conditions of the social system, which allows them to perform their operational activities (Heidbrink 2012). Actually, this is an idea of self-maintenance of the whole economy. On the level of Corporate Identity we can observe the developments of guidelines, Rules of Conduct, with which certain values (like sustainability, whatever it may mean, the principles of "the honorable merchant" and others "virtues") serve as orientation for business practices.

7.7.2 Winners, Losers and Dilemmas

On all levels, one can observe a certain instrumentality of ethical argumentation to justify and enforce certain decisions from businesses up to whole economies in a direction where the advantages and disadvantages are not distributed equally. A win-win situation does not necessarily need to be advantageous for parties not involved within the game.

This gives rise to the distinction between the terms of economic responsibility (merely being responsible that an action or decision will have an economically favorable impact for somebody) and responsibility for the economy (being responsible for actions and decisions and the effects, side-effects, and impacts for individuals, groups and institutions potentially involved). This responsibility for the economy is a decisive part of the "social responsibility", i.e. all economic actors should consider the social dimensions of their decisions.[84] The last term of responsibility also includes a responsibility for shaping an "adequate" economic system, e.g. to establish well working institutions *sensu* Homann. The question concerning "adequacy" is often answered by particular interests, which are labeled as values.

The current criticisms of capitalism as an unfair economic system apply moral categories. Nevertheless, stipulating a non-exploitative global economy means more than just expressing a moral value. There is a lot of massive interest behind this statement, e.g. to live in world in which there is no danger to lose one's own economic existence.

Thus, it is morally not allowed to produce a situation like the prisoners' dilemma or other types of dilemmas for people involved. In other words: If a model of the economy offers possibilities to optimize my own situation without knowing what is happening within the whole system when all other are doing the same, then the application of such a model should not be taken into account. Nevertheless, if such models have been developed, they should be discussed openly to avoid potential

[84] This is in difference to Clark who required that scholars in economics should not only care about economic values but also about social values; cf. Clark (1916), p. 220.

applications. To preclude misunderstandings, it should be pointed out that a competitive situation is not yet a dilemmatic situation. To avoid dilemmatic situations should a question of a mature responsibility attitude in everyday business. As a matter of fact, and despite of this, such arrangements are sometimes done in favor of short term advantages.

To demonstrate, the following example may serve: In stores in the check-out area, with queues of clients, one can frequently find the display of confectionery. This is a special attraction to waiting children. Sweets are not very healthy, and the waiting parent has the choice either to buy some sweets for the child in contradiction to his conviction, or to stand a possible noisy conflict in public. This is a dilemmatic situation because both options are undesirable. Usually the parent gives in, and the department store has sold the sweets. The model behind is very simple: One tries to estimate with what probability a parent is inclined to avoid a public dispute about sweets. Additionally, the estimation of probability can be calibrated by observations of the check-out area. Thus, designing models as an instrument with the purpose to produce dilemma situations to the advantage of a third party is an immoral act.

7.7.3 The Principle of Conserving the Conditions for Responsible Behavior

Very often, the decisions of stakeholders may generate dilemmatic situations for competitors, employees, or customers. Frequently they are forced into a gap between needs and demands. It may be advantageous from an economic point of view to transform all imaginable needs into demands, but in certain situations, this may lead to considerable stress on the other side of the line (e.g. the value chain). The same can be observed in the competitive game between big firms with some inclination to product and service imperialism. Each competitive system should answer the question, how to deal with the losers of the game? Losers can be defined by appreciable restrictions in their options, prospects and possibilities to act. Thus, the "authors" of the game and the rules thereof are responsible for possible dilemmatic situations. This has led to the idea, to formulate a new imperative: *Act in way such that the conditions for responsible behavior may be preserved for all parties.*[85] This imperative is compatible with the integrative monism and position (c) mentioned above in Sect. 7.3.

Another, more theoretical, solution would be to widen the concept of instance: Facing a global interconnected economy that cannot be divided into national economies under different economic theories anymore, all decisions should be examined to determine whether they violate the conditions of responsible actions for all people potentially involved. This seems to be a very far-reaching idea. However, it can be obeyed already on a small scale on the level of enterprises up to the level of national policies.

[85] This principle is developed and discussed in Kornwachs (2000).

Some of these conditions to act in a responsible way correspond with values like fairness, justice, freedom, and stability of agreeable living conditions for all. This still allows competition, it allows many business models, but it extends wise advice, which has been developed for technology, i.e. not to do everything that may be possible in the realm of economy. Above all, it is an attempt to avoid dilemmatic situations, and to avoid blackmailing of economic partners.

7.8 Conclusion and Outlook

If one discusses model building in one discipline through the application of criteria from another discipline, there is a severe difficulty: The basic concepts of the main issues of the one discipline may be very different from the other ones, even if they can be formalized with similar or even identical mathematical tools. With the help of philosophy of science, it can be shown that there are different ontologies in physics and economics. In economics, we have to deal with institutional, not with brute facts. Elaborated regularities are not law-like statements, but fact-like statements in that they can be interpreted as action rules, not as causal explanations. Moreover the communication of the models and their results like simulation, explanation or forecast, have a performative character and may in turn change the modelled processes. Therefore, it is reasonable to look for concepts of responsibility in economics when building and communicating models.

Meanwhile, it is a general conviction that in economics the models, along with the neoclassical approach, are too static. Whether there can be found better models with the claim of sufficient causal explanatory force, cannot be decided on the level of philosophy of science. Nevertheless, any new theories should obey a certain correspondence principle: If the results of the old model cover satisfyingly observations with respect to statistics, the old model should be proved to be a particular model of the new model. The new model must explain the observations in a better way, and it must explain more and further observations. Thus, neoclassical models could be considered as borderline cases of other, better models, which have yet to be developed.

To apply a responsibility concept in economics means to take responsibility for building, communicating and the prospective application of the models. This includes the duty to communicate honestly the real and possible limits of economic models.

Acknowledgments For helpful discussions and constructive critiques I am greatly indebted to Michaela Haase, and additionally to the two anonymous reviewers for their fruitful remarks. Moreover I have to thank for the kind invitation to the workshop and the mind-sweeping discussions there. Last but not least I owe many thanks to Steffen Groß, Hans Walter Lorenz and Bernd Küppers for many discussions during our research stay at University of Jena in 2011. The proof reading of Steffen Groß and his colleagues in Oxford is cordially appreciated.

References

Abend, Gabriel. 2013. The origins of business ethics in American universities 1902–1936. *Business Ethics Quartely* 23(2): 171–205.

AEA American Economic Association. 2012. *American Economic Association adopts extensions to principles for author disclosure of conflict of interest*. Press release January 2012. https://www.aeaweb.org/PDF_files/PR/AEA_Adopts_Extensions_to_Principles_for_Author_Disclosure_01-05-12.pdf. Accessed 1 Apr 2016.

Bardi, Ugo. 2011. *The limits to growth revisited*. New York: Springer.

Bayertz, Kurt. 1995. Eine kurze Geschichte der Herkunft der Verantwortung. In *Verantwortung: Prinzip oder Problem?* ed. Kurt Bayertz, 3–71. Darmstadt: Wissenschaftliche Buchgesellschaft.

Bechmann, Gotthard. 1993. Ethische Grenzen der Technik oder technische Grenzen der Ethik? Geschichte und Gegenwart. *Vierteljahreshefte für Zeitgeschichte, Gesellschaftsanalyse und politische Bildung* 12: 213–225.

Becker, Gary. 1976. *The economic approach to human behavior*. Chicago: Chicago University Press (German: Becker, Gary. 1993. *Ökonomische Erklärung menschlichen Verhaltens*, 2nd ed. Tübingen: Mohr Siebeck).

Beinhocker, Eric D. 2007. *The origin of wealth. Evolution, complexity, and the radical remaking of economics*. London: Random House.

Bell, Daniel, and Irving Kristol, ed. 1984. *Die Krise in der Wirtschaftstheorie*. Heidelberg: Springer.

Berninghaus, Siegfried K., Karl-Martin Erhard, and Werner Güth. 2010. *Strategische Spiele. Eine Einführung in die Spieltheorie*. Berlin/Heidelberg: Springer.

Blaug, Mark. 1980. *The methodology of economics or how economists explain*. Cambridge et al.: Cambridge University Press.

Blinder, Alan S. 2000. Life imitates arts: How the economy comes to resemble the model. *Business Economics* 35(January 1): 17–25.

Branco, Manuel C., and Lucia L. Rodrigues. 2007. Positioning stakeholder theory within the debate on corporate social responsibility. *Electronic Journal of Business Ethics and Organization Studies* 12(1): 5–15.

Brodbeck, Karl-Heinz. 1998. *Die fragwürdigen Grundlagen der Ökonomie. Eine philosophische Kritik der modernen Wirtschaftswissenschaften*. Darmstadt: Wissenschaftliche Buchgesellschaft.

Buder, Mei. 2014. *Vergleich der Unternehmensethik mittelständischer Familienunternehmen in Deutschland und China – Probleme und Lösungsvorschläge bei Gestaltung einer interkulturellen Zusammenarbeit (Comparison of business ethics in small and medium-sized family businesses in Germany and China – Problems and solutions in the organization of a cross-cultural cooperation)*. PhD thesis, BTU Cottbus-Senftenberg, Faculty for Mathematics, Natural Sciences and Computer Science. http://opus4.kobv.de/opus4-btu/frontdoor/index/index/docId/2965. Accessed 1 Apr 2016.

Bunge, M. 1967. *Scientific research II – The search for truth*. New York/Berlin: Springer.

Camerer, Colin F. 2003. *Behavioral game theory: Experiments in strategic interaction*. New York: Princeton University Press.

Caspari, Volker, Hans G. Nutzinger, and Victor J. Vanberg. 2009. Theorienbildung in der zweiten Hälfte des 20. Jahrhunderts. In *Handbuch der Wirtschaftsethik, Vol. 1.1: Einführungen und Grundlagen und Strukturen*, ed. Wilhelm Korff et al., Vol. 1.2, 482–523. Darmstadt: Wissenschaftliche Buchgesellschaft.

Cassidy, John. 2009. *Rational irrationality – The real reasons that capitalism is crisis-prone*. The New Yorker, October 5, 30–35. http://www.newyorker.com/magazine/2009/10/05/rational-irrationality. Accessed 10 June 2016.

Cassirer, Ernst. 2004. Kulturphilosophie. Vorlesungen und Vorträge 1929–1941. In *Ernst Cassirer: Nachgelassene Manuskripte und Texte (ECN)*, vol. 5, ed. Rüdiger Kramme. Hamburg: Meiner.

Clark, John M. 1916. The changing basis of economic responsibility. *The Journal of Political Economy* 24(3): 209–229.
———. 1917. Business acceleration and the law of demand. *Journal of Political Economy* 25: 217–235.
———. 1947. Mathematical economists and others. A plea for communicability. *Econometrica* 15(2): 75–78.
Confucius. 1992. The great learning. In *Con Fu Tse: The Four Books* (Chin.-Engl.). Trans. J. Legge, 1–5. Beijing: Hunan Publishing House.
Descartes, René. 1997. *Discours de la méthode. 3ième partie, Franz. Dt.* Hamburg: Meiner, Engl.: Discourse on the method. http://www.gutenberg.org/files/59/59-h/59-h.htm#part3. Accessed 1 Apr 2016.
Davis, Douglas D., and Charles A. Holt. 1993. *Experimental economics*. New York: Princeton University Press.
Edmunds, Bernhard. 2014. *Politische Wirtschaftsethik globaler Finanzmärkte*. Wiesbaden: Springer Gabler.
EFCA European Federation of Engineering Consulting Assocation. 2011. *Engineering consultancy code of conduct*. Released May 2011. http://www.eesc.europa.eu/self-and-coregulation/documents/codes/private/044-private-act.pdf. Accessed 1 Apr 2016.
Engelkamp, Paul. 2013. *Einführung in die Volkswirtschaftslehre*. 5th ed. Wiesbaden: Springer Gabler.
FEANI European Federation of National Engineering Associations. 2006. *Ethics and conduct of professional engineers*. Released September 2006. http://www.feani.org/site/index.php?eID=tx_nawsecuredl&u=0&file=fileadmin/PDF_Documents/Position_papers/Position_Paper_Code_of_Conduct_Ethics_approved_GA_2006.pdf&t=1414142639&hash=0bf0ab8700f350a9d06052836ea3e90f253083cb. Accessed 1 Apr 2016.
Floyd, Christiane, and Heinz Züllighofen, ed. 1992. *Software development and reality construction*. Berlin/Heidelberg: Springer.
Fodor, Janos, Bernard De Baets, and Patrice Perny, ed. 2000. *Preferences and decisions under incomplete knowledge*. Heidelberg: Physica.
Galilei, Galileo: The assayer. (Il Saggiatore 1623). In *The controversy on the comets of 1618*, ed. and transl. by Drake, S. and C.D. O'Malley. 1960, 151–336. Philadelphia: University of Pennsylvania Press.
Gerlach, Jochen. 2009. Das Zuordnungsverhältnis von Ethik und Ökonomik als Grundproblem der Wirtschaftsethik. In *Handbuch der Wirtschaftsethik*, Vol. 1.2: *Geschichtliche Perspektiven, Religion und Wirtschaft, Politisch-Strukturelle Implikationen, Ethik und Ökonomik*, ed. Wilhelm Korff et al., 834–883. Darmstadt: Wissenschaftliche Buchgesellschaft.
Giddens, Anthony. 1976. Functionalism: après la lutte. *Social Research* 43(2): 325–366.
———. 1979. *The class structure of advanced societies*. London: Hutchinson.
Gilboa, Itzhak, and David Schmeißer. 2009. *A theory of decision under uncertainty*. New York: Cambridge University Press.
Gosepath, Stephan. 2006. Verantwortung für die Beseitigung von Übeln. In *Verantwortung in der Zivilgesellschaft: Zur Konjunktur eines widersprüchlichen Prinzips*, ed. Ludger Heidbrink and Alfred Hirsch, 388–408. Frankfurt: Campus.
Gossen, Hermann H. 1927. *Entwicklung der Gesetze des menschlichen Verkehrs und der daraus fließenden Regeln für menschliches Handeln (Braunschweig 1884)*, 3rd ed., ed. F. Hayeck. Berlin: Prager (Engl.: Gossen, Hermann. 1983. *The laws of human relations and the rules of human action derived there from*. Cambridge: MIT Press).
Groß, Steffen W. 1999. *Volkswirtschaftslehre ist Kulturwissenschaft: Ökonomik zwischen theoretischer Fiktion und kultureller Realität*. Würzburg: Königshausen und Neumann.
———. 2011. Vom "Gesetz" zur "Form" – Überlegungen zum epistemischen und methodologischen Status der Volkswirtschaftslehre. *Ordo* 62: 405–424.
———. 2014a. Modellbildung in der Volkswirtschaftslehre. *Merkur* 68(3): 267–272.

———. 2014b. The power of "mapping the territory". Why economists should become more aware of the performativity of their models. *Journal of Business Economics* 84(9): 1237–1259.
Grunwald, Armin. 1999. Verantwortungsbegriff und Verantwortungsethik. In *Rationale Technikfolgenbeurteilung. Konzeption und methodische Grundlage*, ed. Armin Grunwald, 172–195. Berlin et al.: Springer.
———. 2010. *Technikfolgenabschätzung. Eine Einführung*. 2nd ed. Berlin: Edition Sigma.
———. 2011. Synthetische Biologie. Verantwortungszuschreibung und Demokratie. *Information Philosophie*. http://www.information-philosophie.de/?a=1&t=5733&n=2&y=1&c=1#. Accessed 10 June 2016.
———. 2014. Responsible Innovation: Neuer Ansatz der Gestaltung von Technik und Innovation oder nur ein Schlagwort? In *Wissenschaft – Innovation – Technologie*, Abhandlungen der Leibniz-Sozietät der Wissenschaften, Bd. 37, ed. Gerhard Banse and Hermann Grimmeiss, 241–262. Berlin: Trafo.
Gu, Xuewu. 1999. *Konfuzius zur Einführung*. Hamburg: Junius.
Hanke, John E., and Dean Wichern. 2009. *Business forecasting*. 9th ed. Harlow: Pearson.
Hansson, Sven O. 2004. *The structure of values and norms*. Cambridge/New York: Cambridge University Press.
Hayek, Friedrich von. 1967. Degrees of explanation. In *Studies in philosophy, politics and economics*, ed. Friedrich A. von Hayek, 3–21. London: Routledge & Kegan Paul.
Hayes, Calvin. 2009. *Popper, Hayek and the open society*. New York: Routledge.
Hédoin, Cyril. 2015. *Sen's critique of revealed preference theory and its "Neo-Samuelsonian" critique: A methodological and theoretical assessment*. 3rd Draft. https://sites.google.com/site/cyrilhedoin/work-in-progress. Accessed 1 Apr 2016.
Heidbrink, Ludger. 2012. Unternehmen als politische Akteure. Eine Ortsbestimmung zwischen Ordnungsverantwortung und Systemverantwortung. *Ordo* 63: 203–233.
Heisenberg, Werner 1969. *Der Teil und das Ganze*. München: Piper. (Engl.: Physics and beyond. Encounters and conversations. New York: Harper and Row).
Hempel, Carl G. 1965. *Aspects of scientific explanation and other essays in philosophy of science*. New York/London: The Free Press.
———. 1969. Reduction: Ontological and linguistic facets. In *Philosophy, science and method – Essays in honor of Ernest Nagel*, ed. Sidney Morgenbesser, Patrick Suppes, and Mark White, 179–199. New York: St. Martin's Press.
———. 1973. The meaning of theoretical terms – A critique of the standard empiricist construal. In *Logic, methodology and philosophy of science*, ed. Patrick Suppes, Leon Henkin, Athanase Joja, and G.C. Moisil, Vol. IV, 367–378. Amsterdam/London/New York: North Holland.
Hicks, John R. 1937. Mr. Keynes and the classics. *Econometrica* 5: 147–159.
Höffe, Otfried. 1993. *Moral als Preis der Moderne. Ein Versuch über Wissenschaft, Technik und Umwelt*. Frankfurt am Main: Suhrkamp.
Homann, Karl. 1996. Wirtschaftsethik: Angewandte Ethik oder Ethik mit ökonomischer Methode. *Zeitschrift für Politik* 43: 178–183.
———. 2009. Die Relevanz der Ökonomik für die Implementation ethischer Zielsetzungen. In *Handbuch der Wirtschaftsethik, Vol 1.1: Einführungen und Grundlagen und Strukturen*, ed. Wilhelm Korff et al., 332–343. Darmstadt: Wissenschaftliche Buchgesellschaft.
Homann, Karl, and Franz Blome-Drees. 1992. *Wirtschafts- und Unternehmensethik*. Göttingen: UTB.
Homann, Karl, and Christoph Lütge. 2005. *Einführung in die Wirtschaftsethik*. Münster/London: LIT.
Hubig, Christoph, ed. 1982. *Ethik institutionellen Handelns*. Frankfurt am Main/New York: Campus.
———, ed. 2003. *Ethische Ingenieursverantwortung – Handlungsspielräume und Perspektiven der Kodifizierung*. Berlin: Edition Sigma.

Hume, David. 1748. *An enquiry concerning human understanding*. EBook #9662. http://www.gutenberg.org/ebooks/9662. Accessed 1 Apr 2016.

IEDC International Economic Development Council. 2008. *Code of ethics*. Released October 2008. http://www.iedconline.org/web-pages/inside-iedc/iedc-code-of-ethics/. Accessed 1 Apr 2016.

Jackson, William A. 1995. Naturalism in economics. *Journal of Economic Issues* XXIX(2): 761–780.

Johnson, Neil, Guannan Zhao, Eric Hunsader, Hong Qi, Nicholas Johnson, Jing Meng, and Brian Tivnan. 2013. Abrupt rise of new machine ecology beyond human response time. *Nature Scientific Reports* 3, Article nr. 2627. doi:10.1038/srep02627. http://www.nature.com/srep/2013/130911/srep02627/full/srep02627.html. Accessed 1 Apr 2016.

Jonas, Hans. 1984. *The imperative of responsibility: In search of an ethics for the technological age*. Chicago: University of Chicago Press.

Joas, Hans. 1997. *Die Entstehung der Werte*. Frankfurt am Main: Suhrkamp.

Kirchgässner, Gebhard. 2009. Die Krise der Wirtschaft: auch eine Krise der Wirtschaftswissenschaften? *Perspektiven der Wirtschaftspolitik* 10(4): 438–468.

Klir, George J. 1969. *An approach to general systems theory*. New York: Van Nostrand.

———. 1976. Identification of generative structures in empirical data. *International Journal of General Systems* 3(2): 89–104.

Kochenderfer, Mykel J. 2015. *Decision making under uncertainty*. Cambridge: MIT Press.

Korff, Wilhelm, et al., ed. 2009. *Handbuch der Wirtschaftsethik*. Vol. 1–4. Darmstadt: Wissenschaftliche Buchgesellschaft.

Kornwachs, Klaus. 1985. Modellbildung. *FhG-Berichte* 3(4): 9–16.

———. 1998. A formal theory of technology? *Phil & Tech – Society for Philosophy and Technology – An Electronic Journal* 4(1). http://scholar.lib.vt.edu/ejournals/SPT. Accessed 1 Apr 2016.

———. 2000. *Das Prinzip der Bedingungserhaltung: Eine ethische Studie*. Münster/London: LIT.

———. 2004a. Ethics and engineering – An analytical approach. *Periodica Polytechnica – Social and Management Science* 12: 17–40.

———. 2004b. System ontology and descriptionism – Bertalanffy's view and new developments. *tripleC*. e-journal for Cognition, Communication, Co-operation 2(1):47–62. http://triple-c.at/index.php/tripleC/article/view/15/14. Accessed 1 Apr 2016.

———. 2008. Nichtklassische Systeme und das Problem der Emergenz. In *Selbstorganisation*, 7. Ulmer Humboldt-Kolloquium. Bausteine der Philosophie Bd. 28, ed. Renate Breuninger, 181–231. Ulm: Universitätsverlag.

———. 2012. *Strukturen technologischen Wissens*. Berlin: Edition Sigma.

Kornwachs, Klaus, et al. 2013. Technikwissenschaften: Erkennen – Gestalten – Verantworten, ed. *National Academy of Science and Engineering* (acatech), München: Herbert Utz. (Engl.: Technological sciences. Discovery – Design – Responsibility). http://www.acatech.de/fileadmin/user_upload/Baumstruktur_nach_Website/Acatech/root/de/Publikationen/Stellungnahmen/acatech_IMPULS_Technological_Sciences_WEB.pdf. Accessed 1 Apr 2016.

Koslowski, Peter. 1991. Ethische Ökonomie als Synthese von ökonomischer und ethischer Theorie. In: *Jahrbücher für Nationalökonomie und Statistik/Journal of Economics and Statistics* 208(2), ed. Peter Winkler et al.: 113–139.

Krishnan, Ranjani, Joan L. Luft, and Michael D. Shields. 2005. Effects of accounting-method choices on subjective performance-measure weighting decisions: Experimental evidence on precision and error covariance. *Accounting Review* 80(4): 1163–1192.

Krugman, Paul. 2000. How complicated does the model have to be? *Oxford Review of Economic Policy* 16(4): 33–42.

Küng, Hans. 1991. *Global responsibility: In search of a new world ethic*. London/New York: SCM Press/Crossroad.

Küng, Hans, Günter Gebhardt, and Stephan Schlensog. 2012. *Handbuch Weltethos*. München: Piper.

Kutschera, Franz von. 1982. *Grundlagen der Ethik.* New York/Berlin: de Gruyter.
Lenk, Hans. 1987. Über Verantwortungsbegriffe und das Verantwortungsproblem der Technik. In *Technik und Ethik*, ed. Hans Lenk and Günter Ropohl, 12–148. Stuttgart: Reclam.
———. 1991. *Technikverantwortung. Güterabwägung – Risikobewertung – Verhaltenskodizes.* Frankfurt am Main/New York: Campus.
Lenk, Hans, and Günter Ropohl, ed. 1987. *Technik und Ethik.* Stuttgart: Reclam.
Lorenz, Hans-Walter. 1993. *Nonlinear dynamical economics and chaotic motion.* 2nd ed. Berlin/Heidelberg/New York: Springer.
Luhmann, Niklas. 1985. *Soziale Systeme. Grundzüge einer Allgemeinen Theorie.* Frankfurt am Main: Suhrkamp. (Engl. Luhmann, Niklas. 1995. *Social systems.* Redwood City: Stanford University Press).
Mäki, Uskali, ed. 2002. *Fact and fiction in economics: Models, realism and social construction.* London/New York: Cambridge University Press.
Marshall, Alfred. 1895. *Principles of economics*, An introductory volume. 3rd ed. London: Macmillan.
Maring, Matthias. 2001. *Kollektive und kooperative Verantwortung. Begriffs- und Fallstudien aus Wirtschaft, Technik und Alltag.* Münster/London: LIT.
Marx, Karl. 1965. *The capital*, vol. 3. https://www.marxists.org/archive/marx/works/download/pdf/Capital-Volume-III.pdf. Accessed 1 Apr 2016. (German: Karl Marx. 1965. *Das Kapital*, 3. Band, MEW 25, Berlin: Deietz).
Mayer, Hans. 1932. Der Erkenntniswert der funktionellen Preistheorien. In *Die Wirtschaftstheorie der Gegenwart.* 4 Bände, ed. Hans Mayer et al., vol. 2, 147–239. Wien: Springer. (Engl. In Israel Kirzner, ed. 1994. Classics in Austrian economics, vol. 2: The Interwar Period, 55–168. London: Pickering).
Meadows, Dennis L., Donella H. Meadows, Jorgen Landers, and William W. III Behrens. 1972. *The limits to growth.* Washington, DC/New York: Potomac Association/Universe Books. http://www.donellameadows.org/wp-content/userfiles/Limits-to-Growth-digital-scan-version.pdf. Accessed 1 Apr 2016.
Mehlberg, Henry. 1980. *Time, causality and quantum theory.* Dordrecht: Reidel.
Mesarovic, Michael D. 1972. A mathematical theory of general systems. In *Trends in general systems theory*, ed. George Klir, 251–269. New York/London/Sydney/Toronto: Wiley-Interscience.
Morgan, Mary S., and Tarja Knuuttila. 2012. Models and modelling in economics. In *Handbook of the philosophy of economics. Vol 1 of handbook of the philosophy of science*, ed. Dov Gabbay, Paul Thagard, and John Woods. Amsterdam: Elsevier.
Morgenstern, Oskar, and John von Neumann. 1953. *Theory of games and economic behavior.* Princeton: Princeton University Press.
Münch, Philipp A. 2015. *Die Ordnungsethik der globalen Finanzkrise. Eine Analyse anhand von Dilemmastrukturen.* Heidelberg: Springer VS.
Nida-Rümelin, Julian. 1996. Wert des Lebens. In *Angewandte Ethik. Die Bereichethiken und ihre theoretische Fundierung*, ed. Julian Nida-Rümelin, 832–861. Stuttgart: Kröner.
Noll, Bernd. 2010. *Grundriß der Wirtschaftsethik.* Stuttgart: Kohlhammer.
Nutzinger, Hans G. 2009. Theoriebildung im 20. Jahrhundert. In *Handbuch der Wirtschaftsethik, Vol. 1.2: Einführungen und Grundlagen und Strukturen*, ed. Wilhelm Korff et al., 461–523. Darmstadt: Wissenschaftliche Buchgesellschaft.
Obermeier, Paul-Otto. 1988. *Zweck, Funktion, System: Kritisch konstruktive Untersuchung zu Niklas Luhmanns Theoriekonzeptionen.* Freiburg: Alber.
Padulo, Louis, and Michael A. Arbib. 1974. *System theory – A unified state-space approach to continuous and discrete systems.* Washington, DC: Hemisphere Publishing Corporation.
Pieper, Annemarie. 1992. Ethik und Ökonomie. Historische und systematische Aspekte ihrer Beziehung. In Sozialphilosophische Grundlagen ökonomischen Handelns, eds. Bernd Bievert, Klaus Held und Josef Wieland, 2nd, 86–101. Frankfurt am Main: Suhrkamp.

Pies, Ingo, and Henry Meyer zu Schwabedissen. 2005. *Ethik und Ökonomik: Ein Widerspruch?* WiWi-Online.de, Hamburg. http://www.wiwi-online.de/fachartikel.php?artikel=234. Accessed 1 Apr 2016.

Pies, Ingo, Stefan Hielscher, and Markus Beckmann. 2009. Moral commitments and the societal role of business: An ordonomic approach to corporate citizenship. *Business Ethics Quarterly* 19(3): 375–401.

Popper, Karl R. 1947. *The open society and its enemies*. London: Routledge.

Porstmann, Reiner. 1986. *Wissenschaftstheoretische Grundlagen in den Wirtschaftswissenschaften*. Berlin: Duncker und Humblot.

Poser, Hans. 2001. *Wissenschaftstheorie – eine philosophische Einführung*. Stuttgart: Reclam Junior.

Pribram, Karl. 1992. *Geschichte des ökonomischen Denkens*. Frankfurt am Main: Suhrkamp.

Rawls, John. 1999. *A theory of justice*. London: Harvard University Press.

Richmond, Peter, Jürgen Mimkes, and Stefan Hutzler. 2013. *Econophysics and physical economics*. Oxford: Oxford University Press.

Romer, David. 2002. Keynesian macroeconomics without the LM curve. *Journal of Economic Perspectives* 14(2): 149–169.

Ronge, Bastian. 2015. Das Elend der krisenfokussierten Ökonomiekritik. Zum Verhältnis von Kritik und Krise bei Karl Marx und Adam Smith. In *Über Krise und Kritik*, Studia Philosophica, ed. Anton Hügli and Janette Friedrich, Vol. 74, 75–250. Basel: Schwabe.

Ropohl, Günter. 1987. Neue Wege, die Technik zu verantworten. In *Technik und Ethik*, ed. Hans Lenk and Günter Ropohl, 149–176. Stuttgart: Reclam Junior.

———. 1994. Das Risiko im Prinzip Verantwortung. *Ethik und Sozialwissenschaften* 5(1): 109–120.

———. 1996. *Ethik und Technikbewertung*. Frankfurt am Main: Suhrkamp.

——— 2009. *Allgemeine Technologie: Eine Systemtheorie der Technik*. 3. Aufl. Leipzig Fachbuchverlag. http://digbib.ubka.uni-karlsruhe.de/volltexte/1000011529. Accessed 1 Apr 2016.

Ross, Don. 2014. *Philosophy of economics*. London: Palgrave MacMillan.

Roubini, Nouriel, and Stephen Mihm. 2010. *Crisis economics: A crash course in the future of finance*. New York: Penguin Press.

Samuelson, Paul A. 1938. A note on pure theory of consumer's behavior. *Economica, New Series* 5: 61–71.

Schwaninger, Markus, and Christoph Mandl. 2012. Understanding the dynamics of high-technology markets: Pólya processes with positive feedback, path dependence and lock-in. In *EUROCAST 2011*, Part 1, LNCS 6927, ed. Ricardo Moreno-Díaz, Franz Pichler, and Alexis Quesada-Arencibia, 129–136. Berlin/Heidelberg: Springer.

Searle, John R. 1969. *Speech acts*. New York: Cambridge University Press.

Selten, Reinhard. 1971. Reexamination of the perfectness concept for equilibrium points in extensive games. *International Journal of Game Theory* 4(1): 25–55.

Sen, Amartya. 1999. Rationale Trottel: Eine Kritik der behavioristischen Grundlagen der Wirtschaftstheorie. In *Motive, Gründe, Zwecke – Theorien praktischer Vernunft*, ed. Stephan Gosepath, 246–263. Frankfurt am Main: Fischer.

———. 2002. *Rationality and freedom*. Cambridge: Harvard University Press.

Simony, Károly. 1995. *Kulturgeschichte der Physik*. Thun/Frankfurt am Main: Harry Deutsch.

Slanina, Frantisek. 2014. *Essentials of econophysics modelling*. Oxford: Oxford University Press.

Smith, Adam. 1977. *An inquiry into the nature and causes of the wealth of nations*. Chicago: University of Chicago Press.

Smolinsky, Dieter. 1968. *Bedeutung eines Diagnose- und Prognosemodells (MIDI-Verfahren) für Wirtschafts- und Finanzpolitik*, Forschungsberichte des Landes Nordrhein-Westfalen Nr. 2002. Opladen: Westdeutscher Verlag Köln.

Stachowiak, Herbert. 1973. *Allgemeine Modelltheorie*. Wien/New York: Springer.

Starr, Martha A., ed. 2011. *Consequences of economic downturn: Beyond the usual economics*. London/New York: Palgrave MacMillan.
Strange, Susan. 1986. *Casino capitalism*. Oxford: Blackwell Publishers.
———. 1998. *Mad money*. Manchester: Manchester University Press.
Thielemann, Ulrich. 1998. *Auf der Suche nach dem moralischen Subjekt im wirtschaftsethischen Ansatz Karl Homanns*. St. Gallen: Unveröffentlichtes Manuskript. http://www.mem-wirtschaftsethik.de/fileadmin/user_upload/mem-denkfabrik/AlteTexte/Homann4c.pdf. Accessed 1 Apr 2016.
Thielmann, Ulrich, Tanja von Egan-Krieger, and Sebastian Thieme. 2012. *Towards a renewal of economics as a social science*. Berlin. http://www.mem-wirtschaftsethik.de/memorandum-2012/das-memorandum/the-memorandum/. Accessed 1 Apr 2016.
Tichy, Gunther. 2010. War die Finanzkrise vorhersehbar ? *Perspektiven der Wirtschaftspolitik* 11(4): 356–382.
Ulrich, Peter. 1992. Unternehmensethik – Führungsinstrument oder Grundlagenreflexion ? In *Unternehmensethik*, ed. Horst Steinmann and Albert Löhr, 189–210. Stuttgart: C. E. Poeschl.
———. 1993. *Transformation der ökonomischen Vernunft. Fortschrittsperspektiven der modernen Industriegesellschaft*. 3rd ed. Bern/Stuttgart/Wien: Haupt.
———. 2008. *Integrative Wirtschaftsethik. Grundlagen einer lebensdienlichen Ökonomie*. 4th ed. Bern/Stuttgart/Wien: Haupt.
Veblen, Thorstein. 1899. *The theory of the leisure class. An economy study in the evolution of institutions*. London: Macmillan.
VDI Verein Deutscher Ingenieure (Association of German Engineers). 1991. *VDI Richtlinie 3780 Technikbewertung. Begriffe und Grundlagen*. Düsseldorf: VDI-Verlag.
———. 2000. *Ethische Ingenieursverantwortung. Handlungsspielräume und Perspektiven der Kodifizierung*, VDI report 31. Düsseldorf: VDI-Verlag.
———. 2002. *Fundamentals of engineering ethics*. http://www.vdi.de/fileadmin/media/content/hg/17.pdf. Accessed 1 Apr 2016.
Weber, Karl. 1996. *Wirtschaftsprognostik*. München: Vahlen.
Weber, Max. 2002. *The Protestant ethic and "the spirit of capitalism"*. Trans. S. Kalberg. Los Angeles: Roxbury Publishing Company.
Weidlich, Wolfgang. 2002. *Sociodynamics – A systematic approach to mathematical modelling in the social sciences*. London: Taylor & Francis.
Weißenberger, Barbara, and Bernhard Hirsch. 2013. *Auch Irrationales kann rational sein*. Frankfurter Allgemeine Zeitung, No. 65, 18.3.2013. Der Betriebswirt: 18.
Weizsäcker, Carl Christian von. 1999. *Logik der Globalisierung*. Göttingen: Vandenhoeck & Ruprecht.
Wellas, Patrick. 2012. *Die Allgegenwart kontraintuitiver Folgen moralisch intendierten Handelns in der modernen Weltgesellschaft – Inwieweit trägt ein Denken in normativistischen Fehlschlüssen dazu bei, dass die Lösung globaler Probleme wie Armut, Klimawandel und Finanzmarktkrise sowie nationalstaatlicher Herausforderungen wie Arbeitslosigkeit, demographischer Wandel und Bildungsgerechtigkeit systematisch erschwert wird?* Book series: Philosophie und Ökonomik, vol. 10. Berlin/Münster/London: LIT.
Werhane, Patricia H. 2007. Corporate social responsibility, corporate moral responsibility and systems thinking: Is there a difference and the difference it makes. In *The debate over corporate social responsibility*, ed. Steven K. May, George Cheney, and Juliet Roper, 459–474. New York: Oxford University Press.
Ylikoski, Petri N., and Emrah Aydinonat. 2014. Understanding with theoretical models. *Journal of Economic Methodology* 21(1): 19–36.
Zeigler, Bernhard P. 1978. *Theory of modelling and simulation*. San Francisco: Addison-Wesley.
Zeigler, Bernard P., Herbert Praehofer, and Tag Gon Kim. 2000. *Theory of modelling and simulation: Integrating discrete event and continuous complex dynamic systems*. 2nd ed. New York: Academic.

Zimmerli, Walther. 1991. Verantwortung des Individuums – Basis einer Ethik von Technik und Wissenschaft. In *Technikverantwortung,* eds. Hans Lenk und Matthias Maring, 78–89. Frankfurt am Main: Campus.

Zimmerli, Walther C., and Michael Aßländer. 1996. Wirtschaftsethik. In *Handbuch der Angewandten Ethik*, ed. Julian Nida-Rümelin, 290–345. Stuttgart: Kröner.

Chapter 8
Economic Responsibility Revisited

Michaela Haase

Abstract This article addresses economic responsibility at the intersection of economics, business ethics, and corporate social responsibility (CSR) studies. We argue that Caroll's influential CSR models draw on a concept of economic responsibility that is only loosely or indirectly connected to economics. These CSR models are compared with Milton Friedman's economic approach to social responsibility that does not add much to the business ethics or CSR agendas. We show that John Maurice Clark's approach to economic responsibility is different from that. His article *The Changing Basis of Economic Responsibility* (J Polit Econ 24(3):209–229, 1916) is indicative of the early discussion of the social responsibilities of individuals and businesses in the U.S. Clark's approach to economic responsibility is based on two pillars: the economics of responsibility and the responsibility of economic actors. Drawing on institutional-economic knowledge about what he called *significant and responsible causes*, Clark aimed at the development of an economics able to address economic change and to inform the working business ethics of economic actors. Clark delineated a vision about a future economy based on responsible economic action and moderate, well-informed public control. Clark's economics of responsibility can adjust the CSR models in two respects: First, it is an economic approach to economic responsibility more suitable than Friedman's approach. Second, it criticizes charity as a form of Band-Aid measures and the idea that social responsibility can be conducted voluntarily or as an add-on to economic responsibility. The article concludes that the ideas underlying Clark's approach are still of importance for understanding economic and social responsibility.

8.1 Introduction

This article addresses economic responsibility at the intersection of economics, business ethics, and corporate social responsibility (CSR) studies. We argue that influential CSR approaches have implemented a concept of economic responsibility harking back to the shareholder approach in neoclassical economics and the theory

M. Haase (✉)
School of Business & Economics, Marketing Department,
Freie Universität Berlin, Berlin, Germany
e-mail: michaela.haase@fu-berlin.de

M. Haase (ed.), *Economic Responsibility*, Ethical Economy 53,
DOI 10.1007/978-3-319-52099-5_8

of the firm. The criticisms of Milton Friedman's (1912–2006) approach to social responsibility and shareholder ideology in business ethics and CSR studies have not changed that. Some strands of CSR studies, i.e. those drawing on the definitions of CSR of the EU Commission (EU Commission 2011), have gotten rid of economic responsibility in general. This documents a separation of the economic and the social and can lead to the exclusion (or confinement) of the study of economic action and economic affairs as objects of responsibility or research objects in CSR studies. We argue that economic responsibility is essential for CSR models and the economic foundation of economic responsibility as well. John Maurice Clark's (1886–1963) approach to economic responsibility is remarkable in two respects: First, because his objective is to develop an economics of responsibility that can be considered as a foundation of the concept of economic responsibility from an economic perspective; second, what he developed is an alternative to the shaky foundation of economic responsibility in today's CSR models.

With respect to the understanding of economic responsibility, we focus on John Maurice Clark's *The Changing Basis of Economic Responsibility* (Clark 1916). Clark was an important representative[1] of institutional economics (Rutherford 2000). It was his aim to substitute an economics of responsibility for the laissez-faire economics that he criticized as "economics of irresponsibility." Clark was of the opinion that economic theory and "working business ethics" are not independent of each other. What Clark called "the creation of inappropriable values" or of "unpaid damages"[2] is indicative of, or related to, problems in the working business ethics in his time that are still of importance today.

Abend (2013) illustrates that there was a business ethics prior to the second half of the last century in the U.S. In the first decades of the last century, economics was an established academic discipline, but this did not hold true for what we know today as business administration, management studies, or business ethics. Economics may have influenced the development of these fields of study. Remarkable is how the business schools in those days tried to gain legitimization as part of the U.S. university system: Business schools promised to educate students in a manner so that they are, as economic actors, able to consider the good of society in the course of their economic activities: "Can business be taught? If so, should it be taught at a university? One way for advocates of the business school to strengthen their case was by linking it to moral and social objectives and 'service to society'" (Abend 2013, p. 177).

---

[1] Clark was president of the American Economic Association (1935–1936) and a founding member of the Econometric Society (Markham 1968). He received several honorary doctorates and in 1951 the Francis A. Walker Medal "awarded every five years 'to the living American economist who in the judgement of the awarding body has during his career made the greatest contribution to economics'." After the establishment of the Nobel Memorial Prize for economics, the awarding of the Francis A. Walker Medal stopped in 1977. https://www.aeaweb.org/honors_awards/ walker_medal.php (accessed 14 March 2016).

[2] "We have begun to realize the many inappropriable values that are created and the many unpaid damages that are inflicted in the course of business exchanges" (Clark 1916, p. 218).

It can be assumed that Clark took cognizance of the developing business schools in the U.S.[3] and their attempt to legitimate their inclusion into the university infrastructure by reference to the social good they contribute to society. The University of Chicago (UoC) that Clark joined in 1915 was one of four leading institutions included in Abend's (2013) analysis. Leon C. Marshall, institutional economist (Rutherford 2015, p. 2) and associate professor for political economy at UoC, was assigned in 1909 to function as the dean of UoC's business school (Abend 2013, pp. 182 f.). At the end of *The Changing Basis of Economic Responsibility*, Clark (1916, 229) concludes: "(T)he world is familiar enough with the conception of social responsibilities. These do not need to be rediscovered in the year of the Lord 1916."

The business ethics of the first half of the century has been forgotten[4] (Abend 2013) and Clark's article on economic responsibility as well. No economics of responsibility emerged from the institutional economics and also the responsibility of economic actors seems to have not reached the level in the U.S. and other countries that Clark might have wished-for. Instead, in the second half of the last century a debate emerged on business and society that was considered as a new phenomenon (see Abend 2013), and environmentalism and CSR appeared on the stage as well (McMahon 2003). While the Clarkean conceptualization of economic responsibility passed out of mind, CSR and sustainability increasingly attracted public interest. With it, economic responsibility was a partner on stage, but it was not conceived as a theoretical concept of economics or at the intersection of economics and ethics. In the emerging CSR literature, the meaning of "economic responsibility" drew in part on everyday knowledge or business philosophies (Jones 1960) concerning the tasks and objectives of business in society. This literature encouraged the idea that businesses have to provide a "service to society" (Abend 2013, p. 177). This idea is still present in Archie B. Caroll's (1979, p. 470) explication of "economic responsibilities:" "The first and foremost social responsibility of business is economic in nature. Before anything else, the business institution is the basic economic unit in our society. As such it has a responsibility to produce goods and services that society wants and to sell them at a profit. All other business roles are predicated on this fundamental assumption." From our point of view, however, it is open to discussion if "to produce what society wants" is equal to "service to society."

About a decade later, Caroll (1991) presented the CSR pyramid that is "...probably the most established model of corporate social responsibility" (Crane and

[3] Wharton, founded in 1898, was the first one (Abend 2013). Interestingly, this is exactly the date the first German business school came in to being, the Handelshochschule Leipzig (http://www.hhl.de/de/hhl/im-ueberblick/ [accessed 10 January 2016]). See Göschel (2008).

[4] Caroll (1979, p. 497) acknowledged that "(c)oncepts of corporate social responsibility have been evolving for decades." However, "the modern era of social responsibility (...) may be marked by Howard R. Bowen's 1953 publication of Social Responsibilities of the Businessman" (ibid.). Caroll and Shabana (2010, p. 85) point out "The idea that business enterprises have some responsibilities to society beyond that of making profits for the shareholders has been around for centuries. For all practical purposes, however, it is largely a post-World War II phenomenon and actually did not surge in importance until the 1960s and beyond. Therefore, it is largely a product of the past half century."

Matten 2007, 49). In Caroll (1979) and (1991), ethical responsibility and, with it, ethical reflection on economic activities and processes (and their consequences) is detached from economics in form and content and shifted to another "category" or "group" of responsibilities (Caroll 1979, p. 499); or to another "layer" of the pyramid, i.e., ethical responsibility (Caroll 1991). Since then, in the business ethics as well as the CSR literature, "economic responsibility" is usually equated with "be profitable:" "*(B)e proftitable.* The foundation upon which all others rest" (Caroll 1991, p. 42; italics in the original).

This is the starting point of the article at hand that has two main objectives: First, to identify and discuss the origins of the concept of economic responsibility implemented in the CSR models. Second, to introduce Clark's approach to economic responsibility in whose light the shaky foundations of the concept of economic responsibility in business ethics and CSR studies become visible. In section two, we address Caroll's two CSR models and Friedman's understanding of economic and social responsibility. Both approaches stipulate the firm's obligation to profit, maximum profit, or shareholders. After that, we discuss the relation of responsible and profitable economic action. Section three introduces two models of responsibility originating from the ethic of responsibility. Clark's approach to economic responsibility is discussed in section four. This section begins with Clark's views on individual and social responsibility, followed by his criticism of laissez-faire economics. After that we relate the economics of responsibility to the ethic of responsibility and conjecture that an explication of the concept of economic responsibility as well as the development of an economics of responsibility may be based on a broader framework of analysis composed of empirical, philosophical, or ethical theories. This section ends with a brief comparison of Caroll's and Clark's approaches to social responsibility. The last section concludes.

8.2 Economic and Social Responsibility

In this section, we contrast Caroll's and Friedman's understandings of economic and social responsibility. From Caroll's perspective, economic responsibility is a sub-dimension of social responsibility, while from Friedman's point of view, economic and social responsibility fall into one. In two articles in 1979 and 1991, Caroll unfolded what we call *models of social responsibility*.[5] In CSR studies and beyond, the understanding of social responsibility cannot be limited to these two models. As Lindgreen and Swaen (2010) point out, the development of CSR "reflects the influence of various theories, including agency theory, institutional theory, the resource-based view of the firm, stakeholder theory, stewardship theory and the theory of the firm (…), which results in various conceptualizations of CSR."

[5] Notice that Caroll and Shabana (2010, p. 86) relate the approach presented in Caroll (1979) to "the concept of corporate social performance (CSP) (that, author) has become an established umbrella term which embraces both the descriptive and normative aspects of the field (…)."

Caroll's models are selected from the various conceptualizations because of their reference to economic responsibility in their discussion of social responsibility and their relevance for the unfolding CSR discourses (Caroll and Shabana 2010; Crane and Matten 2007).

In 1970, Friedman's newspaper article *The social responsibility of business is to increase its profits* was published. The attention attracted by this article results from the objections it lodges against *social* responsibility and not from Friedman's understanding of "*economic* responsibility." In particular, it does not result from a rejection of the concept of economic responsibility as advocated by Friedman. The majority of the literature on *economic* responsibility in business ethics, CSR, and beyond, seems to have brought what we consider a limited understanding of economic responsibility. From the perspective of today, this discourse has led to two specifications of the concept of CSR: a narrow version that can be equated with Friedman's position and a broader view maintaining that there is, beyond economic responsibility, a wider social responsibility – meaning that firms should go "beyond profits" (Schwartz and Saiia 2012). The debate's focus on *social* responsibility has deflected attention from *economic* responsibility, as well as from the criticism of Friedman's position concerning *social* responsibility. This is mirrored in the definitions of the EU Commission, which do not refer to economic responsibility at all: "The Commission puts forward a new definition of CSR as 'the responsibility of enterprises for their impacts on society'" (EU Commission 2011). Notice that we do not criticize the orientation of businesses's actions at society; rather, we criticize the disconnection of the economic and the social sphere mirrored by this and previous definitions of the concept of CSR. According to Clark (1916), businesses are actors and therefore they have to be as responsible as any other actor. And as economic actors, they are (have to be) economic responsible actors.

8.2.1 Caroll's Models of Social Responsibility

In Caroll's models, the meaning of "economic responsibility" is influenced by the understanding of "social responsibility" in business ethics on the one hand, and the interpretation of the vocabulary in the conceptual frameworks of economic theories (in particular neoclassical microeconomics and welfare economics) on the other hand. With the development of American business ethics (McMahon 2003 puts 1777, the year after the publication of Adam Smith's *An Inquiry into the Wealth of Nations*, as the reference date) and CSR in North America, questions arouse asking for the role of businesses in society and the social responsibilities of corporations toward society (McMahon 2003). An expression of the broad concern of this perspective is that the term "social," but not the term "economic" or "ethical," is represented prominently in the acronym "CSR" – a characteristic that also became a source for the notoriously vague meaning of "CSR" (for references see Schwartz and Saiia 2012).

As the "C" in the acronym "CSR" is indicative of, the emergence of the "modern era of social responsibility" (Caroll 1979) is viewed as being related to the attention paid to the impact of collective action units that contrasts with the traditionally individualistic understanding of business responsibility in the U.S. (Blowfield and Murray 2011, p. 7). However, when it comes to the determination of "economic responsibility," the corporation, as an economic actor, was not differentiated from other legal forms of collective action or business organizations:

> Historically, business organizations were created as economic entities designed to provide goods and services to societal members. The profit motif was established as the primary incentive for entrepreneurship. Before it was anything else, the business organization was the basic economic unit in our society. As such, its principal role was to produce goods and services that consumers needed and wanted and to make an acceptable profit in the process. At some point the idea of the profit motive got transformed into a notion of maximum profits,[6] and this has been an enduring value ever since (Caroll 1991, pp. 40f.).

Caroll (1999, p. 283) explains his early assumption concerning the meaning of "economic responsibility": "The economic component of the definition (of the concept of CSR, author) suggests that society expects business to produce goods and services and sell them at a profit. This is how the capitalistic economic system is designed and functions." Notice the difference between the reasons given for the need for making profits in Caroll (1991) and Caroll (1999): In the former article, it is seen as a motif for entrepreneurial activity; in the latter as an expectation of society. Caroll (1998, p. 2) states that "good corporate citizens ... are expected to (b)e profitable (carry their own weight or fulfill their economic responsibilities)." "(B)e profitable," that is, the ability of the corporation to "carry its own weight,"[7] is equated with "economic responsibility." The idea that an entity has to "carry its own weight" is expressed in Clark's discussion of the changes in the understanding of "economic responsibility" in the two decades prior to 1916 as well. Clark (1916, p. 209) begins as follows: "Twenty years ago an economist writing under this title[8] would have been expected to deal chiefly or solely with the responsibility of the individual for his own economic destiny: his responsibility for paying his debts and keeping out of the poor-house. Economic responsibility meant self-reliance and self-dependence."

There is a difference in the meanings of "economic responsibility" between Caroll (1979) and (1991) that can be related to the increasing impact of shareholder ideology on management studies and beyond. In Caroll (1979), the meanings of the four responsibility "groups" or "categories" and their interactions (as, e.g., the "trade off" of legal and economic responsibility) were still open to development. About a decade later, with the invention of the CSR pyramid (Caroll 1991), the "semantic space" had gained in "structure" and became more "determined." Caroll (1991, p. 40, Figure 1) puts "economic responsibility" on a par with five stipulations

[6] Caroll and Shabana (2010, p. 90) point out: "Caroll (1991) observes that the profit principle was originally set in terms of 'acceptable profits'; however, the principle transformed to 'profit maximization'."

[7] Caroll (1998, p. 2) ascribes this formulation to U.S. president Theodor Roosevelt.

[8] Clark referred to the title of his article.

concerning the economic components. In five short sentences, each beginning with "It is important," Caroll states that economically responsible firms have "to perform in a manner consistent with maximizing earnings per share"; "to be committed to being as profitable as possible"; "to maintain a strong competitive position"; "to maintain a high level of operating efficiency"; and "that a successful firm be defined as one that is consistently profitable." The content of the five short sentences listed above extends the simple truth that a firm that cannot cover its costs will cease to exist and has no chance to practice responsible economic action. They can be read as a commitment to the shareholder value approach. No wonder, then, that, for example, Salzmann (2013, p. 566), with reference to Caroll (1991), concludes: "Economic responsibility: It is important to perform in a manner that is consistent with maximizing shareholder value."

Caroll's (1979) visualization of the four dimensions of the CSR concept grants them equal importance. In the pyramid model, Caroll (1991, p. 41, Figure 3) explains: "Be profitable. The foundation upon which all others rest." The visualization of the CSR concept by means of the pyramid has furthered the view that the respective responsibilities (economic, legal, ethical, and philanthropic) have to be fulfilled "one after the other" (for such an understanding of the CSR pyramid, see Visser 2006). The layers of the pyramid were interpreted in terms of relevance – with the bottom layer (economic responsibility) as the most and the top layer (philanthropic responsibility) as the less important one.[9] In the CSR pyramid, economic responsibility underlies all other responsibilities, that is, it is assumed to be the basic obligation of firms. In a strict or logical sense, views about the "basic obligation" of firms were not derived from positive economic theory[10]; rather, they seem to be consistent with prevalent business philosophies (Jones 1960). Sun (2013, p. 927) pointed out that "CSR cannot be separate or isolated from the social, cultural and political value systems of a society in which corporations operate." Caroll's (1991) discussion of "economic responsibility" expresses a change in economic ideology from the evolutionarily inspired idea of the survival of the firm (Alchian 1950) to the neoclassical idea of profit maximization (Roth 1999) and the shareholder approach in the theory of the firm (Sundaram and Inkpen 2004).

Sundaram and Inkpen (2004) point out that a shareholder approach to the corporation was already applied in the U.S. in 1919. They quote the ruling of a Michigan court that agreed with the Dodge brothers, minority shareholders in Ford Motor Company: "The business corporation is organized and carried on primarily for the profit of stockholders. The powers of the directors are to be employed for that end" (Sundaram and Inkpen 2004, p. 351). The authors further explain the reason for the

[9] As Caroll (1999, p. 289) clarified with respect to the four dimensions, "that business should not fulfill these in sequential fashion but that each is to be fulfilled at all times." This does not exclude that there is a difference in the relevance of each dimension. Visser (2006), in his CSR pyramid for developing countries, has changed the order of the layers.

[10] According to Caroll and Shabana (2010, p. 90), the "'responsibilities' are the expectations placed on the corporation by corporate stakeholders and society as a whole." That these views do not derive their origin from theory does not mean that they are not consistent with theory or communicated by the advocates of a theory.

legal case: "Henry Ford wanted to invest Ford Motor Company's considerable retained earnings in the company rather than distribute it to shareholders (ibid.)." Notice the court's ruling is not equivalent to Caroll's (1991) five "it-is-important sentences" about economic performance in an alleged shareholder sense. The court did not talk about maximum profits. Profit maximization, reflecting the assumptions of neoclassical models (Roth 1999), may have found its way later into the business philosophies. More recent strands in the theory of the firm allow for imperfect competition or "market structures (…) not characterized by perfect competition" (Morroni 2006, p. 97). In situations of imperfect competition, "business organizations may have various possible aims" (ibid.). Thus, in line with the development of economic (and other) theories, the meaning of "economic responsibility" can change. Theories and models provide diverging descriptions of "theoretical worlds."

After World War II, neoclassical economics became the dominant economic approach. Institutional and Austrian economics paled into insignificance while Keynesian economics became the main opponent to neoclassical economics. The battlesome Chicago economist and Nobel Prize winner Milton Friedman not only fought against Keynesian fiscalism, but also against the view that there is a social responsibility of firms beyond striving for profits.

8.2.2 The Economic Foundations of Friedman's Newspaper Article

In the decades after the "rise of social issues in business ethics 1962–1970" (McMahon 2003, p. 348), two things happened. First, the responsibility dimensions subsumed to "*social* responsibility" and their respective relationships were elaborated to a greater extent. Second, Friedman's notorious New York Times Magazine article *The Social Responsibility of Business is to Increase its Profits* was published (Friedman 1970). This article did not add much to Friedman's (1962) *Capitalism and Freedom.* This book was already popular; the newspaper article, however, reached a much larger public. Business is seen as having to act within the rules of law and ethical custom (Cosans 2009), and within these "rules of the game," *The Social Responsibility of Business is to Increase its Profits* (Friedman 1970). For firms this means that striving for profits is *the* responsible *social* activity. As Champlin and Knoedler (2004, p. 548) point out, "Friedman's position was not that corporations should not act according to legal and social conventions but that businesses should not engage in 'social responsibility.'"

Thus, Friedman's approach to social responsibility ($SR^{Friedman}$) is narrower than Caroll's (SR^{Caroll}). Friedman did not deny that there may exist other socially responsible activities such as those neglected in $SR^{Friedman}$ and included in SR^{Caroll}. However, according to Friedman's view, it is not the task of firms, but of other actors (individuals) or of the state to conduct them. From the perspective of McMahon (2003, pp. 345 ff.), this view corresponds to the early U.S. American approach to business ethics between 1891 and 1963. In this regard, it seems that Friedman's view was in harmony with the contemporary business ideologies in the U.S. Or, to put it otherwise, economic ideology and business ideology were in tune with each other.

In the newspaper article, Friedman provided rather superficial references to the economic foundation of his argumentation. His rejection of an "extra" social responsibility of firms, i.e. of a view equivalent or at least similar to SR^{Caroll}, is grounded in, among others, political liberalism and property rights theory (see Lodge 1982, p. 86). Shareholder approach and property rights theory, combined with a narrow interpretation of methodological individualism[11] furthered the view that individuals only, and not firms, can be held responsible for their deeds (Blowfield and Murray 2011, p. 7). Managers are considered to be responsible only for the fulfillment of their contractual and fiduciary obligations toward the shareholders of the firm they are working for. The idea that a firm's management is obligated to do "good" with money that it does not own runs contrary to this view.

Friedman's position is theoretically well-derived and, within its framework, sound. With respect to the ends, which shareholders may want to achieve or strive for, Friedman referred to the standard approach in microeconomics (Bowles 2004, pp. 93 ff.). The standard interpretation is grounded in assumptions of economic models according to which individuals strive for utility or firms strive for profit, respectively (Bowles 2004; Roth 1999, p. 1). However, even if one takes this neoclassical framework for granted, there is a weak point in Friedman's argumentation: In harmony with the view of not empirically testing the assumptions underlying individual behavior in the process of theory application (Friedman 1953), Friedman had probably neglected the possibility that "real world" shareholders can develop preferences different from those assumed by neoclassical economic models.[12] Thus, he did not address the consequences accruing from non-standard preferences for the principal-agent relationship between shareholders and managers (Bowie and Werhane 2005, 31; Schwartz and Saiia 2012). Law and custom, as well as the formation and change of individual preferences, was not among the main topics of neoclassical economics at the time Friedman had published his article (Friedman 1970).

Notice that Friedman's approach to "economic responsibility" ($ER^{Friedman}$) has nothing to add to the meaning of "economic responsibility" already included in Smith (2003 [1776]) (Hillinger 2012, p. 3). More precisely, $ER^{Friedman}$ can be traced back to the neoclassical reading of Adam Smith's epoch-making work *Inquiries into*

[11] There are different strands of methodological individualism (Heath 2015). Note that there are views in methodological individualism that do not exclude that firms can be held responsible.

[12] Roth (1999, p. 1) lists assumptions of „received, neoclassical theory" ignoring uncertainty or imperfect information, which say, with respect to the individual consumer: "His preferences are both exogenously determined and stable, and defined on objects of choice whose qualitative and other properties are known with certainty." In the meantime, these assumptions have been put into perspective, in part by information economics (e.g., Stigler 1961; Akerlof 1970), in part by works critical to "received" rational choice (Hargreaves Heap 2009).

the Wealth of Nations (1776) which cuts off economics from moral philosophy (Sen 1987, p. 2)[13]:

> It is not from the benevolence of the butcher, the brewer, or the baker, that we expect our dinner, but from their regard to their own interest. We address ourselves, not to their humanity but to their self-love, and never talk to them of our own necessities but of their advantages (Smith 2003 [1776], p. 22).

This is one of the most cited quotes of *The Wealth of Nations*, and it usually serves as legitimization of self-interest. This quote is used for spelling out the beneficial effects of the pursuit of self-interest on society – viz. that pursuing one's own interest and only one's self-interest is an ethical act since it increases the welfare of society uno actu: "Attracted by their own interests, individuals will do what serves the common good, for in that all will gain and prosper."[14] Friedman's (1970) dictum that the only social responsibility of the firm is to increase its profits must be understood in this light.

The relationship between individual action and societal welfare described above is the ethical dimension of economics that has attracted the highest degree of attention in economics and beyond (see Krause-Junk 2010, p. 99; Witzum 2008, p. 401; Scherer and Palazzo 2007, pp. 1100 and 1106). Yet, the metaphor of the invisible hand seems to include a "hidden" or "implicit" understanding of "economic responsibility" at best.[15] From the perspective of approaches to rational action in ethics (Frankena 1983; Nida-Rümelin 2005; Schatzki 2007, p. 97), the idea is not convincing that, because of the working of the "invisible hand," individuals can follow their self-interest, and only their self-interest, without reflection on their motives. According to the invisible-hand metaphor, individuals can contribute to the "common good" without explicitly aiming at or reflecting on this. The new social welfare theory draws on neoclassical behavioral and technical assumptions; it insists on its value-free character that also applies to its main evaluative standard – efficiency. The neoclassical economist Frank Knight (1922, p. 193) has found clear words for this practice:

> Economists who pretend to eschew ethical problems, to confine themselves to 'price economics,' or contrast price economics and welfare economics, or pecuniary and social efficiency, have in general merely worked in terms of unformulated, unconscious ethical standards, and hence, in the literal sense, unintelligently.

---

[13] In Adam Smith's work, this division is presented in his writings *Inquiries into the Wealth of Nations* (2003 [1776]) and *The Theory of Moral Sentiments* (2000 [1759]).

[14] Introduction to Smith (2000 [1759]), author unknown. See Zaman (2012, n.p.)

[15] Notice that the invisible-hand metaphor has not been proved worthlessly; in fact, the content of this metaphor adds to insights into the functioning of a particular type of macro systems. As a metaphor cannot be "true" or "false," it can however be argued that this metaphor is less useful for the understanding of "economic responsibility." For the solution of problems requiring the economic responsibility of an actor, this metaphor remains relevant insofar it is a starting point for the development of alternative perspectives.

Note that self-interest and only self-interest as an action motif was perhaps not "Adam Smith's Message" (Hayek 1978, p. 267 [1976]).[16] For Hayek (ibid., 268) the view is an "error that Adam Smith preached egotism"; instead, Smith was interested in the recognition of the functioning of modern, post tribal societies.[17] Hayek sees in Smith's work a "clear recognition of the central problems of science" (ibid.), an approach "to the most simple and universal elements"[18] which was then applied to markets:

> The recognition that a man's efforts will benefit more people, and on the whole satisfy greater needs, when he let himself be guided by the abstract signals of prices rather than by perceived needs, and that by this method we can best overcome our constitutional ignorance of most of the particular facts, and can make the fullest use of the knowledge of concrete circumstances widely dispersed among millions of individuals, is the great achievement of Adam Smith (Hayek 1976 [1978, p. 269]).

For Hayek, the working of the "invisible hand" or of market coordination, with all its implications for societal welfare, is superior to planning.

According to Caroll, firms have a basic obligation to conduct profitable economic action; more precisely, they are obliged to follow the idea of maximum profit for shareholders. From this perspective, profitable economic action is tantamount to responsible economic action. The two expressions are interchangeable. Read this way, the expression "responsible economic action" adds nothing to "profitable economic action." Every action motif that goes beyond the achievement of "maximum profit," has to be addressed in other terms such as legal, ethical, and discretionary (philanthropic) responsibility. This reduces the potential objects of responsibility for economics to one. In Caroll (1979) and (1991), economic responsibility is at least a dimension of social responsibility; in the EU Commission's definition (2011) this connection has got lost altogether.

In the next section we wonder what happens if the relation between responsibility and profitability is not given by definition, but is conceived of as a contingent consequence of economic action. In (business) economics, profitability is a positively assessed consequence of economic actions traced back to sources as different as innovation, prudence, alertness, reputation, or monopoly power.

8.2.3 *On the Relation of Profitable and Responsible Economic Action*

In the CSR models detailed above, "economic responsibility" is equal to "profitability." In the following, we put "responsible economic action" and "profitable economic action" on a par. We wonder what happens if the equalization

---

[16] The article "Adam Smith's Message in Today's Language" was taken from the Daily Telegraph, London, 9 March 1976, and published in Hayek (1978 [1976]).

[17] Hayek used the term "open society."

[18] Hayek quotes Francis Jeffrey, editor of the Edinburgh Review, a statement from 1803.

(equivalence) of economic responsibility (or responsible economic action, ER) and profitability (or profitable economic action, P) is broken into its components and discussed in terms of two material conditionals.[19] In order to give the reader a rough idea what is meant by "responsible economic action" and "profitable economic action," we introduce the following stipulations: A profitable economic action is an economic action that, for whatever reason, leads to a surplus over the costs. A responsible economic action is one that by intent attempts to avoid or delimit action consequences that hurt society or nature. Two conditionals express the different connections between P and ER: (i) P → ER (read: "If there is profitable economic action, then there is responsible economic action" or "Every profitable economic action is a responsible economic action")[20] and (ii) ER → P (read: "If there is responsible economic action, then there is profitable economic action" or "Every responsible economic action is a profitable economic action"). Notice that a material conditional does not express a causal relationship; that is, the if-component does not express a cause for the then-component. This means that, e.g., in case of ER → P, responsible economic action and profitable economic action take place together on a regular basis, but responsible economic action does not cause profitable economic action. In addition, (i) and (ii) express general sentences; that is, the appearance of one instance embodying contrary evidence falsifies them.

(i) expresses that profitable economic actions are performed in a responsible manner; in other words, it says that it cannot happen that a profitable economic action was not performed in a responsible manner. Profitability presupposes economic responsibility although not all responsible economic actions are profitable. This is the description of a desirable world in that *only* responsible economic action can lead to profitability. The conditional P → ER is wrong only in the case that profitability is given but not responsibility: P and non-ER. It is obvious that there are situations can be described by sentences that truly state "P and non-ER." For example, Champlin and Knoedler (2004) who observe that customers do not (or do not effectively) punish the misbehavior of business firms is indicative of that.

According to (ii), responsible economic action is sufficient for profitable economic action and profitable economic action is a necessary condition for economic responsible action. This is perhaps close to the view underlying the CSR pyramid or a saying like "profitability is the basis for everything else:" Only profitable economic action can be responsible economic action. This is a description of a world in which economic responsible action is always profitable, but there are profitable actions not conducted in a responsible manner as well. This conditional seems to be

[19] The conditional connects two sentences in the "if …, then …" form (Suppes 1957). If a conditional with a wrong antecedens is interpreted as true (sic), then the "if …, then …" sentence is named a "material conditional" (Quine 1969, p. 39).

[20] In (i) and (ii), we abstract from information concerning time and space, for example: if there is profitable economic action in the 20th century in the United States, then there is responsible economic action in the 20th century in the United States. As Quine (1969, p. 38) points out, if the antecedent (the if-part) of the conditional is true, then we are committed to its consequent (the then-part). In other words, in case of (i) we want to say: it cannot happen that *P and non-ER* occurs, and if it happens, then we are no longer committed to the conditional.

wrong, too. In other words, there are instances or events that can be described by "ER and non-P." Many examples are available which document that customers have not accepted the offerings of firms that result from responsible economic action. Acting economically responsible is not tantamount to being able to market a product or service that is subjectively valuable to customers *and* higher valued by them as comparable offers by competing firms. One reason for that may be that a competitor has an – in terms of economic value – better or a cheaper offer. That a firm acts economically responsible is one aspect that customers might and (from the perspective of normative ethics) should consider throughout their decision-making process. It does imply that customers take into account self-interest *and* the common good, but it does not mean that they sacrifice their self-interest (or subjective value) for the sake of a particular firm's profit.

If we recall Caroll's (1991) five short sentences stating that for economically responsible firms "(i)t is important to perform in a manner consistent with maximizing earnings per share"; or "to be committed to being as profitable as possible"; or "to maintain a strong competitive position"; "to maintain a high level of operating efficiency"; and "that a successful firm be defined as one that is consistently profitable," then we can conclude that this list of recommendations misses the point at best. It provides no hint useful for the establishment of a connection between economics and ethics. Although the brief discussion in the preceding paragraph has shown that both (i) and (ii) are wrong, as there are instances that can lead to the formulation of sentences which contradict them, this result does not exclude that there are observations (instances) that can confirm (i) and (ii). The main point is that at the given point of time, there is no regularity expressing a connection of responsible and profitable economic action. Without the invisible-hand mechanism in the background, there seems to be no basis for the empirical truth of (i) and (ii) and, with it, of the equivalence ER $\leftrightarrow$ P.

Caroll (1991) argued that profitable economic action is the main pillar for the social responsibility of the firm and constitutes the basic layer in the pyramid model on which the other responsibilities draw. In case of ER $\rightarrow$ P, there are other sufficient conditions for P. A number of actions that might be classified as "irresponsible economic actions" can be related to profitable economic actions as well. Profitability can result from short-term "milking a plant" (Jackall 2010, p. 96) and other forms of questionable economic or even unethical behavior (exploitation, wage dumping, etc.).

Notice that what is called the "business case for CSR" (Baron 2001) is not touched by the discussion of the two conditionals. The reason for this is that, according to our interpretation of the conditional "ER $\rightarrow$ P," "ER" requires moral action. Compared to that, the business case is an example for profitability that can be achieved by non-ethical (as opposed to *un*-ethical) behavior. The "business case" instrumentalizes CSR for the sake of profit making. According to the "business case," firms pursue CSR only for strategic reasons, not because of their motifs or values (see Sun 2013, p. 926). Ethically, this is less demanding than Friedman's narrow CSR concept (Cosans 2009). Irrespective of its self-assessment as "value free," and despite the criticism it faces, new social welfare theory is a moral theory.[21] Considering the wealth-creating social mechanism, striving for profit *is* socially responsible, that is, ER = SR. In the light of the business case for CSR, corporate social performance is only a means for the achievement of the good of the manager or company (Beisbart 2012). Ethical motives or self-reflection is not required, simply self-interest. Stripped of its social-theoretical dimension, this view falls behind that of Adam Smith. The economist[22] Adam Smith was interested in the "basic mechanisms" or "minimum conditions," which are built on the division of labor and exchange relationships among anonymous parties and make post-tribal societies work. Action on the basis of self-interest is one of these "minimum conditions."

The preceding analysis suffers from the indetermination of the meaning of the concept of responsibility. How can "economic responsibility" be understood if there is no explication and definition of "responsibility"? For this reason, we introduce two models of responsibility which originate from the ethic of responsibility. After that, Clark's discussion of individual and social responsibility is interpreted against the backdrop of these models.

8.3 Two Models of Responsibility

The concept of responsibility began to mature after the separation of economics and ethics expressed in the two major works by Adam Smith: *The Wealth of Nations* (1776) and the *Theory of Moral Sentiments* (1759). The concept of responsibility gained in importance both in ethics and in the public debate not earlier than in the second half of the nineteenth century and it was an invention of political rather than economic science (Bayertz 1995, p. 40). No wonder, then, that important contributions to the contemporary discussion about responsibility originate from political science (Young 2004, 2006, 2011). Prior to the 1850s, responsibility was discussed in terms of imputation, guilt, or duty (Bayertz 1995, p. 24).[23] The concept of responsibility is explicated on the basis of theoretical frameworks which developed in the last 150 years. Bayertz (1995) names these frameworks "models" and distinguishes a "classical model" from a "modern model" of responsibility. Each model is built on two pillars: description and valuation. Because of the first pillar, the ethic of responsibility is related to the social life world and empirical science as well. The second pillar constitutes the ethic of responsibility as part of ethics.[24]

---

[21] According to Roth (1999, p. 2), the new social welfare theory is „a hybrid moral theory incorporating elements of goal- and rights-based moral theories."

[22] The moral philosopher Adam Smith was interested in more than in this in basic mechanism.

[23] Clark (1916, p. 209) noticed that there was a change: "The ideas of obligation which embody the actual relation of man to man in the twentieth century, and answer the needs of the twentieth century, are radically different from the ideas which dominated the nineteenth."

[24] If the ethic of responsibility cooperates with empirical science, then normative content accrues from the latter as well.

The classical model is built on two metaphysical assumptions: intentionality and causality (Bayertz 1995, p. 21). The model assumes that actors – via their actions – are able to bring certain – intended – effects about, and because they can take into consideration the consequences of their actions they can be held responsible for them (imputation). In addition, the classical model assumes that the relationships in question are face-to-face relationships. As Bayertz (1995) argues, this model combines description and normative assessment. The meaning of the concept of responsibility is not independent from the knowledge available in the domains of ethics and economics or their intersections. Based on description and normative assessment, actors can be held responsible for their deeds. The model draws on a description of (parts of) social reality, selected for several reasons, and (based on normative assessment) it selects action consequences of interest. In this vein, the classical model focuses on descriptions of actions which have already taken place and whose consequences are negatively assessed. Thus, as Bayertz (1995) has emphasized, judgments of responsibility are a result of interpretation and construction.

The two basic components of the "classical" model of responsibility, description and normative assessment, are in need of adaptation. Bayertz (1995, pp. 43 ff.) provides a sketch of what he calls the modern model of responsibility. There are five main characteristics of this "modern" model of responsibility[25]: (1) responsibility has grown beyond face-to-face relationships and has become an important factor in the provision of public goods; (2) the reversal of the direction of time: it is more important to avoid harm than to make someone responsible for the harm after its occurrence; (3) the responsibility for future generations or ecological responsibility includes the maintaining of actual states or the generation of future states; (4) the act of omission is equally as important as the conduct of an act; (5) in case of actions which are put into effect via organizational structures and technological systems, an increase of the relevance of objective knowledge concerning action consequences can be found.

That social reality has changed and, with it, the conditions of applicability for the classical model eroded, was a starting point for Clark's article published in 1916. From the perspective of today, it can be ascertained that the shrinking of the range of application of the "classical model" has continued and the idea of linear causality or controllability has further lost in importance (Kersting 2003). The decrease in the relevance of face-to-face relationships in "modern" industrialized societies and the increase of problems (or the increasing awareness of these problems) accruing from unwished-for action consequences or negative externalities has attracted attention in economics, CSR, business ethics, and sustainability research. The identification and assessment of negative action consequences is no – substantial – problem for the before mentioned disciplines, while the ascription of these action consequences to single actors or actions is. This "gap" in its descriptive foundation is a weakness of the classical model of responsibility. The attempt to maintain or substantiate the relevance of the ethic of responsibility in face of the solution or avoidance of problems related to the provision of global public goods addressed in terms of

[25] For a detailed description, see Haase (2015a).

sustainability or justice, has led to the development of approaches that try to cope with that (e.g., Young 2004, 2006, 2011).

Notwithstanding, the modern model provides fruitful starting points for the conceptualization of economic responsibility; in particular, the future-oriented perspective in connection with the orientation toward the maintaining of states, or toward the bringing about of wishful states, is relevant. From that can be learnt that an explication of the concept of economic responsibility has to recognize the objective knowledge that has its source in economics and potentially influences the actors' decision-making processes.

In the next section, we address *The Changing Basis of Economic Responsibility* by John Maurice Clark (1916). Clark did not create a model of responsibility appertaining to the ethic of responsibility; however, he pioneered many thoughts which characterize the modern model of responsibility. Although he did not refer to the ethic of responsibility, the article provides evidence for the shrinking range of applicability of the classical model as early as hundred years ago. In addition, Clark was well aware of the knowledge foundation of what Bayertz (1995) later called models of responsibility and, without doubt, he saw economics as being under the obligation to provide this knowledge.

8.4 Clark's Approach to Economic Responsibility

Clark analyzed economic responsibility from an economic point of view. From his perspective, economic responsibility has a theoretical and a practical dimension. The first dimension leads to the development of a *responsibility of economics*, the second addresses the *responsibility of economic actors* or their "working business ethics," respectively (Clark 1916, p. 210). The latter needs the "input" from the former, that is, economic knowledge is conceived of as a source for responsible economic action. One could argue that both, empirical and normative knowledge is of importance for the "working business ethics." The tasks of theory or of theorists, respectively, are as follows: first, "to reveal those causes and consequences of things men do which transcends the scope of three exchange" (Clark 1916, p. 220); second, "to substitute an economics of responsibility for the economics of irresponsible conflict" (ibid.); third, "furthering the growth of willing cooperation" (ibid.).

Clark does not neglect the complexity of the social world and the influence of the man-made social environment on individuals. However, if knowledge gaps prevent individuals from linking actions and action consequences because of the increasing complexity of the environment and the myriads of unintended action consequences, then economics can play a positive role in filling these gaps. In a way, scientific knowledge is a compensation for the limitations individuals' cognitive capacities face in modern times. We do not have to give up our "purpose … to shape the world – or a little bit of it – 'nearer to the heart's desire'" (Clark 1916, p. 214). Two aspects are important in this regard: first, to gain knowledge about significant causes of events of interest; second, to be able to control the causes and, with it, the events themselves. Controllable causes are called "responsible causes." New knowledge extends the range of responsible action for human beings: "(N)ew ideas of causes and effects" (Clark 1916, p. 213) lead to "new ideas of responsibility" (ibid.). To have generated this knowledge, however, is not sufficient for responsible economic action. Actors need to be able and willing to make use of this knowledge. And they need to know what knowledge is of importance for their purposes and for the achievement of what purposes they can or should strive towards. In other words, actors require normative knowledge or the ethical advice of economics as well. Actors need to be aware that, by economic action, they can create both value for themselves and others who come into view because of the social responsibility of actors.[26] For example, Clark criticized efficiency as being too narrow a focus for the achievement of social value. This is not a question of belief or disbelief in something; it is a question of the knowledge required in order to decide about what can be reasonably believed.

Compared with Caroll's approach discussed in the previous section, and expressed in terms of the ethic of responsibility, one can conclude that Clark's approach identifies a potentially larger number of objects of responsibility than the CSR models do.

8.4.1 Individual and Social Responsibility

As mentioned above, Clark did not neglect the influence of the social sphere on the individual; however, he was convinced that this is not tantamount to "staying helpless" on the evidence of the complexity and impact of the man-made social environment (cp. Clark 1916, p. 213). "The only way the environment can overcome a man completely is by persuading him that it can do so" (ibid.). In particular, "laying responsibility on the environment cannot take it of the shoulders of persons so long as the environment of each of us consists chiefly of the rest of us" (ibid.). There is an individual (personal) responsibility and a collective responsibility – and the latter is "personal responsibilities reflected in the social mirror" (Clark 1916, p. 217).

Clark (1916, p. 229) held the view "that a large part of them (social responsibilities, author) are business responsibilities." This seems to be in harmony with the understanding of "social responsibility" in CSR studies. However, what the responsibility of corporations toward society is according to the CSR discourses, that is social responsibility, is from Clark's perspective the economic responsibility of a collective actor or business (an expression of what Clark calls *collective* or *joint*

[26] We exclude from our discussion a third category of value amending economic and social value: ecological value. Notice that Clark's discussion of negative action consequences includes the creation of value that, if measurable and measured, leads to negative measures (or destruction of value) of what we call "ecological value" (Haase 2015b). Clark did not use contemporary vocabulary, for example, the expression "negative externalities" in the discussion of such issues, but formulations such as "inappropriable values that are created" or "the many unpaid damages that are inflicted in the course of business exchanges" (Clark 1916, p. 218).

responsibility). It is the responsibility of an economic actor to contribute to the creation of social value or to act in the public interest. However, it is not left to the actors' subjective beliefs or subjective knowledge what social value is, but research object of the economics of responsibility.

Thus, Clark (1916) has to be read in connection with Clark's (1915) article on the concept of value or social value, respectively (Clark 1936). In early publications in the field of American business ethics the idea prevailed that businesses have to provide something to society or have to "serve society." Insofar Clark addresses the objectives of businesses, he doubts that the social value of businesses' activities is limited to the provision of goods and services. For one example, Champlin and Knoedler (2004) point out that the maintenance of sophisticated faculties of the workers may result in higher social value than the sheer existence of certain products or services. According to Champlin and Knoedler (2004, p. 546), Clark criticized as well "the familiar orthodox premise that consumption is the end of all economic activity, with production simply as a means to that end." This view "considers only individual sensation and ignores 'social interest'" (ibid.). It is not important that we produce but how as "the quality of the activity involved in work is more important as a positive social value than the quantity and quality of consumption" (ibid.).

Clark opposed the "denial of any responsibility for the public interest" as well (Champlin and Knoedler 2004, p. 545). His "vision of an economics of responsibility was one in which business recognized and accepted its responsibility for the public interest and in which the rest of the society worked toward the same end" (Champlin and Knoedler 2004, p. 547). What Champlin and Knoedler describe is an economic practice guided and informed by an economics of responsibility. Economic knowledge is created for the good of society, for building a "'great society' on the combined basis of freedom and progressive social morality" (Clark 1947, quoted by Sharfman 1947, p. 292[27]). Clark (1916, p. 223) formulated an idea, an ideal of economic action that harmonizes with this line of thought: "The ideal is to pay one's way, not to hurt others without compensation, to get value for value given, and to leave the world in other respects just as one found it, or at least not to leave it worse for one's presence."

Clark's (1916) understanding of both "social responsibility" and "economic responsibility" differs from the use of the words in the CSR literature and in business ethics. Economic responsibility is no dimension of social responsibility, but something that is detailed on the basis of the economics of responsibility. Table 8.1 summarizes the different views of the approaches discussed in this article.

As we have argued above, the conduct of socially responsible economic action requires, at least in part, economic knowledge. That knowledge is available is not the end of the story, however. First of all, this knowledge is an offer. Economic actors can use it as input to their social constructions of reality. We read Clark's approach to social responsibility in this interpretative, "social constructivist" manner; it is what comes out of processes of reflection: "For what is collective responsibility but personal responsibilities reflected in the social mirror?" (Clark

[27] Sharfman refers to a lecture given by Clark in 1947 and published in Clark (1948).

Table 8.1 Comparison of four approaches to economic and social responsibility

	Economic responsibility (ER)	Social responsibility (SR)
Caroll	Produce goods and services and sell them at a profit (1979)	"Social responsibility" is the name of a group of responsibilities. All responsibilities (expectations of stakeholders) have to be fulfilled
	"Be profitable" (1991)	
Friedman	ER = SR	SR = ER (within the "rules of the game"
EU Commission	–	Business has to take into account its impact on society
Clark	ER is the responsibility of individuals and collective action units for the social environment or the social structure	Social responsibility is a perspective, a form of interpretation of the social word that helps economic actors to establish self-control and to extend individual control to public control that includes paying attention to the public or social interest
	Economic actors are responsible for	
	the creation of economic and social value;	
	the avoidance of creation of inappropriable values and the bringing about of damages	
	Examples for social value created by responsible economic action are:	
	Sophisticated faculties of workers are valuable for society	
	Paying attention to "public" or "social interest" is part of every economic action calculus	
	The quality of products and services is important, not their amount (refers to the objectives of economic action)	

1916, p. 217). As we are "jointly responsible for the general social environment (…) our personal responsibilities are being broadened" (ibid.). This means that there is no division between individual (personal) and joint responsibility. Social responsibility accrues from the joint responsibility addressing (in Clark's terms) the social environment.

8.4.2 Clark's Criticism of Laissez-Faire Economics

Clark's understanding of responsibility mirrors the historical circumstances of the changes that took place between 1896 and 1916. He analyzed the insufficient potential of contemporary neoclassical economics for the understanding of "economic responsibility" and he brought institutional economics to the fore for the conduct of an adequate analysis of the issue. From his point of view, the business system of free contract and laissez-faire is a system of irresponsibility and the economic theory behind it an “economics of irresponsibility” (Clark 1916, p. 218). Clark (1916, p. 222) made it very clear that a certain type of economic system affects the creation of social value detrimentally:

> Science has made available for society’s use an amount of knowledge of what is happening to its members vastly greater than they can ever absorb individually and use individually in the daily course of looking out for their interests. No one who appreciates this fact can hold that a system of free contract normally protects all interests, and that every free business transaction is automatically self-supporting and productive for society as a whole.

Clark doubts the neoclassical view that the common good results regularly from the myriad of individual actions coordinated by the price mechanism and conducted without paying attention to the public interest. As a matter of fact, not every business transaction creates social value: Inadequate values are created and negative effects of business are clearly recognizable. For this reason, business does not (or shall not) act in an “extra cosmos” ruled, for example, by the “laws of the market” separated from the “rest of life” and in that “bad behavior by business is bad for business” (Champlin and Knoedler 2004, p. 548).

A solution to these problems cannot draw on a dichotomic view of markets and state or a disjunctive vision concerning these entities (Wagner 2007). The market does not punish misbehavior or the creation of inadequate value; government regulation is no solution per se; and law and custom cannot substitute for ethics. Clark (1916) did not neglect the problems related to the public control of business affairs which can accrue from the limited knowledge and the self-interest of the ruler. In addition, government regulation has often not led to the effects desired-for: “Government regulation of business expanded significantly during the twentieth century. However (…) there is a considerable gap between passage of regularly law and effective enforcement” (Champlin and Knoedler 2004, p. 549). For Clark, the solution to this problem is not “more control” or “better control” by the state, but the establishment of self-control by the ruled and public control on the basis of adequate information. Clark can be read as an early critic of “public choices (…) framed in a dualistic fashion: free markets versus government regulation” (ibid, p. 550). According to Clark, there is a “third possible solution to corporate misconduct: public opinion” (ibid.).

Clark anticipated some of the ideas of the modern model of responsibility: the ideas of joint responsibility for social and economic affairs; of forward looking with regard to the creation of social value and the avoidance of harm and, with it, the omission of acts; and finally, the emphasis put on the relevance of objective knowledge. That Clark does not reject the idea of individual responsibility “because collective responsibility is becoming greater” (Clark 1916, 216), can be interpreted in a way that he overruled the classical model of responsibility only in part, he does not deny it any relevance in the modern times.

The next sub-section discusses the development of the concept of economic responsibility within a research framework constituted, among others, of economics and ethics.

8.4.3 Toward a Framework for the Explication of the Concept of Economic Responsibility

Clark's (1916) foundational article can be read as the starting point for the development of an economics of responsibility. Until today, there is no *economic theory* of economic responsibility or an economics of responsibility, respectively. The economics of responsibility is a source both for responsible economic action and the explication of the concept of economic responsibility.

Clark's seminal article in 1916 notwithstanding, the concept of economic responsibility is still under-conceptualized. Several reasons may be given for that: First, the concept of responsibility began to mature after the separation of economics and ethics; and its invention is rather related to political science than to economics. Second, in neoclassical economics, which turned into mainstream before World War II, the memory of the common action-theoretical foundation of economics and ethics in reason and rationality got lost or eroded, at the least (Sen 1987, pp. 2 ff.; Van Staveren and Peil 2009). Third, in ethics, the ethic of responsibility went into a crisis more or less at the same time the responsibility rhetoric in business ethics, inspired by the CSR discourses, exploded (Heidbrink 2003). Fourth, the CSR discourse is still influenced by Caroll's models of social responsibility and the reactions to Friedman's article on the social responsibility of business.

From Clark's work we can conclude that an understanding of the concept of economic responsibility has to be embedded in a broader framework. Economics and the ethic of responsibility are important constituents of such a framework. In line with Bayertz' (1995) models of responsibility which are considered as being based on description, analysis, and normative assessment, this framework entails descriptive-analytical and normative components. There is, however, no clear separation between the normative and the non-normative and assignment to a particular discipline. The economics identifies the subjects (actors) and objects of responsibility (activities, affairs, problems, etc.) and, furthermore, it can propose instances of responsibility (e.g., shareholders) and explicitly or implicitly advocate certain values (efficiency, effectiveness, justice).

Clark's rejection of the laissez-faire economics makes clear that not every economic approach has the potential to become or to be the source of an economics of responsibility. This necessitates a choice among more or less adequate approaches. One important criterion that could be brought to the fore in this regard is the connectivity of the economic approach with other approaches within the framework selected for some reason. For example, rationality theories and theories of value (and value creation) in economics as well as theories of value in ethics (axiology) influence the understanding of the concept of economic responsibility. Friedman formulated his ideas in the language of neoclassical theory that embodies some of Smith's ideas but rejects broader conceptions of rationality (Sen 2002). A theory of value and a concept of rationality is implied even in theories, which conceive of themselves as value-free. Reference to utility or profit maximization as behavioral assumptions and efficiency as standard or norm are an expression of a narrow interpretation of the rationality principle related to both $ER^{Friedman}$ and Caroll's CSR models. If a narrow interpretation of the rationality principle is excluded from the framework, the approaches drawing on it are excluded as well.

The dominance of neoclassics notwithstanding, economics is no monolithic strand of thought but splits into different strands and schools of thought. Thus, economic theories specify different types of problems and, based on these differences, distinct approaches to economic responsibility can arise. Consequently, the semantics of the concept of economic responsibility can vary in reaction to the implemented economic approach. Depending on the constituents of the framework, the meaning of "economic responsibility" can change because approaches may identify differing subjects, objects, and instances of responsibility (Friedman considers individuals as subjects of responsibility; profit maximizing as the main or only object of responsibility; and shareholders as instances of responsibility). Clark's (1916, p. 209) article is indicative of the potential changes in the semantics of the concept of responsibility. The article begins with a statement about the meaning of "economic responsibility" in the nineteenth century: "Economic responsibility meant self-reliance and self-dependence." His message is: we need to change this interpretation because of the changes in the economy, the inadequacy of laissez-faire economics, and the problems observable if one looks at the working business ethics. New knowledge incorporated by new theory or more adequate theory (institutional economics) modifies the meaning of "economic responsibility."

8.4.4 Clark's View of Some Ideas Embodied in Today's CSR Models

Caroll and Shabana (2010, p. 90) refer to McGuire's (1963) distinction between traditional and new responsibilities of the corporation. As Clark did in *The Changing Basis of Economic Responsibility*, these authors react to a change. According to them, the "new" responsibilities are the "essence of CSR: ethical and philanthropic responsibilities" (ibid.). Although the authors, perhaps against the backdrop of the recent economic and financial crisis, strike a milder tone with respect to the profit principle, they maintain the "notion of economic responsibility in terms of financial profit to stockholders" (ibid., p. 91). If compared with these views, drawing on what the authors labelled "stakeholder expectations" toward the corporation, Clark's concept of economic responsibility focuses on responsible economic action in individual and public interest. In this vein, the creation of social value draws on economic knowledge.

Caroll's CSR models separate social and economic responsibility and make "ethical responsibility" a sub-dimension of social responsibility. Although Caroll points out that all responsibilities have to be fulfilled, these responsibilities are separated and prioritized. From Clark's point of view, there is no such separation. The social environment is an object of responsibility and the individual or business is responsible for it toward the collective, the group, the community, etc. Ethical knowledge is part of the knowledge that actors need to have available in the decision-making process. In this regard, Clark seems to have been inspired by Kant: "John Smith is still a law onto himself, whatever the statistics may tell us about the thousand" (Clark 1916, p. 217).

Charity is not equal to but may be related to the philanthropic dimension of social responsibility. Clark rejected charity in the form of a Band-Aid put on the negative action consequences that could be avoided as well: "To many the word 'charity' is a red rag to a bull, and this will never be otherwise as long as much that passes for charity is merely repairing the damage or salvaging the wreckage for which industry is the chief responsible cause; the same industry which distributes the dividends out of which charity funds so freely come" (Clark 1916, p. 229). According to Clark, "justice, not charity" (ibid.) is the right way. Rutherford (2000, p. 286) points to "Hamilton's and Clark's references to the relevance of institutional economics for the solution of social problems." This makes clear that "institutionalism was always linked to a progressive social reform agenda" (ibid.). Clark was not opposing to "help the unfortunate" (compare Clark 1916, p. 229); however, help should not substitute responsible economic action. In contrast, voluntariness undermines responsibility.

8.5 Conclusions

Milan Quentel, who was awarded the Mark Blaug Student Essay Prize for *The History of Economic Thought and its Role for Rethinking Economics*,[28] points out: "Economic ideas do often depend on their historical context and are, thus, contingent" (Quentel 2015, p. 4). With this in mind, one could argue, if an idea proves to be "true" or relevant beyond a context, then it makes its originator a "classic." Clark, a leading representative of the institutional economics in the U.S. and a member of the first Chicago School in economics, is a classic in the economics of responsibility.

It was Clark's objective to sketch the domain and tasks of an economics of responsibility in *The Changing Basis of Economic Responsibility*. Clark's economics of responsibility, however, remained a rough sketch. In his long and successful

[28] The Foundation for European Economic Development (FEED) awards this prize. http://www.feed-charity.org/essay-prize.htm (accessed 30 March 2016).

career, Clark worked on many parts of the big picture that is necessarily incomplete. From the contemporary perspective, Clark's legacy is seen in the foundation of social economics (Lutz 2009) or behavioral economics (Stewart 2005) while the expression "economics of responsibility" seems to have quit the scene in its entirety. However, an interest in the study of problems put on the table by Clark can be observed. For example, in 1981, Rohrlich bemoaned that there is still no "coherent theory of social value" (Rohrlich 1981, p. 347). From the perspective of today, we observe increasing interest in social value and its determination or measurement (Cole 2015; Mang and Reed 2015). Interestingly, the provision of solutions to social problems has become an issue in the recent business economics, social entrepreneurship, and CSR literature (e.g., Caroll and Shabana 2010; Dees 2012; Porter and Kramer 2006, 2011, 2014).

Against the backdrop of Clark's analysis, it can be concluded that business ethics and CSR studies backed the wrong horse. It is time to pay attention to the neglect of economic responsibility or its inadequate understanding in parts of the CSR literature that suffers from its affinity to neoclassical economics and the theory of the firm. A re-conceptualization of "economic responsibility" should take into consideration the plurality of knowledge sources in economics. It is obvious that Clark's approach needs to be critically reflected on and, in dependence of the results, further development. One "adequacy condition" for the framework discussed in the previous subsection is its openness for the inclusion of different economic theories. It is, thus, possible that there may be one day more than one economics of responsibility. A second adequacy condition is its connectivity to other empirical, philosophical, or ethical theories. A third adequacy condition is the contribution of the concept to the understanding and solution of problems arising at the intersection of economics, business ethics, CSR, or other fields of interest.

One hundred years after the publication of *The Changing Basis of Economic Responsibility*, it is obvious that it is worth the effort to engage in the analysis and discussion of this article. The rejection of laissez faire and the invisible hand means that there is no mechanism linking economic and social value that is working behind the actors' back. If the actors want to create social value, they need to take action toward this objective. This is the lesson learned from Clark (1916). Clark's vision was that economics is able to provide the actors with the knowledge they need for pursuing this task and that the actors make use of this knowledge. To put effort into the explication of an economic concept of economic responsibility is an important step in this direction.

References

Abend, Gabriel. 2013. The origin of business ethics in American universities, 1902–1936. *Business Ethics Quarterly* 23(2): 171–205.

Akerlof, George A. 1970. The market for "lemons": Quality uncertainty and the market mechanism. *Quarterly Journal of Economics* 84(3): 488–500.

Alchian, Armen A. 1950. Uncertainty, evolution and economic theory. *Journal of Political Economy* 58(3): 211–221.
Baron, David P. 2001. Private politics, corporate social responsibility and integrated strategy. *Journal of Economics and Management Strategy* 10(1): 7–45.
Bayertz, Kurt. 1995. Eine kurze Geschichte der Herkunft der Verantwortung. In *Verantwortung: Prinzip oder Problem?* ed. K. Bayertz, 3–71. Darmstadt: Wissenschaftliche Buchgesellschaft.
Beisbart, Claus. 2012. Varieties of goodness at work: The relationship between business and morality. *Inquiry* 55(4): 405–430.
Blowfield, Michael, and Alan Murray. 2011. *Corporate responsibility*. Oxford/New York: Oxford University Press.
Bowie, N.E., and P.H. Werhane. 2005. *Management ethics*. Malden: Blackwell.
Bowles, S. 2004. *Microeconomics: Behavior, institutions, and evolution*. New York/Princeton/Oxford: Princeton University Press.
Caroll, Archie B. 1979. A three-dimensional conceptual model of corporate performance. *Academy of Management Review* 4(4): 497–505.
———. 1991. The pyramid of corporate social responsibility: Toward the moral management of organizational stakeholders. *Business Horizons* 34(4): 39–48.
———. 1998. The four faces of corporate citizenship. *Business and Society Review* 100(1): 1–7.
———. 1999. Corporate social responsibility: Evolution of a definitional construct. *Business & Society* 38(3): 268–295.
Caroll, Archie B., and Kareem N. Shabana. 2010. The business case for corporate social responsibility: A review of concepts, research and practice. *International Journal of Management Reviews* 12(1): 85–105.
Champlin, Dell P., and Janet T. Knoedler. 2004. J.M. Clark and the economics of responsibility. *Journal of Economic Issues* XXXVII(2): 545–552.
Clark, John M. 1915. The concept of value. *The Quarterly Journal of Economics* 29: 663–673.
———. 1916. The changing basis of economic responsibility. *The Journal of Political Economy* 24(3): 209–229.
———. 1936. Toward a concept of social value. In *Preface to social economics: Essays in economic theory and social problems*, 44–65. New York: Farrar & Rinehart.
———. 1948. *Alternative to serfdom*. New York: Knopf.
Cole, Raymond J. 2015. Net-zero and net-positive design: A question of value. *Building Research & Information* 43(1): 1–6.
Cosans, Christopher. 2009. Does Milton Friedman support a vigorous business ethics? *Journal of Business Ethics* 87(3): 391–399.
Crane, Andrew, and Dirk Matten. 2007. *Business ethics*. 2nd ed. Oxford University Press: Oxford.
Dees, J. Gregory. 2012. A tale of two cultures: Charity, problem solving, and the future of social entrepreneurship. *Journal of Business Ethics* 111: 321–334.
EU Commission. 2011. *Communication from the commission to the European Parliament, the Council, the European Economic and Social Committee and the Committee of the Regions*. A renewed EU strategy 2011–14 for Corporate Social Responsibility. http://eur-lex.europa.eu/legal-content/EN/TXT/?uri=CELEX:52011DC0681. Accessed 22 Feb 2016.
Frankena, William K. 1983. Concepts of rational action in the history of ethics. *Social Theory and Practice* 9(2/3): 165–197.
Friedman, Milton. 1953. *Essays in positive economics*. Chicago/London: The University of Chicago Press.
———. 1962. *The capitalism of freedom*. Chicago: The University of Chicago Press.
———. 1970. The social responsibility of business is to increase its profits. *New York Times Magazine*, September 13.
Göschel, Hans. 2008. *Die Handelshochschule in Leipzig*. Leipzig: Handelshochschule Leipzig.
Haase, Michaela. 2015a. Marketing theory and the concept of responsibility: A story of three interpre-tations. In *Handbook on ethics and marketing*, ed. Alexander Nill, 125–149. Cheltenham/Northhampton: Edward Elgar.

———. 2015b. Values-based value creation and responsibility: On the relationship of "doing business" and "doing CSR". *Journal for Business Economics and Ethics (zfwu)* 16(3): 339–368.

Hargreaves Heap, Shaun P. 2009. Rationality. In *Handbook of economics and ethics*, ed. Jan Peil and Irene van Staveren, 416–425. Cheltenham/Northampton: Edward Elgar.

Hayek, Friedrich A. 1978. *New studies in philosophy, politics, economics and the history of ideas*. London/Henley: Routledge & Kegan Paul.

Heath, Joseph. 2015. Methodological individualism. In *The stanford encyclopedia of philosophy* (Spring 2015 Edition). http://plato.stanford.edu/archives/spr2015/entries/methodological-individualism/. Accessed 13 Apr 2016.

Heidbrink, Ludger. 2003. *Kritik der Verantwortung: Zu den Grenzen verantwortlichen Handelns in komplexen Kontexten*. Weilerswist: Velbrück.

Hillinger, Claude. 2012. *Adam Smith's argument for the existence of an 'invisible hand.'* SSRN. http://ssrn.com/abstract=2168777. Accessed 6 Apr 2016.

Jackall, Robert. 2010. *The world of corporate managers – Twentieth anniversary edition*. New York: Oxford University Press.

Jones, Manley H. 1960. Evolving a business philosophy. *Journal of the Academy of Management* 3(2): 93–98.

Kersting, Wolfgang. 2003. Verantwortliche Verantwortung. Prologue to *Kritik der Verantwortung: Zu den Grenzen verantwortlichen Handelns in komplexen Kontexten*, ed. Ludger Heidbrink, 9–16. Weilerswist: Velbrück.

Knight, Frank H. 1922. Round table conference on the relation between economics and ethics. *American Economic Review* 12(3): 192–201.

Krause-Junk, Gerold. 2010. Moral und Gesetz – einige Anmerkungen zu Volker Arnold. *Perspektiven der Wirtschaftspolitik* 11(1): 99–102.

Lindgreen, Adam, and Valérie Swaen. 2010. Corporate social responsibility. *International Journal of Management Studies* 12(1): 1–7.

Lodge, George C. 1982. The connection between ethics and ideology. *Journal of Business Ethics* 1(2): 85–98.

Lutz, Mark A. 2009. Social economics. In *Handbook of economics and ethics*, ed. Jan Peil and Irene van Staveren, 516–522. Cheltenham/Northampton: Edward Elgar.

Mang, Pamela, and Bill Reed. 2015. The nature of positive. *Building Research & Information* 43(1): 7–10.

Markham, Jesse W. 1968. Clark, John Maurice. In *International encyclopedia of the social sciences*, ed. D. Stills, 508–511. New York: Macmillan and the Free Press.

McGuire, Joseph W. 1963. *Business and society*. New York: McGraw-Hill.

McMahon, Thomas F. 2003. A brief history of American business ethics. In *A companion to business ethics*, ed. Robert E. Frederick, 342–352. Cambridge, MA: Blackwell.

Morroni, Mario. 2006. *Knowledge, scale and transactions in the theory of the firm*. Cambridge et al.: Cambridge University Press.

Nida-Rümelin, Julian. 2005. *Über menschliche Freiheit*. Stuttgart: Reclam.

Porter, Michael E., and Mark R. Kramer. 2006. Strategy and Society: The link between competitive advantage and corporate social responsibility. *Harvard Business Review* 84(12): 78–92.

———. 2011. Creating shared value. *Harvard Business Review* 89(1–2): 62–77.

———. 2014. A response to Andrew Crane et al.'s paper by Michael E. Porter and Mark R. Kramer. *California Management Review* 56(2): 149–151.

Quentel, Milan. 2015. *The history of economic thought and its role for rethinking economics*. http://www.feed-charity.org/essay-prize.htm. Accessed 30 Mar 2016.

Quine, Willard V.O. 1969. *Grundzüge der Logik*. Frankfurt am Main: Suhrkamp.

Rohrlich, George F. 1981. John Maurice Clark's unmet challenge. *Review of Social Economy* 39(3): 343–348.

Roth, Timothy. 1999. *Ethics, economics, and freedom: The failure of consequentialist social welfare theory*. Aldershot et al.: Ashgate.

Rutherford, Malcolm. 2000. Understanding institutional economics: 1918–1929. *Journal of the History of Economic Thought* 22(3): 277–308.
———. 2015. *Chicago and institutional economics.* Becker Friedman Institute for Research in Economics Working Paper. SSRN. http://ssrn.com/abstract=2714082. Accessed 28 Jan 2016.
Salzmann, Astrid J. 2013. The integration of sustainability into the theory and practice of finance: An overview of the state of the art and outline of future developments. *Journal of Business Economics* 83(6): 555–576.
Schatzki, Theodore R. 2007. Introduction. *Human Affairs* 17(2): 97–100.
Scherer, Andreas G., and Guido Palazzo. 2007. Toward a political conception of corporate social responsibility: Business and society seen from a Habermasian perspective. *Academy of Management Review* 32(4): 1096–1120.
Schwartz, M.S., and D. Saiia. 2012. Should firms go "beyond profits"? Milton Friedman versus broad CSR. *Business and Society Review* 111(7): 1–31.
Sen, Amartya. 1987. *On ethics and economics*. Cambridge, MA: Blackwell.
———. 2002. *Rationality and freedom*. Cambridge, MA: Blackwell.
Sharfman, I.L. 1947. "Alternative to serfdom". Five lectures delivered in March by Professor John Maurice Clark of Columbia University. *Michigan Alumnus Quarterly Review* LIII(21): 288–292.
Smith, Adam. 2000, 1759. The theory of moral sentiments. Amherst: Prometheus.
———. 2003, 1776. Introduction. In *The wealth of nations*, ed. Alan B. Krueger. New York: Bantam Classic.
Stewart, Sharla A. 2005. Can behavioral economics save us from ourselves? *University of Chicago Magazine* 97(3). http://magazine.uchicago.edu/0502/features/economics.shtml. Accessed 10 Aug 2015.
Stigler, George J. 1961. The economics of information. *Journal of Political Economy* 69(3): 213–225.
Sun, William. 2013. Embedded CSR. In *Encyclopedia of corporate social responsibility*, ed. Samuel O. Idowu, Nicholas Capaldi, Zu Liangrong, and Ananda Das Gupta, 926–931. Berlin/Heidelberg: Springer.
Sundaram, Anant K., and Andrew C. Inkpen. 2004. The corporate objective revisited. *Organization Science* 15(3): 350–363.
Suppes, Patrick. 1957. *Introduction to logic*. New York et al.: Van Nostrand Reinhold Company.
Van Staveren, Irene, and Jan Peil. 2009b. Introduction. In *Handbook of economics and ethics*, ed. Jan Peil and Irene van Staveren, xvi–xviii. Cheltenham/Northampton: Edward Elgar.
Visser, Wayne. 2006. Revisiting Caroll's CSR pyramid: An African perspective. In *Corporate citizenship in a development perspective: New partnership perspectives*, ed. Mahad Huniche and Esben R. Pedersen, 29–56. Copenhagen: Copenhagen Business School Press.
Wagner, Richard E. 2007. *Fiscal sociology and the theory of public finance*. Cheltenham: Edward Elgar.
Witzum, Amos. 2008. Smith's theory of actions and the moral significance of unintended consequences. *Journal of the History of Economic Thought* 15(3): 401–432.
Young, Iris M. 2004. Responsibility and global labor justice. *The Journal of Political Philosophy* 12(4): 365–388.
———. 2006. Responsibility and global justice: A social connection model. *Social Philosophy & Policy*: 202–230.
———. 2011. *Responsibility for justice*. Oxford: Oxford University Press.
Zaman, Asad. 2012. *Death of a metaphor: The invisible hand.* http://ssrn.com/abstract=2094930. Accessed 25 July 2012.

Appendix

M. Haase (ed.), *Economic Responsibility*, Ethical Economy 53,
DOI 10.1007/978-3-319-52099-5

THE JOURNAL

OF

POLITICAL ECONOMY

VOLUME 24 *March 1916* NUMBER 3

THE CHANGING BASIS OF ECONOMIC RESPONSIBILITY

I. FORECAST OF THE ARGUMENT

Twenty years ago an economist writing under this title would have been expected to deal chiefly or solely with the responsibility of the individual for his own economic destiny: his responsibility for paying his debts and keeping out of the poor-house. Economic responsibility meant self-reliance and self-dependence.[1] Today any treatment of the subject from such a limited standpoint would be an anachronism. The ideas of obligation which embody the actual relations of man to man in the twentieth century, and answer the needs of the twentieth century, are radically different from the ideas which dominated the nineteenth.

Some have failed to realize what the change means and have resisted it uncomprehendingly. Interdependence means no more to them than it did in the days when free exchange seemed adequate to organize the world, and enlist the far islands of the seas

[1] Cf. Hadley, *Economics*, chap. ii. Cf. also Henry C. Adams, *The Relation of the State to Industrial Action*, pp. 80–85. Here the dominant note is reliance on free competition wherever free competition naturally prevails. Action by the state is urged, (1) to enable the majority in a trade to decide what the plane of their competition shall be, and (2) in the case of natural monopolies. The author announces the theory of responsibility as the keynote of this policy, using the term "responsibility" none too definitely, but in a strongly individualistic sense.

to furnish London breakfast tables. That was one kind of interdependence, marvelously far-reaching and marvelously effective—but not the interdependence that is putting its peculiar stamp on the life of the present generation.

Some have gone to the other extreme and have lost their old sense of personal accountability in an easy philosophy that lays the burdens on the impersonal state, and the blame on heredity and environment. But most of us have not gone so far as that. We do not want a state that shall prohibit all our vices, syndicate all our virtues, and render old-fashioned self-reliance obsolete, if indeed that were remotely possible! Instead, many men are honestly seeking to know what their obligations are in this new era, that they may meet them on their own initiative. More knowledge is wanted, that men may guide themselves. The modern prayer is not so much for strength as for wisdom.

In the economic world this issue is presented more clearly perhaps than anywhere else. We have inherited an economics of irresponsibility. We are in an economy of control with which our intellectual inheritance fits but awkwardly. To make control really tolerable we need something more; something which is still in its infancy. We need an economics of responsibility, developed and embodied in our working business ethics.

II. THE SWING OF THE PENDULUM

We have gone through a revolution of late in many realms of thought and policy. We have swung far away from narrow individualism toward a sense of solidarity and social-mindedness. In religion the dominant ideal is no longer a narrowly personal salvation granted from above as a reward of personal faith, but rather an attitude of love and service to one's fellows which are in themselves salvation. The old idea of free will is giving way to determinism, individualism to public control, personal responsibility to social responsibility.

This changed attitude shows itself in economic matters in a hundred ways. The common law treated industrial accidents as matters of personal responsibility and attempted to fix a personal blame. The results were intolerable. Something was wrong.

Contrast the attitude of a system of compulsory compensation which blames nobody, and seems almost to take away all responsibility, distributing it between the state and the employer and treating the employer impersonally, as the representative of the industry. This policy expresses a new idea of responsibility.

Not long ago we were almost morbidly afraid to do anything to relieve distress, for fear of undermining people's independence and perpetuating the disease we aimed to cure. If these unfortunates could not quickly be put in a condition of doing for themselves there was danger in doing too much for them. Anything looking toward permanent assistance was a confession of failure in the present and an omen of evil to come. Meanwhile poverty continued to breed poverty. Now free meals for school children are becoming more and more common, the minimum wage in a mild form is being seriously tried out, and we seem to be on the threshold of similar experiments with old-age pensions, mothers' pensions, and insurance against unemployment.

The old-time lumber-gang boss or division superintendent promoted men or discharged them at will. He was responsible to his superior officer for getting results, and to his conscience, if he had one, for the rights and wrongs of his actions. Often he adopted a policy of rewards or punishments that were sudden, unexpected, and intentionally arbitrary, his object being to keep the men in proper awe of what might happen, and to keep them on their good behavior in little things: things so small in themselves that only the momentary impulse of an arbitrary autocrat would take any notice of them. It was every man's own lookout that the blow did not fall on his head. This system could work tolerably well in a young country, so rich in opportunity that most men could "fall on their feet" whatever happened and whenever and wherever they might be cast adrift.

But today the consequences are too serious to be treated thus cavalierly. Compare the situation of the modern official dealing with a strong union. He cannot discharge men without the possibility of having to face a committee of their fellow-laborers who will make him give an account of his actions. A group has assumed responsibility for its members and a new responsibility of an individual toward the group is being enforced. How shall the group, the union, have brought home to it its own responsibility to the larger group of which it is a part? That is the next chapter of the story, and the end is not yet written.

Unemployment used to be considered largely a matter of personal fitness and willingness to work; now it is spoken of as a disease of our economic system. Criminals and prostitutes used to be regarded quite simply as wicked people. Now they are quite as often looked upon as victims of the social order. In fact this explanation is so much in the air that it has become a habit, an unthinking reaction to anything and everything that goes wrong, and anyone and everyone who goes to pieces. There is little room to question that our habit of overworking this conveniently impersonal scapegoat is closely connected with what Miss Repplier has called our national "loss of nerve." It is all a most disquieting phase of the spread of deterministic ideas among people ready to absorb them one-sidedly.

But it is all part of a movement we cannot escape, with its successes and its failures, its inspiration for the man big enough to catch it, and its enervating effect on those without the vision. It is the product of new situations and new knowledge, and we must use the knowledge to make the best of the situations. We must take what it gives and fight to keep whatever of good it threatens to take away.

It is the product of many things, from psychology to life insurance and from bacteriology to large-scale manufacturing. The bottom facts are, first, that we are becoming interdependent in new and unforeseen ways, and, second, that we are finding out more about the remote causes of things, which we used to take for granted.

Psychology shows us our minds as products of inherited tendencies and the environment to which they react. This makes the living conditions of the slum responsible for the gangster's criminal tendencies and many lesser personal faults and failures. Mortality tables show us occupational environments as killing so many men out of a thousand every year, and statisticians correlate hot weather and suicide, and attempt to correlate crime and heredity.

Indeed, statistics, together with the mass-phenomena they measure, have been the instrument of a surprising deal of altered thinking. When we are looking at John Smith alone, we cannot tell just what he will do in a given situation or what a change in environment will do to him. He is still an independent personality and a law unto himself. But we can tell in advance what such a change will do to a thousand John Smiths. It may kill so and so many, or save so and so many alive, and we become accustomed to the idea that enfeebling environments have made so and so many criminals, and so and so many good-for-nothing idlers, who would otherwise have remained on the safe side of respectability and self-support. The environment has become responsible for John Smith.

But at the same time John Smith has become responsible for the environment. A knowledge of bacteria makes criminal neglect out of what were once matters of purely private concern, and the outcome is to make medicine more and more a matter of maintaining a healthful environment and hence a matter of public prevention rather than of private cure.

Man is ever in the presence of powers too strong for him to cope with, and never knows when they may reach out and take his life. Where the environment that threatens and the powers that kill are the environment and the powers of nature, he worships and watches his priming, learns to sleep lightly, to read footprints, and to know the signs of water. Where the environment is man-made and the powers are those of machinery, he ceases to worship, and he may begin instead to resent, to protest, and ultimately to revolt. Large-scale industry puts the laborer in surroundings, no more dangerous perhaps than the forest or desert which faced the old-time frontiersman, but surroundings which, dangers and all, are the work of human hands and human brains. All these things have given us new ideas of causes and effects, and these have given us new ideas of responsibility. We are finding out that many things are not to be taken for granted as of old, because they are things over which someone can exercise control, and that means they are things for which someone is responsible.

III. CAUSATION

If we try to trace the causes of anything fully, we are overwhelmed. Everything is a joint result of so many contributing causes that the whole universe may seem to have conspired to make one commuter miss the four-thirty train. So that when we talk about the "reason why," we never mean more than a few out of an infinite series of reasons. How do we go to work to pick out those few?

We are likely to look first at the cause that is closest to the event and gives the most obvious push or offers the most obvious resistance. The teacup broke because the maid dropped it. The workman lost his fingers through a moment of carelessness at his machine plane. The panic was precipitated because of such and such failures.

Of course we shall never get anywhere on any such superficial principle. And yet we cannot go wandering through the mazes of infinity looking for the ultimate and the fundamental. We have a purpose: to shape the world—or our little bit of it—"nearer to the heart's desire." We want to know two things: "Which are the causes that are really important in deciding the exact nature of the outcome?" These are the significant causes. Also, "Which are the causes over which we have some control and before which we do not stand entirely helpless?" These we may call the responsible causes.

The failure of such and such a bank may have precipitated the panic, but the panic would have arrived and run much the same course in any case. Sun-spots may cause crises, or they may be symptoms of something else which causes climatic changes and these may be a cause of crises, and statistics may support this with its most convincing proofs. But these climatic cycles are not the only things that disturb the smooth running of the machinery of production and consumption, and the essential thing seems to be that we have an industrial system in which misfits work cumulatively, regardless of the source from which the original disturbance arises. In a system of private production with enormous use of capital, involving the staking of industrial fortunes on a distant future, any irregularity is intensified in some quarters. An unexpected weakening of demand is felt more keenly by wholesalers than by retailers, since the retailer not only has sold fewer goods, but is allowing his stock to diminish. For the time being he buys even less than he sells. For the same reason the manufacturer feels the slackening of demand more keenly still, and the machine industries and construction industries most of all, since new construction is suspended and even maintenance is likely to be postponed. Those engaged in these industries can buy less, and this may lead to a slackening of demand for many products. Even in active times contractors may be squeezed by a rise in the price of their materials, and their profits turned to losses. Their failures, in turn, embarrass their creditors and may spread a feeling of panic to the whole financial community. The part played by banks in making both expansion and contraction cumulative is too well known to call for comment here.[1]

Compared to these qualities of our industrial organization the exact nature of the one most regular disturbance of production would seem to have little to say in determining the exact nature of the outcome. We should in all probability have panics without sun-spots or climatic cycles, but with a different industrial system sun-spots could come and go without producing anything like the present type of panic. Sun-spots may help us to predict the time of stress, but apart from this they are probably not the most significant cause for our purposes. Moreover, we cannot do anything about sun-spots, while we can change our credit system. Sun-spots are therefore not a responsible cause of panics.

One of the greatest things that the progress of science and industry has done for us is to give us responsible causes of a social and environmental sort. We used to think we could change men more easily than their environment, and we preached thrift, industry, and all the economic virtues, and let the rest stand as "natural laws," unchangeable. Now we are finding that to change the individual we must change his environment, and that preaching is not usually a big enough environmental change to get the desired results. We are coming to take a certain amount of human carelessness for granted and demanding safeguarded machinery and

[1] For a full treatment of these and other causes contributing to crises, the reader is referred to W. C. Mitchell's *Business Cycles*.

shortened hours with a view to securing an environment in which the natural weakness will be guarded against and the limited endurance not overtaxed.

When a man is discharged because he is not worth a living wage and the employer seeks another in his place his personal shortcomings are certainly the cause of his trouble, whatever we may think about the ultimate causes of his inefficiency. But when a railroad or an industrial corporation turns off thousands of men at a time because a cut of a certain per cent is deemed necessary or advisable, how does the case stand? It is still the least competent who go and their incompetence is the cause of their being the ones selected. But it is not absolute incompetence in this case, but relative incompetence: merely the fact that they are at the bottom of the list.

If some are absolutely incompetent, that is an evil to be remedied. But something tells us that no amount of personal effort and no amount of education or hygiene can hope to prevent 10 per cent of the men from being less efficient than the other 90 per cent. In such a case the incompetence of the men may well cease to be the responsible cause in our minds, and instead the industrial situation, under which an industry wants now 10 per cent more men and now 10 per cent less, may come to stand as the thing we try to change, the thing we hold responsible for the evil of unemployment.

Not that personal efficiency does not make a difference, but opinion is unfortunately divided between those who think that the laborer ought to try to solve the problem by improving his efficiency and those who think that this would only make matters worse and that if the men increase their capacity 10 per cent there will be fewer men needed. In this disagreement the economist takes the side of those who emphasize individual self-dependence and would hold the laborers to the duty of making the utmost of whatever capacities they have and whatever situation they may find available.

In this case as in all other cases anyone who thinks that individual responsibility is becoming less because collective responsibility is becoming greater is making a mistake somewhat like that of the dog in the fable, who dropped his piece of meat to catch the other which he saw reflected in the water. For what is collective responsibility but personal responsibilities reflected in the social mirror? We need all the sense of responsibility we can arouse, of all kinds, organized and directed into the most intelligent and efficient channels, to make even moderately satisfactory headway with the increasingly complex problems that are piling up ahead of us.

The scope of personal responsibility is broader than ever before, not narrower. It is a false notion of the meaning of determinism which interprets it in such a way as to undermine the responsibility of the individual for his own choices. John Smith is still a law unto himself, whatever the statistics may tell us about the thousand. We cannot predict him, for the determining causes of his destiny lie partly in his own personality. The power over his environment of a man who does not know when he is beaten is the last thing we can afford to belittle or ignore. It is only too obvious what a difference it makes whether men who are free to act as they will, choose to act with courage, self-reliance, and generosity or not. The only way the environment can overcome man completely is by persuading him that it can do so.

And laying responsibility on the environment cannot take it off the shoulders of persons so long as the environment of each of us consists chiefly of the rest of us. The responsibility is harder to bring home to the subject, and the duties it imposes are harder to fulfil effectively, for "what is everybody's business is nobody's business." But that simply means that our first obligation is to organize machinery by which these most difficult of obligations can be first effectively brought home and, second, effectively performed. This means, again, that we are facing the difficult task of keeping the sense of obligation alive while delegating to specialists the bulk of the active work involved in meeting our obligations and fulfilling them.

But it is not alone by making us jointly responsible for the general social environment that our personal responsibilities are being broadened. We are coming to see that our everyday business dealings have more far-reaching effects than we have ever realized, and that the system of free contract is by itself quite inadequate to bring home the responsibility for these effects. We have begun to realize the many inappropriable values that are created and the many unpaid damages that are inflicted in the course of business exchanges. New possibilities at once of parasitism and of service are here revealed, and here at least is a field in which responsibility is being concentrated instead of diffused. Instead of unearned increments which come from a shadowy social environment, and wastes for which an impersonal "system" is responsible, we are making some beginnings at tracing these things home to the policies of particular enterprises and the doings of particular individuals. Unemployment is being traced partly to seasonal trades, as one of their unpaid costs of production.

IV. RESPONSIBILITY AND THE LIBERAL ECONOMICS

By comparison with the scope of responsibility as it has been conceived and presented here the laissez-faire economics may well be characterized as the economics of irresponsibility, and the business system of free contract is also a system of irresponsibility when judged by the same standard. Of static theory we must simply say that while it does not deny social responsibilities it does to a large extent ignore them. Since its abstract premises leave out most of the facts on which they are based, they are left to be taken account of in other departments of the science. Liberal economics or business economics in general accomplishes much the same result by separating business sharply off from the rest of life.

"Business is business," and while men are unselfish and recognize many kinds of obligations to their fellows beyond the letter of the law, their unselfishness is not carried into business relations, and the extra-legal responsibilities are not business responsibilities, except such as have become so firmly established in business morals as to have the binding force of laws. In business, men do not render services without being paid such price as they are willing to accept nor undergo sacrifices except for a consideration which they deem sufficient. From this it may be concluded that both parties are better off for every business transaction, at least in their own minds at the moment, than if the transaction had not been made.

With this dangerously inadequate idea of bargaining and contract, and with the equally inadequate idea of business competition as a sort of Darwinian struggle for survival, constantly tending toward the natural selection, of the fit, it is small wonder if the business man is willingly convinced that in the struggle for financial success he is fulfilling the whole duty that society can reasonably impose upon his business hours. In other words, theory and practice combine to further an irresponsible attitude among leaders of industry and laborers alike.

Meanwhile the demand for control has grown with amazing speed, and in every direction experiments are being tried. This should properly be regarded as a recognition of special kinds of responsibility which the business economics leaves out of account and which the machinery of free contract furnishes no way of bringing home to the proper persons. But instead, this regulation is looked on by too many as a phase of the old irresponsible struggle, merely translated from the field of business into the field of politics. It is under suspicion as being mere irresponsible class legislation, and unfortunately the suspicion has some justification.

Hence employers often feel either contemptuous or deeply injured when laws begin to interfere with customary business practices, and when investigating committees ask prying questions which imply a demand for a righteousness that shall exceed the righteousness of the scribes and Pharisees. Business men with this point of view oppose the growth of public control with a resistance that is now adroit and now stubborn but nearly always powerful. The economics of control is at war with the economics of irresponsibility.

Beyond all the special issues of this struggle there stand out certain general questions of attitude and interpretation that are most real and most vital. Are these new policies of regulation to be regarded as exceptions to our general economic philosophy or are they an integral part of it? Are they special and disconnected cases or are they phases of one consistent program whose central features can be formulated? And above all, are they mere matters of political struggle and political compromise; matters to be temporarily settled by a show of hands, or of teeth, and perpetually unsettled again with every real or fancied change in the strength of the contending parties? Or are they matters of economic law, with a solid foundation in real relationships of cause and effect which no party in the many-sided struggle can permanently ignore? Do our economic regulations mean merely the creation and attempted enforcement of arbitrary requirements or do they mean the recognition and bringing home of existing and very real responsibilities? And, if the answer to this last be in the affirmative, is there a twilight zone of obligations not yet enforced by law or custom but no less real for that? If there is such a twilight zone, how shall we act toward it?

It is good and necessary that new proposals should be first treated as exceptions to economic theory, for they need to be settled on their merits, but it is not good that they should remain permanently unassimilated. It is good and necessary that they be urged by men intensely devoted, each to his special cause, but it is also good ultimately to absorb them all into a broadly constructive plan. It is good when political force breaks down stereotyped codes and precepts masquerading as "natural rights" and natural law, but it is not good to imagine that there are no laws to which men and groups of men are responsible other than the law of getting all they can.

The task of economic theory in these matters is clear, and the importance of this task is often too little realized. There are principles underlying our multifarious social policies—principles as general and far-reaching as those underlying the "theory of value and distribution." In fact, they are all phases of one process, social housekeeping. And until "free exchange" and "social reform" are both interpreted as governed by one consistent set of laws, they are not interpreted correctly. The crucial task of such a theory is to unify, to reveal those causes and consequences of things men do which transcend the scope of free exchange. These create responsibilities which, in turn, the policy of regulation is attempting to enforce. In a broad sense the great task of the theorist of our tremendously dynamic age is to substitute an economics of responsibility for the economics of irresponsible conflict. That is his part in furthering the growth of willing co-operation in the endless process of adapting our organization and industrial ways to the unforeseen needs and relationships which machinery and science are continually thrusting upon us.

V. DIFFICULTIES OF PUBLIC CONTROL

Any system of regulation of private industry needs a well-developed basis of agreement as to what in general the mutual obligations of the parties are, or else the system will not work. For without it confidence is lacking and as a result co-operation is crippled. It is expensive when the people distrust the leaders of industry and are in turn distrusted by them: it is only less expensive than trust misplaced. It is hard enough for those familiar with trade practices to adopt rules for their own observance; it becomes well-nigh impossible when the rules are passed by outsiders, themselves unfamiliar with the details of the situation, who are forced to interpret all advice from the interested parties in the light of those parties' interests and to suspect it of subtly aiming to thwart the ends of public policy. This is not a complete picture of our present situation, fortunately, but it is a true picture of one most exasperating phase of it, showing itself particularly, perhaps, in legislation on banking and on unfair competition.

Another weakness of regulation of private enterprise is, that while it consists largely in forbidding things, it often describes these things in terms of form, not of spirit and essential effect. The result is the widespread feeling that useful ways of doing business are being outlawed because they are capable of abuse.

Attempts to limit speculation and capitalization, for example, are so regarded, with how much or how little justice we need not stop here to inquire. All of this leads to a hostile public opinion on the part of a large and solid class, and against such a solid and sincere opinion laws cannot be profitably enforced. Indeed, regulation would not now be able to show its present record of success unless this hostile opinion had been to some extent convinced and won over to a belief in the need and the justice of control.

This attitude is in itself a clear recognition that the business economics is inadequate and needs revising, at least at certain points. But many fail to see what a far-reaching change of attitude is involved in this simple admission, though they may feel uneasily that there is a camel's head inside the tent. The conservative expects things to continue on the principle that "business is business," meaning that it is a self-regarding business, and that his only business obligations are those enforced by law and settled custom. They have been added to somewhat, but that is all, and wherever the law has not yet spoken there is no reason for taking any but the old irresponsible attitude. Further responsibilities there may be of a social or charitable sort, but not further business responsibilities.

This view might be more convincing if only every business transaction were a wholly isolated fact, concerning only one buyer and one seller at one moment of time, and having no possible effect on other people or on other transactions. Only if that were true, most of our existing body of business regulations would be wholly unnecessary, so that the question at issue would not be likely to arise at all. But to argue about modern industrial dealings as if they could be so insulated in their effects from all other relationships would seem to imply a certain lack of insight.

After what has been said already, it is only necessary to point out that, thanks largely to modern machinery and the complex organization that goes with it, every act has numberless effects on others, furthering or thwarting their purposes in ways often unknown to them personally, but known to someone nevertheless. These by-products may often be far more important in the aggregate than the one service or the one sacrifice over which a voluntary bargain happens to be struck. And thanks to science, the specialist can find out about these matters on which the man in the street could never by any possibility inform himself. And not only could he not inform himself, but he cannot even understand if he is told. Science has made available for society's use an amount of knowledge of what is happening to its members vastly greater than they can ever absorb individually and use individually in the daily course of looking out for their interests. No one who appreciates this fact can hold that a system of free contract normally protects all interests, and that every free business transaction is automatically self-supporting and productive for society as a whole.

Now we can expect the employer—a specialist—to watch his own business and to know what it is doing, though we could not expect the same man in his rôle of unspecialized consumer to watch with the same effectiveness every producer whose policies affect his welfare. And if men are responsible for the known results of their actions, business responsibilities must include the known results of business dealings, whether these have been recognized by law or not. Indeed, when they have passed into the statute books they are no longer responsibilities at all in the highest sense: of obligations which the individual must himself decide how to meet. The decision is made for him by government and he has only to obey or take the consequences. But where the law has not spoken, every man must decide on his own initiative.

Now if men are to follow this out in the simplest way, if they are merely to make good as nearly as possible all actual damage they cause, they will find themselves going far indeed before the task is accomplished. The ideal is to pay one's way, not to hurt others without compensation, to get value only for value given, and to leave the world in other respects just as one found it, or at least not to leave it the worse for one's presence.

In other words, it is a static idea of business we are discussing. But it is simply impossible for anyone to leave the world just as he found it, especially if he is one whose decisions have any importance. As Professor Veblen says: "Invention is the mother of necessity" in the most unexpected ways. The necessity for writing these words (if there be any such necessity) is a by-product of the mechanical inventions that gave us the industrial revolution and the subsequent vast "advances" in scientific production and large-scale industry. Every lumberman in the Mississippi Basin is jointly with others a cause of the new flood conditions that are inflicting so much damage and calling for so much expenditure of money and thought to devise methods of prevention. Some few have managed their property so as to avoid increasing the danger of floods; others have contributed to relief funds and studies in flood prevention. But whether they have met the responsibility or not, it is there.

To the extent that each of us is a factor in economic evolution, be it only that his presence adds one member to the population, he shares in all the increasing difficulties which economic evolution brings with it. He cannot do anything so far-reaching as building a house without affecting other people's property interests for better or for worse. Unless he affects them for the better he is pretty sure to affect them for the worse. And unless he leaves society stronger in its power to master the manifold troubles of modern industry he will leave it relatively weaker by just so much as those troubles have grown in size and complexity. Modern industry gives a new meaning to the text, "He that is not with me is against me," and is constantly showing new ways in which, whether we like it or not, we are our brothers' keepers.

In many such matters, such as the policy of lumbermen toward the danger of floods that comes with deforestation, or the employer's attitude toward the unemployment that arises from the seasonal nature of his trade, the responsibility is one which we are not yet ready to crystallize into a legal obligation. Law and custom can at best never keep pace with the needs which they are made to meet, for the simple reason that the need must be there before it can be felt, and it must be felt in a substantial way to be worth making a law about, and felt for a long time and by a considerable number to give rise to a custom. These agencies which prescribe just how a man shall take upon himself the consequences of his acts can never cover more than a few of the more direct and the more obvious. By far the greater number must always remain in a sort of extra-legal borderland.

If they are neglected, the result may be evils which will ultimately call forth legislation of an experimental sort, ill-informed and inept perhaps, and usually not calculated to improve the morale of our attitude toward goverment. But if these matters are treated as public obligations by those most directly responsible, much of this friction and waste motion can be avoided. The interested parties may ultimately want a law to help control them, for the sake of controlling also the bolters in their own ranks. But it will be a law asked for by the governed, not imposed on them from outside.

We have become accustomed to the idea that nineteen men who want good conditions may be coerced by one competitor whose standard is more unscrupulous. They may actually be unable to do as they wish unless commanded by law. We have not always seen that this is a two-edged doctrine. It has been used to show how far regulation can go without transgressing the principle of industrial freedom and the natural right of the business man to run his enterprise as he sees fit. It has been used by the individualist to set limits on the sphere of government.

But surely the more significant thing about it is the fact that it takes for granted that competitive standards and standards of public good are not one and the same, whether the majority in the trade are awake to that fact or not. And it further takes for granted a widespread sense of responsibility on the part of a majority of business men, not limited to the letter of the law. If this sense of responsibility is to be a guide to legislation, it must go before the law and be independent of it.

This is one great reason why the state cannot afford to assume all responsibility for the outcome of the business system and leave individuals to look after their own interests with a single eye and a clear conscience. Some feel that the state has taken the responsibility, once for all, of a system in which individuals are supposed to look after their own interests and that while there may be abuses it does not fall on the individual to correct them. Moreover, they hold that the state is the only agency that can effectively bear the burdens and perform the tasks of correcting the miscarriages of free contract. Men who are under the compelling force of competition must seek their own interests foremost and all the time or go to the wall. If they try to correct abuses, to follow fairer tactics and leave off using competitive weapons that do damage, the general practice will not be changed, they will simply be forced out of business and their place will be taken by others less scrupulous.

We have seen that the state cannot well do all that this attitude would demand of it. Let us look at the idea further. It is possible that free contract would do more good than harm even in the hands of a wholly selfish and irresponsible population, though nowadays there is more and more evidence to the contrary. But there can be no doubt that enough harm would be done to offset much of the good, and it is quite possible that the strain of conflicting selfish interests might ultimately rack the system to pieces.

Indeed, this is just what the Socialists think is now happening before our unseeing eyes. What with the unmeasured wastes of competition where it remains active, the exploitation where competition has ceased to act, the parasitism which is so inextricably bound up with the guidance of sound production, and the disintegrating effects of the distrust and hostility that rule between large bodies of the population, roused by the sense that each is reckless of the interests of the others—with all these to combat it often seems that we need all the saving sense of public obligation we can possibly muster, merely to keep the machinery running at all.

It is often raised as a conclusive objection to Socialism that it relies on altruism, while the present system harnesses to our service the more reliable force of self-interest. The fact is that in this respect the contrast between the two systems is a matter of degree only. Socialistic industry would find many ways of enlisting and utilizing selfish motives, and we cannot say how great its demands on altruism would be without more extensive experiments than have yet been tried. But we do know that the present system also calls for a great deal of public spirit to make it run properly, and this fact is daily becoming more prominent, and is driven home afresh by every reading of the morning paper.

Suppose the state does take its chances of the harm which business selfishness can work, and with its eyes open sanctions a system which it knows to be capable of abuse. Does it thereby tacitly approve all abuses, or take for granted that men will commit as many (always inside the law) as they see fit? Does not its very act impliedly make every man responsible for the balance of good or harm that may come from his own efforts?

And as for the argument that private persons cannot do anything effective, there are three reasons why that is not conclusive: First, when we are speaking of human relationships, "impossible" is a relative term, and we may occasionally find ourselves forced to choose between two courses, both of which seemed impossible till one was forced upon us. Secondly, we have seen enough to realize fully the well-nigh fatal weakness of state action without a strong sense of responsibility in the people at large to make the way as easy as possible. Thirdly, private individuals can act collectively where one alone is helpless and get results which would be impossible for the official machinery of government.

Is it not probable that more could be done to check unfair competitive practices by trade organizations regulating their members and adjusting relations between each other's members than by any number of special laws and court decisions? If only we could trust such bodies to act truly in the public interest, and not merely to eliminate competition for their own benefit or to fortify a wastefully numerous class of middlemen against the competition of more direct and efficient methods!

VI. RESPONSIBILITY AS AN ACTUAL FORCE

And this brings us to the final point, which is that business responsibility beyond the law is not an ideal only but to a considerable extent a fact. Business men's associations are the very effective embodiment of it. The retailer and manufacturer take the responsibility for not short-circuiting the wholesaler, and in return the wholesaler does not "poach" on the retailer. This is responsibility to a group, enforced by mutual interests. All that is needed is to make it cover a larger group—to make it general.

The sense of general responsibility is a fact, also, though it is weaker than the tie that binds a class, a trade, or a profession. In proportion as it grows in strength we can rely on it more and more to guide public policy. Perhaps in some future century we may even venture to ask business men's advice on proposed laws for the prevention of unfair competition without the uneasy feeling that their only purpose in giving of their wisdom is to make the laws ineffective and keep things as they are.

With the idea generally accepted that "wealth is a trust" the next order of development is a gradually broadening revelation of how far the trusteeship extends. It most surely extends to the earning of the wealth as well as the spending of it. It extends to a sincere effort to make labor conditions as nearly right as possible in plants from which one draws dividends, and conditions of competition as fair and free from waste as they can be made.

In fact, one of the most serious objections to the present degree of concentration of wealth is that the largest capitalists are interested in so many industries that they cannot do by any of them what their position demands. They have undertaken, or have had thrust upon them, responsibilities utterly beyond their power to fulfil.

Still more effective in bringing about this result is the corporation, which holds out a standing invitation to every man of considerable means to split his investments with a view to greater safety. Sometimes this is carried so far as to defeat its own end. The eggs are in many baskets and the baskets cannot all be watched. But long before this point is reached the watching is reduced to the bare essentials necessary to knowing if the investment is profitable and safe. And when a man's familiarity with his own money-making enterprises—and every investment comes under this head—when his familiarity dwindles to the irreducible money-making minimum, something has evaporated, and that something is a social interest of incalculable importance. Private fortunes may be safer, but not without cost to the nation. Has the principle of limited liability been carried too far? If a moderate curtailment of that privilege should result in concentrating each man's investments in fewer enterprises, the commonwealth would be the gainer in a very real way.

From the same point of view one of the worst features of the internal organization of corporations is its wonderful aptitude for dividing responsibility, concealing it from outside observers and even from the members themselves, and making it thoroughly ineffective for other than "business" purposes. To an economics of irresponsibility this might appear as an incidental blemish; to an economics of responsibility it is one of the very roots of evil.

Many men would fulfil their responsibilities in a very different spirit if they were put before them in present and tangible shape: for example, if they had to bargain with their laborers directly. But it is an unusual stockholder who will so instruct his paid officials that they shall feel free to lessen dividends if necessary to make the industry truly a source of gain for the other participants, laborers, and others. And yet they usually have it in their power to make it either a source of gain or a source of net loss to those whom it affects by its operations.

VII. CONCLUSION

In conclusion: the world is familiar enough with the conception of social responsibilities. These do not need to be rediscovered in the year of our Lord 1916. But the fact that a large part of them are business responsibilities has not yet penetrated, and this fact does need to be brought home to a community in which business men and theoretical economics alike are still shadowed by the fading penumbra of laissez-faire. This issue is deeper and more far-reaching than anyone can realize who has not tried earnestly to understand the sources of the deep sense of injustice that animates the discontented classes. The trouble is not that the unfortunate are not helped, but that they are helped in the name of charity, regardless of whether they are victims of their own weakness or of the misfit grindings of our none-too-perfectly-adjusted industrial machine. To many the very word "charity" is as a red rag to a bull, and this will never be otherwise as long as so much that passes for charity is merely repairing the damage or salvaging the wreckage for which industry is the chief responsible cause; the same industry which distributes the dividends out of which charity funds so freely come.

The cry for "justice, not charity" may cover a deal of hysteria and wrong-mindedness, but it also has a solid basis in scientific fact, and the way to quench the hysteria is to investigate sanely just what that solid basis is. Such studies are the task of experts and specialists. All that is here attempted is to show the important place which such work has to fill in our scheme of social management and social interpretation, and to do whatever may be done to hasten by ever so little the growth of a broadened attitude toward the responsibilities of business relationships.

J. MAURICE CLARK

UNIVERSITY OF CHICAGO

About the Authors

Markus Feiks (University of Tübingen, Germany) studied Cultural Sciences (M.A.), Communication and Media Science (B.A.) at the University of Leipzig. He currently writes his dissertation about the moral orientations advertising practitioners use in their daily practice. Since 2014 he is research assistant in the DFG-funded project 'Advertising Ethics in Times of Media Change'. Main research areas are methods of empirical research (especially content analysis), historical and sociological aspects of consumption, communication in marketing and advertising as well as the sociology of social practices and pragmatism.

PD Dr. Michaela Haase (Freie Universität Berlin, Berlin, Germany), Head of the Center for Marketing Ethics at the Freie Universität Berlin, studied economics, philosophy of science and political science at the Freie Universität Berlin. She hold positions in and beyond academia such as the Freie Universität Berlin and the Friedrich-Alexander-Universität Erlangen-Nürnberg. Her areas of expertise include marketing theory, business ethics, institutional economics, and philosophy of science.

Carsten Herrmann-Pillath Research Professor of Economics and Evolutionary Sciences at Witten/Herdecke University, Germany, Long Term Fellow of the Max Weber Center for Advanced Cultural and Social Studies, University of Erfurt, Distinguished Visiting Professor of Schwarzman Scholars at Tsinghua University, Beijing. After completing education in economics, linguistics and Chinese studies at the University of Cologne, Professorships in Chinese economic studies, economics and evolutionary/institutional economics at Duisburg University, Witten/Herdecke University and Frankfurt School of Finance and Management. Major fields of research: Economics and philosophy, institutional change and economic development, international economics, Chinese economic studies. 300+ academic papers and 16 books. His magnum opus 'China's Economic Culture: The Ritual Order of State and Markets' is forthcoming with Routledge.

M. Haase (ed.), *Economic Responsibility*, Ethical Economy 53,
DOI 10.1007/978-3-319-52099-5

Dr. Stefan Hielscher (University of Bath, School of Management, UK) holds a position as a Prize Fellow in Business and Society. He received his PhD in Economics from Martin-Luther-University Halle-Wittenberg, Germany. His research interests are in Corporate Social Responsibility, the Sharing Economy and Corporate Citizenship, as well as in Institutional Economics, Rational-Choice Theory and Systems Theory.

Prof. Dr. Klaus Kornwachs former Chair for Philosophy of Technology at Brandenburg Technical University of Cottbus (1992-2011), since 1990 Honorary Professor for Philosophy at University of Ulm, studied Physics, Mathematics and Philosophy. He was Lecturer at Universities of Freiburg and Stuttgart, Senior Research Fellow at the Fraunhofer-Institute for Industrial Engineering, Stuttgart (1979-1992). Guest Professor at Technical Universities in Budapest, Vienna, and Dalian (China), Alcatel-Lucent Fellowship at IZKT, University Stuttgart. Since 2004 Full Member of the National Academy for Science and Engineering (acatech), since 2013 Honorary Professor at Intelligent Urbanization Co-Creation Center at College for Architecture and Urban Planung, Tongji-University, Shanghai. His main fields in research are: Analytical Philosophy, Philosophy of Pure and Applied Sciences, General System Theory, Theoretical Philosophy, Ethics. Numerous publications; for more see: www.kornwachs.de (in German).

Jutta Krautter (University of Tübingen, Germany) studied General Rhetoric and philosophy at the University of Tübingen. From 2010 till 2013 she was a member of the Research Training Group 'Bioethics' at the International Centre for Ethics in the Sciences and Humanities at the University of Tübingen (IZEW) with the dissertation project "'Neuro-Enhancement' in focus – reasons and aftermaths of its medial appearances". Since 2014 she is research assistant in the DFG-funded project 'Advertising Ethics in Times of Media Change'. Her research areas are ethical and rhetorical aspects of media communication.

Helge Löbler is Professor of Management and Marketing and director of the Institute for Service and Relationship Management at the University of Leipzig, Germany. He studied Cybernetics and Economics at the universities of Stuttgart and Bonn holds an PhD in Economics. He received an award for his outstanding contributions to the 12th International Colloquium in Relationship Marketing. He has lectured at different international Universities. His main research area is social constructionism, second order cybernetics, and their impact on service and communication and other social interactions.

Dr. Uta Müller (University of Tübingen, Germany) Director and Coordination of the Department of Ethics and Education at the International Centre for Ethics in the Sciences and Humanities at the University of Tübingen (IZEW). She studied Philosophy and Political Sciences in Heidelberg and Munich and graduated with her dissertation in 1990. Since 2002 she is research assistant at the IZEW, and since 2014 she is, in cooperation with Prof. Dr. Guido Zurstiege, the supervisor of the DFG-funded project 'Advertising Ethics in Times of Media Change'. Her research focusses on applied ethics, corporeality and aging and furthermore questions of ethical justifications.

Farah Naz is a doctoral candidate at the Department of Sociology Alpen Adria University, Klagenfurt, Austria. She holds a position of lecturer at the Department of Sociology at University of Sargodha, Pakistan. Her major research interests are gender, development and business ethics. At present she is conducting her empirical research on global football production networks. She intends to analyze the way global production processes and market systems interact with local gender norms and cultural practices.

Prof. Dr. Ingo Pies holds the Chair in Economic Ethics at Martin Luther University Halle-Wittenberg. He was appointed in 2002. Before, he studied economics at Münster University, received his doctoral degree from Catholic University Eichstätt and his venia legendi in economics from Münster University. He is working out an „ordonomic" research program. His areas of expertise include normative institutional economics, business ethics, sustainability management, and the political responsibilities of business firms ("corporate citizenship").

Prof. Dr. Guido Zurstiege (University of Tübingen, Germany), Professor for Media Studies (focus on empirical media research), studied Communication Science, Anglistics, and Economic Policy at the University of Münster. After his dissertation (1997) he habilitated in the area of communication studies. He has been a lecturer and (visiting) professor in Münster, Berlin, Greifswald, Zurich, and Vienna. Since 2014 he is, in cooperation with Dr. Uta Müller, the supervisor of the DFG-funded project 'Advertising Ethics in Times of Media Change'. His areas of expertise cover advertising and consumption.

Index

M. Haase (ed.), *Economic Responsibility*, Ethical Economy 53,
DOI 10.1007/978-3-319-52099-5

If you have any concerns about our products,
you can contact us on
ProductSafety@springernature.com

In case Publisher is established outside the EU,
the EU authorized representative is:
Springer Nature Customer Service Center GmbH
Europaplatz 3, 69115 Heidelberg, Germany

Printed by Libri Plureos GmbH
in Hamburg, Germany